Simon Quail MA B.Ed Master Mariner

Simon Quail went to sea as a deck apprentice in 1966 when the British Merchant Navy was at its height. Employed by eleven very different shipping companies, serving on three dozen ships over twenty years, he sailed the five oceans of the world, crossed countless sea, touched almost every continent as he experienced life as a deck officer on general cargo ships, passenger ships, chemical tankers and bulk carriers.

GANGWAY is an engaging mix of personal account and technical data. The author describes life aboard ships crewed by fifty men which fell to only eleven. And life ashore during weeks in port. He explains the traditional techniques used by navigators to find their way across the oceans, long before the advent of GPS.

A ship's gangway is the link between the solidity of the land and the mysterious, often dangerous, instability of the seas and oceans that circle our planet. To climb a gangway is to seek life beyond.

'The Last Grain Race' described life at sea in the age of sail. 'Gangway - a Life at Sea' is a maritime memoir which describes the challenges faced by cadet, navigator and chief officer in the last age of the motor ship, before the age of the super ship.

Simon Quail is a Liveryman of the Honourable Company of Master Mariners.

GANGWAY

A Life at Sea

Simon Quail

Copyright © Simon Quail 2019

The moral rights of the author have been asserted

All rights reserved

For Jo, Pippa and Robert, but especially for a mariner's wife par excellence, Marilyn.

PHOTO CREDITS

Unless otherwise stated below, all photos and map sketches are by the author.

The Cadet Years: Cadets by FB pool: Alan Provan©. Cadet at the wheel, taking sights, in jolly boat, FB Captain, Stoppering Off: all from 'A Career in the Elder Dempster Fleet.' Photographer Carl Hughes.

MV Marsina: Photos Licensed under Creative Commons.
Ref: http://www.wikiswire.com/wiki/Papuan_Chief_I

Map of North Sea Routes taken from A Link with Tradition: the Story of Stevenson Clark Shipping Ltd 1730 – 1980

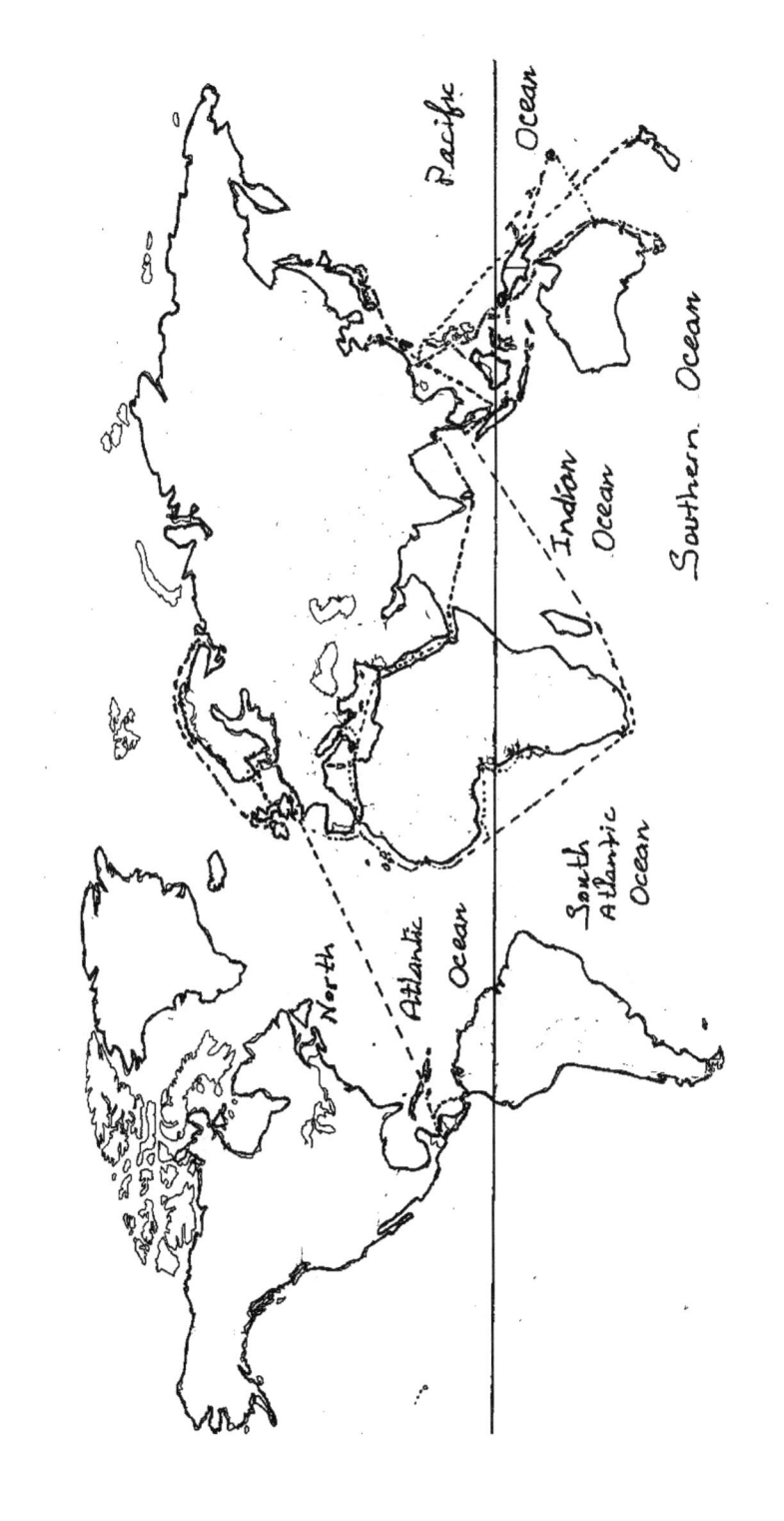

OCEAN ROUTES FOLLOWED BY THE AUTHOR 1966-1988

UK to West Africa Routes

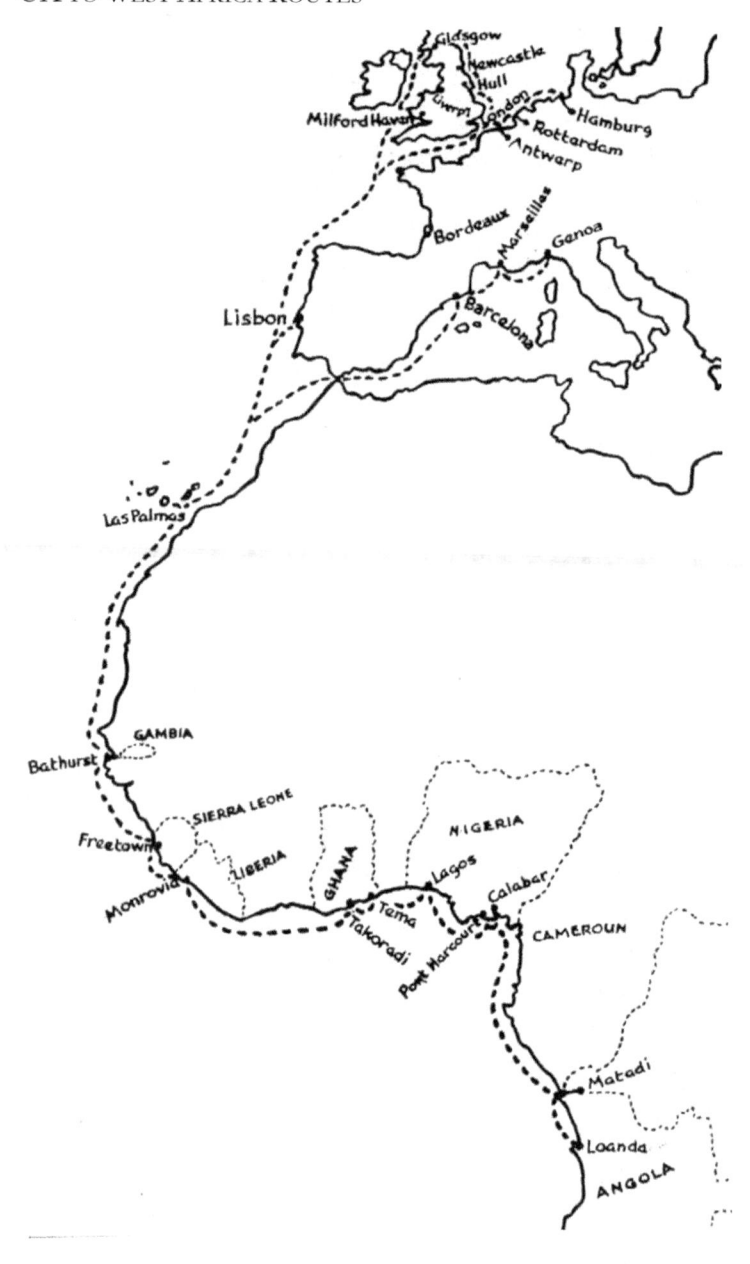

INTRODUCTION

Fifty years ago I boarded the first of thirty seven merchant ships and went to sea. I experienced a way of life no longer available to the modern mariner.

In August 2019 the world's largest container ship, the *MSC Gülsün* arrived in Europe from China. At 1,300 feet long, she is three times the length of my first ship, *MV Deido*. And carries twenty six times more cargo. 248,000 dwt. *Deido* needed a crew of fifty. *Gülsün* needs a crew of just 26.

This scaling up of vessel size and scaling down of crew numbers is a dramatic illustration of the vast changes experienced in the world of marine transport.

And of the life at sea—and long days in port—experienced in my day? All gone. In fifty years.

I have witnessed myriad sunrises and sunsets over steel grey horizons and smoky headland and stood lookout under a canopy of glittering stars. From bridge or bow I had a grandstand view of dancing dolphin pods, shocks of flying fish and stuka-diving gannets. Snug in a hammock rigged on the monkey island I have been lulled to sleep by a gentle swell. Like a wild horse in bucking seas, the kick of the deck has sent me sprawling. I have been covered with choking cargo dust, been threatened by rope, wire or heavy block. I survived. But three ships and many of their crew did not. They sank into the deeps, lost forever.

Gangway

To me ships are not a prosaic construction of steel and machinery. Every time I read that a ship has been broken up, it hurts. It hurts because these ships were my *home*; the home where I ate, rested, worked, played, sometimes drank too much, sometimes enjoyed parties on board. Slept. Woke up to another day as *my* ship sailed inexorably onward, laying a silvered wake across a carpet of deepest blue.

We crew lived together for months on end, shared good times and bad times, in rough weather and glorious. Went ashore together. Came back to *our* ship. Glad to be back after a good run ashore. But sometimes sad to be stuck on board and wishing to be home.

The older the ship the greater the character. The *Glenorchy*, built in 1941, had twenty seven years of history rammed into her deck caulking when I joined her and countless thousands of marine encounters under her keel. Ships built in the 1980s had less charm, built to be efficient steel boxes but they still carried the freight of mariners' lives; their hopes and fears, their dreams and sodden realities.

'Scrapped at Kaohsiung' may be an acknowledgement of a commercial reality but it was a heartless epitaph, a kick in the teeth to the sentiment we mariners felt about *her*, our ship. It wasn't about economic turnover for the sailor. Her loss was a loss of memory, a loss of shared experience, of a voyage safely completed. 'Finished with Engines' was only meant to be for now, this port, not for ever. I felt that most strongly when leaving that old rust bucket, *Rogate*. I was the last man aboard. The last to feel her as a living vessel before she became a steel hulk and was razor bladed.

These ships also made a ship owner a minimal profit. When that thin margin vanished, the sentence was to suffer the ultimate indignity of being scrapped, taken to the knacker's yard in Europe, India or Taiwan.

Some ships arouse feelings of unreasonable dislike, usually due a Master careless of his crew, or when poorly maintained. Ships have to be cared for, by Captain to cabin boy, from bridge to keel, from cable locker to propeller. Or they turn nasty on you.

In seeking to discover meaning in my own life I have discovered that ships have a life of their own, worthy of celebration. And commemoration. These ships and men have vanished from the seas. I tell my tale so that the vessels and those who lived on board will not be erased from our national memory.

To climb up a gangway is to commit yourself to the ship, trusting her (for a ship is always feminine) to complete the voyage safely, to survive the unknown encounters ahead, be it storms or hidden rocks.

Introduction

To climb a gangway is to seek life beyond.

To step down the gangway, onto solid land is to give up an unspoken expression of thanks for the voyage safely completed, the biblical chaos of the waters survived.

A ship's gangway is the link between the hidden worlds of life at sea, over the horizon, and the more known world of life ashore. A gangway invokes a complex metaphor of the link between the solidity of the land and the mysterious, often dangerous, instability of the seas and oceans that circle our planet.

The call of the sea was in my blood. I discovered several years ago that my great-grandfather and great-great-grandfather were both master mariners. Thus it was, even though I lived in a Cotswold hamlet one hundred miles from the nearest sea, sea salt flowed in my veins. After the gangway had been hauled in and the ropes let go, and we set sail away from the safe, solid shore, I wanted to discover what lay beyond the distant flat horizon.

Every time I joined my ship, every time I went ashore, from Archangel to Yokohama, the gangway was the link between these two contrasting worlds.

I have learned that once a sailor vanishes over the horizon, he is forgotten by the landlubbers who remain ashore. The mariner is no longer held in close affection by the community memory because so few British men and women go to sea. There are no longer, as in my day, the numerous family connections to those who follow the call to go a-roving; very few left behind who talk about absent fathers and brothers away for up to two years at a time, leaving behind 'grass widows' to bring up families all alone. There is no residual understanding among landlubbers, and the seafarer's life is a lost world.

The wake of life stretches away behind us, silvered by a rising moon of memories, its ghostly illumination casting a pale light on recalled events. This memoir is an evocation of my past. You may have similar memories of a time when the British Merchant Navy was at its peak, when 3,000 British ships under the Red Ensign—the Red Duster—plied the oceans of the world, manned by British officers and sailors, when conditions have never been bettered.

For centuries the ships of the British Merchant Navy carried the lifeblood of Britain, their bulging holds crammed with goods to satisfy every perceived need and luxury, to sate the population's appetite.

Gangway

Not now. These arteries have had a transfusion of foreign bodies. Ships have grown huge and fat. They are rarely sustained by British blood. Their stories belong to other shores.

My story is of seafaring five decades ago, of men like me who filled the fridges of families with groceries, manufactories with raw materials, foundries with base ores, who then sailed away to live their lives over a distant horizon.

So climb up the gangway and glimpse a world long gone, a world which shaped and sustained a nation.

PROLOGUE

Tottering along the narrow slippery deck of the submarine I headed towards the access hatch and scrambled down the ladder. Inside the narrow steel tube all was strange; smells of hot oil, steel and stale air. I peered into the periscope eyepiece. The images of ships in the Solent appeared to be upside down.

After a whirlwind tour we left that claustrophobic, windowless world.

'Do hurry up! And take care!' gasped my mother confusingly, scrambling behind me, her voice full of fear.

I increased my pace along the rolling deck till I gained the boarding ladder hanging down from the curving hull. I jumped nimbly into the boat bobbing below on the choppy waters. Made it.

We returned to a large yacht, our base for the 1953 Queen's Review the Fleet, where we were given a picnic lunch. As we sat on the wooden deck, a big man in a bobble hat offered me a bowl of hard boiled eggs and I lifted one, surprised and distracted by its smooth, cold shell. (I learned afterwards that the kindly egg man was the actor, John Mills.)

It was my first memory of boats and ships and the sea.

I was five years old.

Twelve years later I signed an Indenture of Apprenticeship with Elder Dempster Lines and so joined the British Merchant Navy. One cold January day I made that mystical transition between the shore and sea as I walked up the gangway to board *MV Deido* and set off to see the world.

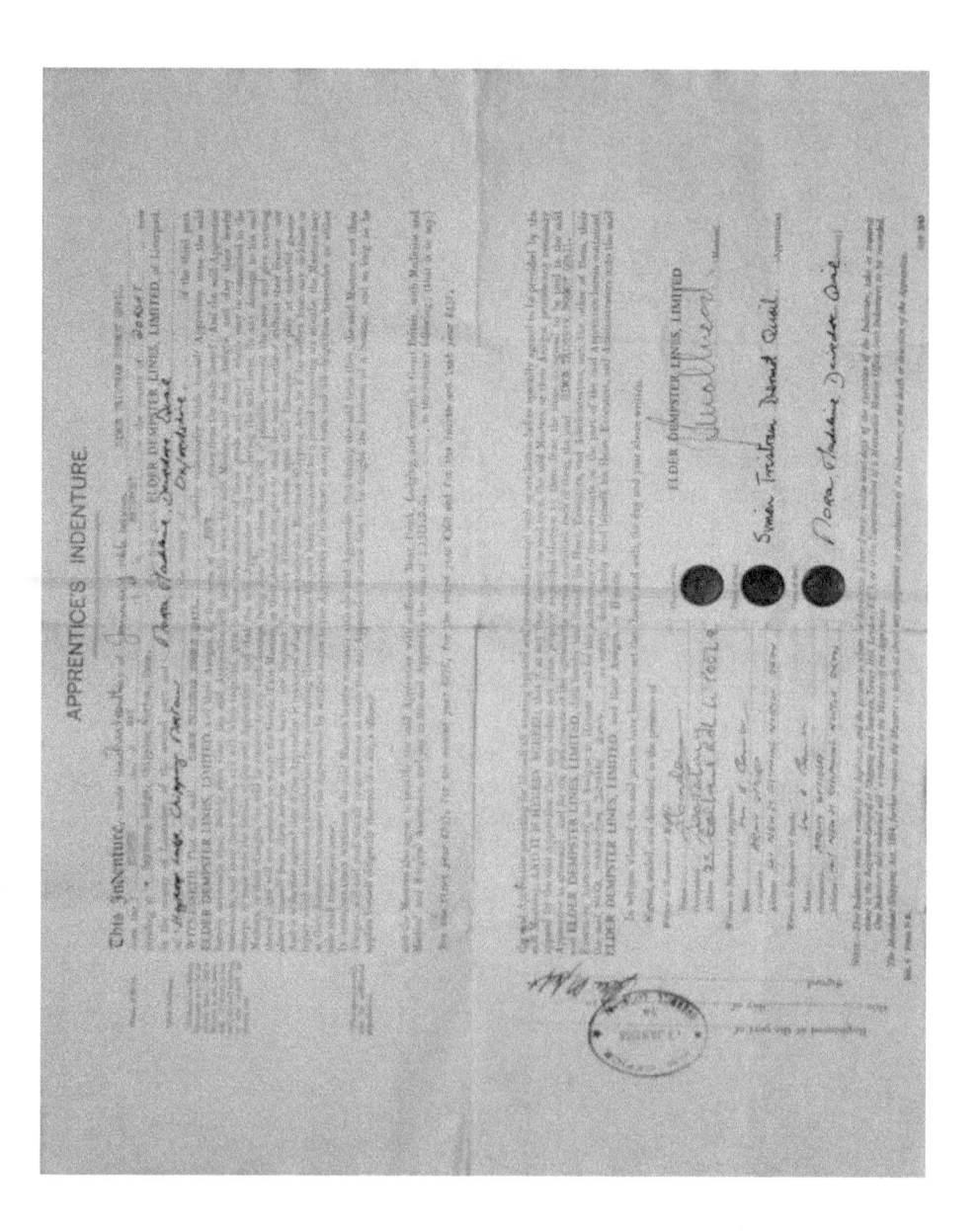

The Indenture of Apprenticeship; the journey begins.

FIRST LIFE

DECK APPRENTICE

IN

ELDER DEMPSTER

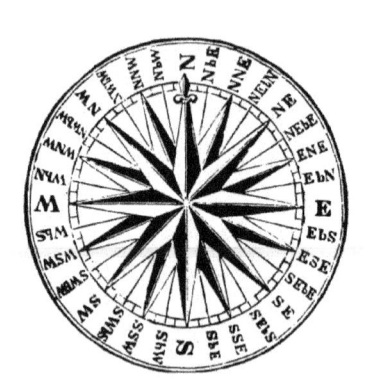

Chapter 1

A Green First Tripper

It was two o'clock in the morning. I should have been in bed. The tide was right but the time was not.

A shadow slid slowly across the black river as gaunt crane ribs drifted astern.

'Stand there and keep out of the way!' ordered a bearded face with three gold stripes on his arm. Keeping well for'ard of a set of fo'c'sle bitts, I looked about, stamping my cold feet on the steel deck. The sharp toot of a tug answered the urgent, deeper notes from the ship's whistle. Shore lights glimmered on oily water. Sailors moved efficiently about their tasks, dealing with mooring ropes and towing lines with a brisk competence that was a total mystery to me, the new deck apprentice on board *MV Deido*, a general cargo ship in transit across the River Thames from the Blue Circle Cement Wharf to Tilbury Docks, where she was to load exports for West Africa.

Three weeks before I had been a mere country boy, a 17-year-old youth trapped by the timetable of the school day. I had grabbed the opportunity to leave behind the boring classroom and embrace the excitement of travelling the world in the Merchant Navy. My letter of acceptance into Elder Dempster Lines had arrived 3 November 1965, releasing me from the prison of school.

Now I was bound by the new bonds of an Apprentice's Indenture, dated 13 January 1966, whereby I promised (as I re-read the terms and conditions fifty years later) in language that had not changed in decades, *'not to frequent taverns or alehouses, unless upon Company business, nor play at any unlawful games.'* The rule about alehouses was universally ignored. What *'Company business'* could possibly have taken me into a pub? Or, indeed, what were those *'unlawful games'*? I never found out.

With real pleasure I had informed the headmaster of Chipping Norton Grammar School that I was leaving at Christmas. The staff, knowing of my academic performance—or lack of it rather—approved of my decision. My headmaster had encouragingly written in my final report, *'I think Simon will make a very good sailor.'*

Would I?

The train from Banbury took me from the depths of the Cotswolds and deposited me into the midst of Liverpool's maritime world. Within the imposing India Buildings on Water Street I met the gruff-mannered, sharp-eyed Captain Smallwood, RN, the Personnel Manager of Elder Dempster Lines. He was my first employer and I was much in awe of him. After some small talk about home life and my hopes for the future, he laid out my career path in the company; what was expected of me in terms of behaviour, my hard work and my progression through the officer ranks. He gave a brief description of the history of the company and its trading pattern between America and Europe and West Africa.

'Right Cadet, give me a salute. Like this,' he demonstrated in the approved Royal Navy manner.

I so did, feeling rather self-conscious in my new uniform so recently acquired at a naval outfitters down in London, thanks to my wonderfully generous Godfather.

'Very good. Now we can start to make an officer out of you,' he said.

And thus began my induction into a life at sea.

Down at the Mercantile Marine Office I clutched a board on which had been slid bold black figures: R832000. The photograph was for my Seaman's Record Book number. Repeated use etched this sequence onto my memory. Details of my indenture of apprenticeship were entered into this book and in time, the record of my qualifications, as a lifeboatman and as an EDH—an efficient deckhand. It would also contain details of

A Green First Tripper

service aboard every ship in which I sailed as a junior officer; date of engagement, date of discharge, rank and description of voyage (Foreign Going or Home Trade). I presented my Record Book to the Captain when joining each vessel. It would become the official record of my life at sea.

My red British Seaman's Card was also issued at this time. It was my essential travel document, used instead of a passport. It had to be produced at dock gate security when going ashore in a foreign port.

'Cough please,' commanded the doctor in a white coat. We were back at India Buildings, high up in the medical department, undergoing full health checks and receiving multiple vaccinations for West Africa. I was taller than the average cadet and failed to fit underneath the height bar measuring stick jutting out from the wall.

'6 feet 3 inches; that will do,' said the doctor as he scribbled down the details that made their way into my official documents. Fourteen years later I had 'shrunk' by an inch when documents were reissued.

During the week we were taken to Huskisson Dock, where behind a high brick wall lay a hidden world. Lines of cargo ships filled the docks, pressed hard up against the narrow quayside. A slab of black steel towered over me and above that a white accommodation block, topped by a large yellow funnel. It was my first sight of an Elder Dempster ship. A forest of derricks and taut rigging wires loomed over the cramped space between ship and warehouse. Men in flat caps and worn clothes, thin cigarettes stuck to thin lips, stabbed vicious cargo hooks into sacks and heaved them into place. A three-wheeled motorised cart piled high with crates trundled along, operated by a driver stood on an open platform at the front, weaving a path between the mayhem. With a squeal of running wires a sling of sacks was hauled rapidly across the sky high above and landed with a thump at the dockers' waiting feet.

Navigating a path between this intense activity, I stepped up the gangway, clambered awkwardly over a storm lintel of the heavy accommodation door, and jumped as it crashed shut behind me. The noisy chaos outside ceased. A low hum of distant machinery filled the air. We were led up more stairs, along narrow alleys lined by cabin doors of dark wood. We followed our guide back outside, up ladders, stepped over a storm lintel and entered the surprisingly confined space of the wheelhouse. This was to be my world for twenty years. This was where I would learn to steer a ship, keep a watch at sea and of course, navigate. I would also learn to rig derricks, varnish taffrails, holy-stone wooden decks and polish brass portholes till they sparkled. Looking down from the bridge dodger I watched, mystified, as far below me the holds were emptied of bags and bales.

'Where have they come from?' I asked.

'West Africa—that's where the ships of Elder Dempster ply their trade,' Captain Smallwood inform me.

Africa. It sounded exotic and far away. And I would sail there in a few days.

Cargo work and ship stability were concepts beyond my comprehension at present but as I passed my professional exams up to Master Mariner, I would become a fully competent deck officer, working my way up through the ranks from junior fourth officer, third officer, second officer, (the navigator) up to chief officer, in charge of loading and discharging cargo. All this was in the future. The prospect before me was so much more exciting than the classroom that I had gladly left behind. I could not wait to get started.

My sailing orders dated 17 January 1966 sent me by train from Liverpool to London to join my first ship, bound for Africa. Our taxi dumped us at 9 pm (2100 hours as I was to learn to say in maritime parlance) at the Blue Circle Cement Wharf opposite Tilbury Docks.

My fellow midshipman and I lugged our heavy seagoing kit through a maze of cranework towards our first ship, *MV Deido*. Reaching the bottom of the gangway we looked up; sloping metal steps spanned the space to the top of a black hull. It looked very narrow, and long. We cautiously clattered our loads into our new world. Shown to our cabins by the duty officer we quickly stowed our gear, and reported to the Captain. After a brief welcome, we were warned to grab a few hours' sleep before we would be called for our first duty.

"Its 1.30! Wake up! Get up! You're on duty!" a voice thundered into my dreams.

Shocked into unexpected wakefulness, I dragged myself from my warm pit, hurriedly dressed and, following the chief officer, took my stations for'ard. My new chum went aft. Mooring lines were let go and *Deido* crossed the river, nudged into position by tugs and slotted into the lock leading to Tilbury Docks. Entering at high water with the lock gates wide open, we were pushed and prodded onto our berth. Once secured alongside, my shipmate and I were allowed back to our cold bunks.

The ship did not sail immediately upon completion of cargo loading. It took several hours to prepare the vessel for sea. The sailors wrestled derricks into their resting crutches. Hatch beams dropped into position, wooden boards slotted into place. Three layers of tarpaulin were manhandled over and secured with locking bars. Five of them. I learned to undertake this dangerous dance later in my cadetship. We took care not to fall into an empty hold, crashing onto unyielding deck sixty feet below. Safety harnesses? What safety harness?

The next high tide was, of course, in the middle of the night. The pilot came on board. I took up station on the fo'c'sle with more confidence, just a little bit wiser than previously, as *Deido* was pulled and pushed out of the dock, through the locks and out into the river. Tooting goodbye to the assisting tugs, we set off down the River Thames, heading for the English Channel. Next stop Casablanca.

Snow was falling heavily as we made our way down the River Thames, down the English Channel and rounded the dangerous rocks off Ushant, marked by its flashing light. Now I encountered the wrath of the Bay of Biscay.

The Bay of Biscay is notorious because it is surrounded on three sides by land, the west side open to the power of an Atlantic storm. The swell enters on one side and is bounced back on three sides. The ship meets a heavily confused swell in the middle and is tossed crazily about. I was a 'green first tripper' struggling to keep my bridge watch. I was green with seasickness and retched until there was nothing left to add to the bucket. The merciless mate on watch had no compassion. I steered the ship for an hour before being sent on to the outer bridge wing to face the sharp salt air gusting straight in from the Atlantic, 'keeping lookout'. Fat chance. The only ship I could see was my own, as I leant my arms wearily on the taffrail. Four hours later my bunk welcomed me back into its warm embrace. Somehow I wasn't interested in food.

Four days after leaving London, I was delighted when we reached safe haven in Casablanca. Here I began to learn how to hold my drink. We walked ashore to the nearest bar and I had a tot from each pretty bottle on the bar shelf: whisky, gin and rum. It was enough.

We called at a run of ports that became very familiar over the years: Freetown, Monrovia, Takoradi, Tema, Lagos, Port Harcourt, Sapele and Warri.

The West African dockers were generally friendly, but so laid back. Work, they felt, was best avoided. They dressed in shorts and T shirt, and wore no gloves, shoes or flip flops; certainly no industrial boots with steel caps—which explained the missing toes. Sleep was also very important, especially on the night shift, of course. The work force tended to evaporate between two and five in the morning and they had to be levered out of dark crevices to keep the cargo coming ashore. Tact was needed to keep them happy and on the job.

I needed more lessons in tact.

It took two weeks to sail 4,000 miles from Lagos back to Tilbury. What do landlubbers do to pass fourteen days? Shop, empty the bins, walk the dog? *Deido* ploughed a creamy furrow through tropical seas across which danced flying fish. Schools of dolphins jumped and dipped under our bows. This was living. This was a new and treasured experience. This was the seafaring about which I had dreamed.

The crew hung cargo cluster lights over the side at night. The flying fish flew over these false moons and crashed on deck, ready to be harvested in the morning. Hung in lines on the poop deck to dry in the sun, these became essential ingredients for hot pepper soup. Too hot and bony for my taste.

After a blur of ports we were homeward bound. Picking up the north-east trades north of the Canaries we entered cooler climes; out of tropical uniform and back into long trousers and thick coats. It was March. Stiff gales followed us up the channel. We were back in home waters, the White Cliffs of Dover on our port bow, my African adventures far astern.

Bowling home to Heythrop by train I felt alive, excited to be back. Home was the sailor with yarns to spin, no longer a schoolboy. Voyaging out from the solid base of my Cotswold stone house I had seen and experienced life over the horizon and on many a foreign shore. I visited my ex-schoolmates at the Grammar School. A-levels exams loomed large but the delights of three-card brag filled their minds. I had moved on.

On a salary of £243 per year, I soon ran out of cash. After nine days leave I was off again. It was time to return to the security of bed and board of my next ship. I was glad to leave the house in the depths of the countryside and return to my chosen world. The mysterious call of the sea continued to exert its pull. At least this time I knew what to expect.

Chapter 2

CRUSHED DUCK

Sitting on the edge of my seat I looked eagerly through the window of the taxi taking me from Lime Street Station back to Huskisson Dock. A bold yellow funnel towered above the far side of the high dock wall. This was *MV Eboe*, 10,000 tons dwt. She was a classic 1950s British-built ship with fine, graceful lines, 500 feet from bow to stern. From her flaring bow to her rounded poop she was a grand sight.

I swung the kitbag onto my shoulder and hauled the heavy cabin trunk up the gangway with both hands. This was becoming routine. I knew what was expected of me. I had shed the embarrassment of being a green first-tripper.

Elder Dempster had been on the West African trade since the mid nineteenth century. We were part of a great trading tradition. Though not aware of this history, I felt the weight of tradition in learning the way things were done aboard a well found ship. I absorbed the standards demanded in discipline, punctuality and loyalty. I was expected to give my all for the good of the ship and the good of the company.

Butting down the Irish Sea into the Western Approaches, *Eboe* encountered a stiff April breeze, catching big sprays over the fo'c'sle as she dipped her head into the increasing westerly swell, shipping occasional solid green waters along the weather deck. The sickening corkscrew motion in the choppy, confused waters of the Bay of Biscay eased as the southerly wind veered west onto the starboard bow.

At last, after four days out from Liverpool, we picked up the north-east trades. Under blue skies and following white horses the temperature rose and we cadets laughed and joked with a new freedom. In ripped shorts and bare backs we worked in the sunshine with a will. We seemed to be forever greasing runners and blocks, holystoning decks, washing down bulkheads, stripping varnish from taffrails and polishing brass portholes. I acquired a good suntan between the grease marks. There was no such thing as paid overtime. We worked as required.

'Right, there is Altair, the bright star in the middle of a row of three and nearby you've got that really bright star, Vega the Swan, just outside the blurry arc of light we call the Milky Way.' The third officer stabbed the dark night sky with his index finger as I craned my neck to stare into deep space.

'And further round you've got the bright star of Deneb inside that D of stars, in the middle of the Milky Way. That's what we call the Summer Triangle. Three nice easy stars to find and remember. Got that?'

'Yeah, I think so…'

'See the curve of stars, the reddish star at the end is Arcturus. The other end of the handle you got a saucepan shape; follow the extended line of those two stars; just to the left in space all by itself, that's Polaris.'

Thus it was I began to learn the names and the positions of navigable stars in the northern sky. Even today it gives me great pleasure to find and identify these special summer stars.

After over 1,600 miles and six days the smudge on the horizon hardened into focus as the island of Gran Canaria emerged from the haze. The pilot came out from Las Palmas and took us into the bunkering area of the port. Taking my station for'ard I continued to grapple with the mystery of mooring as *Eboe* came on to her berth and made fast fore and aft.

The cadets were granted a two hour shore leave. Quickly changing into clean shorts and shirt, we nipped down the gangway to explore this Spanish outpost basking under the hot sun. We did not waste time—or scarce money—in a bar but mooched through the vibrant streets. Sitting on a clean beach framed by a sparking sea and deep blue skies, I licked a cold ice cream and trickled soft sand through bare toes. We were abroad.

Bunkering complete we sailed on to the hot, sticky ports of Africa. *Eboe* was a motor ship and so did not 'sail' of course. It was only twenty seven years since Eric Newby had written the story of the Last Grain Race, when full rigged sailing ships competed to carry grain from Australia to Europe. Maritime terms were still heavily influenced by those not so distant days of sail.

'Come with me, Cadet. Help me stream the Log,' commanded the second officer.

The Log was a braided length of line, set to the correct length calculated according to the length and speed of the ship. This was connected to the Walker Log, a set of dials which sent a signal to an electric repeater on the bridge.

Together we fed the line outside the after end of the bulwark stanchions. I opened the new wooden box and lifted out its precious contents; a compact brass rotator with three curved fins, (about the size of a miniature bomb) and carefully clipped it to the log line. Once set, the rotator, (called a duck) would be dragged through the water and its rotating fins measure off the nautical miles as indicated on the dials. A metal wheel (the governor) was also clipped onto the log line and we were ready to launch. The engines throbbed below us. The propeller thrashed out an angry wake.

'All ready?' asked the second officer.

'All ready!' I cried.

'Release!'

I flung the duck outwards towards the boiling wake. In horrifying slow motion I saw the loop of the rope drag the new, shiny duck into the steel stanchion with a sickening thud. Wearily, and with much concern about the damage inflicted, we hauled the log line back on board and inspected the fins. They were completely bent. This was not a good result. Dead duck. Crushed.

The second officer fixed me with a terrifying glare. 'Go and get the spare rotator, Cadet! Let's try smashing up that one shall we?'

Over the next few weeks we discharged cargo at a run of ports; Bathurst, capital of The Gambia, Freetown in Sierra Leone, Monrovia in Liberia, Takoradi and Tema in Ghana; Lagos, Port Harcourt, Sapele and Warri in Nigeria, Port Victoria in the Cameroons, Matadi and Boma up the Congo River and finally Luanda in Angola.

The Gambia is a smiling mouth under the hook nose of Dakar. This thin wedge of land is thrust into the larger landmass of Senegal. Its width was governed (so I was told) by the distance a cannon ball shot could reach to either bank of the river, an area that could be defended by an 18th century British man-of-war. However, cannon balls lose useful velocity after one mile. As Gambia is about ten miles wide, that would be considerably more than a long shot.

The Portuguese established the Gambia River as a slaving port. In 1765 the British took over, but The Gambia had gained its independence only the year before we sailed into port. Taking a pause from my cargo work duties, I looked over the side at the miserable, uninviting hinterland and had no regrets about not being able to take shore leave. Bathurst was just too hot. Decades later I was astonished to learn that it had become a tourist destination. I cannot think what commends it to tourists.

In Lagos a tailor came aboard and, for a very reasonable sum, ran up two shirts and shorts with legs much shorter than the standard 'knee tremblers' issued by the Miller, Rayner, Haysom, naval outfitters in Liverpool. Another canny salesman who came aboard looking for custom had a nice line in curved occasional tables with detachable legs made of local hardwood which I proudly took home and still use fifty years later.

Luanda at that time was still run by the Portuguese and was considered a very seedy run ashore. The dim blue light in a bar a short walk from the ship failed to hide the girls' raddled complexions. The lazy rhythm of the music and the high price of the warm, watery beer added to the mood of vague threat. I was glad to leave. Each port had its own idiosyncrasies, which provided an educational experience for a naive youth in his first year at sea.

Somewhere off the coast we gave another piece of kit a rare test. The Kelvin Deep Sea Sounding Machine was rigged aft at the poop railings. Approaching land at 150 fathoms the Captain ordered soundings as a cross-check on our dead reckoning position as thick cloud and hazy horizons had prevented decent astro fixes.

The ruddy faced second officer took me aft. 'Don't fuck this up, Cadet,' he swore at me. Unsurprisingly.

Together we attached the twenty eight pound lead weight to the wire and then carefully lowered it to the waterline. Checking the rate of fall with the drum brake, he allowed the piano wire to run free. I held an L-shaped feeler bar hard against the fast running wire. The moment the wire slackened under my fingers I knew that the bottom had been reached, and I cried out 'Slack line!' and the second officer read out the depth from the dial. Inserting two winding handles onto the barrel we sweated up 180 fathoms of wire. Arms aching, we went back to the chart room to cross check our position against the depths on the chart.

On arrival at Freetown *Eboe* picked up twenty extra Krooboys needed for loading logs up the Creek ports, and the dirtier ship maintenance tasks. One Krooboy was the laundry man. Even cadets could send their laundry away to be dhobied. For very little cash our dirty white tropical uniforms were washed, starched, beautifully ironed and delivered to our cabins. One day as we were walking aft, we saw the dhobi man on the poop deck, thrusting thin arms into the soapy suds of his tin tub. He energetically rubbed across a wash board a large mottled object, which he wrung out with a vigorous twisting motion, shaking open a shapeless bundle. I nudged my fellow cadet in the ribs. 'I see the dry cleaner is hard at work on your Harris Tweed jacket, Jim.'

Freetown is an ex-British colony with a legacy of administrative buildings and churches. Walking ashore at eight o'clock on Sunday morning, I arrived at a church at 0900 to discover that I had had a fruitless walk; the service had been held an hour before to beat the heat. Strolling back to the ship I came upon a colourful street market, rather different from Chipping Norton high street. Local women, dressed in brightly patterned dresses, heads swathed in lose, colourful turbans, sat on low stools at the side of the road, guarding low pyramids of dusty fruit and toiletries. The sun slammed into my back and produced an instant sweat which trickled down my armpits. I was too hot to barter in the still, humid air.

We sailed on to Takoradi, but as there were no berths for us we moored to fixed buoys. I learned for the first time the complex procedure involved in hanging off the anchor, whereby the heavy anchor cable could be led out to the for'ard buoy and secured with a massive shackle.

First the anchor was lowered a short distance and hung off with wire ropes and lashed back to the bitts. I was sent over the side on a Bosun's

Chair, and suspended above the anchor. The weight now being released from the cable I was able, with much shouting and direction from above, to locate and split the joining shackle two fathoms above the stock. A light nylon rope was now secured to the end of the anchor cable and hauled away to the buoy by a rope boat. This rope was sent back to the ship, turns taken on the windlass barrel end (warp end) and heaved in, thus hauling out the cable to the buoy, which was shackled on.

The stern was secured with two heavy cable-laid manila ropes run out to the after buoy and secured with two large shackles. Now *Eboe* was safely secured against any West African storms that might sweep through the harbour. If riding only to a single anchor unloading to lighters alongside causes problems for passing traffic when the ship swings to tide or wind.

Whereas the dockers in Takoradi were friendly, helpful workers I found those of Lagos could be intimidating and difficult. We were trading in the middle of the Biafran war, and the Nigerian soldiers gave our Igbo stewards, who came from Biafra, a very hard time. I heard about a steward on *MV Accra,* an Elder Dempster passenger liner, who was arrested in his cabin and shot dead. A fellow cadet said that they had seen the bullet mark embedded in the cabin bulkhead.

Port Harcourt between 1967 and 1970 was the capital of the self-declared state of Biafra. Elder Dempster still ran ships into the Delta. Commerce was king. The war which killed one million people had little impact on us cadets.

A Russian fish factory was in port and a game of football was arranged between us. We got hammered and so had the privilege of inviting the winners on board to a boozy dinner afterwards. The cook prepared a large tuna, fresh out of the sea that day. The beer flowed, our limited cadet ration relaxed for the night. Our honoured guests were excellent singers who entertained us with many folk songs sung in mesmeric bass voices, redolent with Slavic sadness. Our attempt to repay the compliment by singing rugby songs was pathetic by comparison.

Eboe proceeded to Sapele then on to Warri via the dense Niger Delta jungle. On arrival at the Bonny River Bar company regulations required the taking of soundings to confirm depth of water under the Bar. Shifting sands in an estuary can reduce under-keel clearance, threatening safe passage.

The bosun rigged a platform swung out from the hull, protected by stanchions and chains. He prepared the hand lead line, rigged with a nine pound lead weight, carefully arming it with tallow wax on the hollow base. Stepping up onto 'the chains', the bosun grasped a double coil of light manila rope in each hand. Carefully balancing himself, he swung the lead round a couple of times and cast it well for'ard. The sudden slack on the line told him that it had touched bottom. Waiting until the ship was right over the weight, he felt with his fingers for the *mark*, a piece of knotted rope, cloth or leather, which indicated the depth (essential when working in the dark).

'By the mark five!' called the bosun. In his hand was a strip of white calico; five fathoms, (thirty feet) of water lay beneath the hull.

'By the deep four!' he called (four fathoms—*unmarked* depths are called *deeps*). I watched the bosun's easy action, as after each cast, he rapidly gathered the rope in a loose coil and hefted the heavy lead, swinging it far forward to take the next sounding.

The tallow base revealed the type of bottom found; sandy, gravel or shells and so gave an additional piece of information to aid confirmation of position when compared to the chart. (A man who made a mess of the job, or just pretended and so didn't get a good sounding was just 'swinging the lead'.)

Once the ship had crossed the Bonny River Bar, the native pilot approached with his entire family packed into two canoes. A derrick was swung over the side, and the wooden pilot ladder dropped down over the fifteen foot high slab-sided hull. Once the pilot and his little clan had clambered up, the canoes were hoisted aboard and landed on the boat deck. They quickly made themselves at home under the shelter of the lifeboats. It was here that the pilot and his family received their food and slept during the several days that we transited the Delta region. The mate hated the mess they made on his clean, white holy-stoned timber decks.

Rule 14 of the Rule of the Road at Sea (Collision Regulations) states that 'when two power-driven vessels are meeting head-on, both must alter course to starboard so that they pass on the port side of the other.' This also applies in narrow channels. So when the pilot decided to alter course to port to avoid an approaching vessel the Captain could see an imminent collision and strongly countermanded his order.

'Belay that! Hard-a-starboard, Quartermaster!'

At all times the Master is in command and the pilot advises. But it makes for a difficult relationship when one cannot trust the other.

Getting around the sharp river bends required abnormal ship manoeuvring procedures. On the approach to the sharp bend, a ship was deliberately run aground into the soft bank of the mangrove swamp whereupon (old hands enlightened me) dozens of monkeys swung out of the trees and into the rigging and dropped onto the deck. But no monkeys came aboard that trip. Full ahead on the engines, wheel hard-a-port and the ship gradually swung her stern to starboard. Full astern brought her bow sucking wetly from the muddy bank, until clear water permitted 'slow ahead' as we slowly turned to port around the bend. This was repeated many times during a busy trick on the wheel, until arrival at the next creek port. It is not a manoeuvre I observed on the rivers and estuaries of Europe.

We sailed deeper up the creeks with palm thatched village huts set along the shoreline. Small children paddled out in canoes to wave and shout greetings, handling their large canoes with ease. Most impressive.

Sapele is famous for its huge hardwood trees, felled to make musical instruments and car dashboards. We loaded them in vast ten or twenty ton logs. They were lowered into the hold and dragged into position. A wire was lead through a snatch block to obtain an angled purchase back to the winch on deck. The snatch block was secured with a wire grommet (a weak point like a fuse) designed to fail before the overloaded wire shredded. As the huge logs were hauled into place my job was to dodge between the shifting loads and paint a coloured separation mark on each log to indicate its port of discharge. Whilst skipping nimbly over the wet, slippery logs, adding my splodges of paint, a grinding noise indicated the imminent destruction of the wire grommet. Warned by a howl from the dockers on deck, I jumped down into a safe hole as the hauling wire and snatch block zipped across the length of the hold like a cheese wire. Avoiding the cheese-cutter was a close run thing at times. Working in these lively conditions sharpened my senses somewhat.

The ship's bar was run by the Second Steward, who opened up at lunchtimes and in the evenings. The smoke room was a good focus for social gatherings, a welcome space to enjoy a beer at the end of a long working day or when off watch. And prevented secret drinking—and drinking to excess; the curse of later decades when ships lacked a bar and thus a centre to social life.

Somebody would bring out their guitar on board and lead the watch below in singing sea shanties and ballads: *'It was on the Sloop John B, or: 'In South Australia I was born.'*

Movies were shown on large 35 mm reels, usually four to a film. The clattering of projector sprockets signalled the start of the film, and we settled down and forgot the watery world outside for a while to enjoy a beer and shout at the screen. We saw *The Magnificent Seven* twenty times and would recite snatches of the dialogue.

The table tennis table was slotted under the sheltered after-deck. In port furious games released pent up energy. Playing at sea was more challenging. The ship had a habit of dipping the table away from the ball; another winning shot missed.

The cadets' accommodation was situated on the poop deck. Two double bunks filled the compact cabin, mattress and occupant held in place with high-sided wooden boards. There were showers but one room was equipped with a square bath, fitted with a tap labelled *Hot Salt*. Give that a try, I thought. At the end of a long day on deck, I eased my aching muscles into the soothing, hot water. Pleasure quickly changed to disappointment. I took a fresh-water shower to rinse off the bitter, sticky salt deposits.

Landlubbers take water for granted. At sea every drop has to be carried for a voyage that can last for several weeks. After a while the water becomes brackish, with a metallic taste. As the water level reaches the mucky bottom of the storage tank the tap releases a stream of rusty water. Not very appealing. One solution is to generate freshwater from the seawater freely available but when *Eboe* was built in the 1950s this was a primitive science, hence the salt water baths.

Food is a very important part of a cadet's life and happily Elder Dempster were very good feeders. Preservation of food at sea in the 1960s was a more primitive science than today. Breakfast cereals became infected with minute, black crawling insects, too numerous to remove. Old hands soon taught the new boys to disdain the little bugs and just munch the cornflakes, ignoring the rim of dead insects on the edge of the milk. Polar Milk arrived in frozen blocks which didn't taste quite the same as fresh milk. But this was better than the sweet evaporated milk added to coffee and tea.

We sailed from Warri back down the creeks on a day's voyage to Port Victoria, Cameroon. As usual we arrived off port at dawn. The first streaks of sunlight broke the horizon and soon the heat of the tropical sun pressed down on us. Victoria was a surf port. There was no jetty to which the ship could make fast. So we anchored off and secured our stern to buoys. Cargo was offloaded into barges and taken ashore.

Sunday 8 May 1966 was my 18th birthday. No cargo was being worked. Because it was Sunday, not because of my birthday. We were moored in the bay, not comfortably alongside so we felt somewhat marooned. However, the local cricket club challenged us to a match. I preferred cricket and was pleased to be chosen. A liberty boat took us all ashore with whatever gear we could muster and what a motley crew we looked.

When we arrived at the oval, we saw that the only level part of the pitch was the wicket; the outfield looked as wavy and undulating as the sea. We spent a few happy hours whacking the ball about and, due to our burly chief officer scoring over 70, honour was satisfied with a good win and we were royally entertained by the local ex-pats. I was just about to get a glass of champagne in celebration of my birthday, when someone discovered that it was also the wife of Second Engineer's birthday—and not being as pretty as her, I lost out.

Eboe had also put up a football team, but they had lost and had gone back to the ship early, and discovered the case of birthday beer that I had set up for later. When the cricket team piled back on board late that night, tired but thirsty, the case was empty and the culprits fast asleep in bed.

Matadi lies twelve miles up on a sharp bend of the River Congo. The river racing out to seas swirls so strongly round this bend that it creates a powerful whirlpool, the Devil's Cauldron, just a few hundred yards off the jetty. To maintain steerage way against the flow, *Eboe* approached the jetty at full speed to forge though the drag of the whirlpool. 'Full speed astern!' ordered the Captain as she shook herself free of the water's grip and surged towards the jetty, bringing her smartly alongside.

After loading our cargo we set off back down the river. With a strong following current we proceeded at full speed to keep enough pressure on the rudder. *Eboe* slithered round sharp bends, brown stern wave boiling as grassy clods dropped off the banks, collateral damage in the run to the wide ocean.

It was time to return to England with our mixed cargo of African exports. We sailed up the west coast of Africa, cut through the Canary Islands, across the Bay of Biscay, up the English Channel, entered the wide Thames estuary, and followed the river up to Tilbury. Granted ten days leave, I was happy to head home and share my maritime adventures.

My family was still living in the hamlet of Heythrop in the Cotswolds. On 27th May I celebrated my birthday again. By now I had a collection of old flags which I draped around the trees and hedges, a fitting backdrop to lunch outside on a warm spring day. Memorable.

Crushed Duck

In two trips to sea I had changed from schoolboy to well-travelled man. After a short leave I was happy to receive orders to join *MV Pegu* in Liverpool.

SE Asia, China And Japan Routes

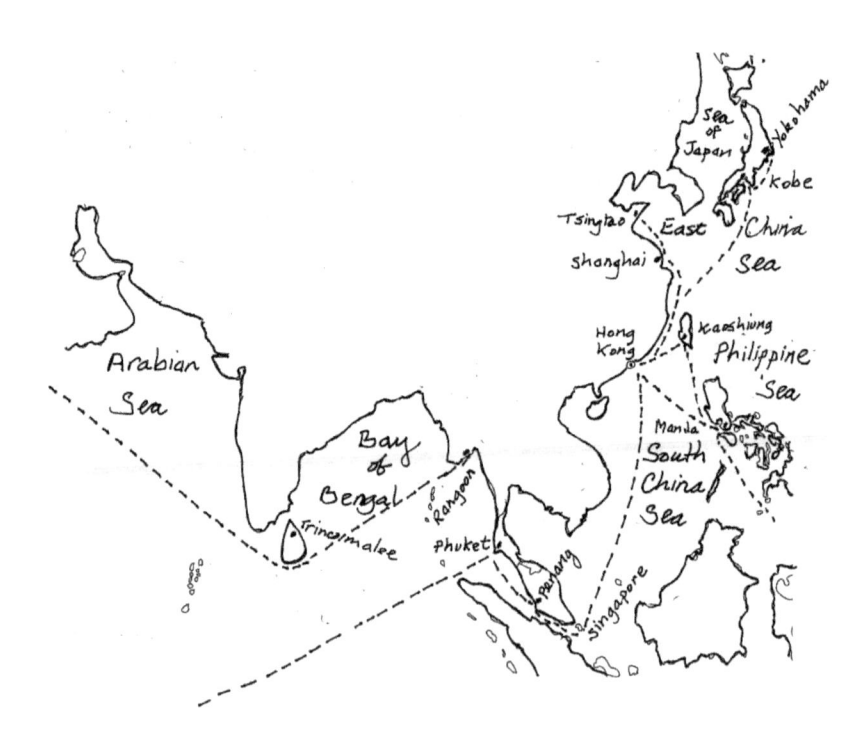

Chapter 3

EAST OF SUEZ

My train from Banbury arrived at Liverpool's Lime Street Station on a hot June afternoon. I jammed my gear in the waiting taxi. 'Huskisson Docks, please,' I called out through the window and jumped in.

I looked up at the *Pegu* and noted her five hatches, the array of derricks, accommodation amidships, her black-topped red funnel; not the big yellow funnel of my two previous voyages. The distinctive funnels of each shipping company were important not just for reasons of commercial identity. They helped establish our loyalty to the company, just as the Army builds up an attachment to a regiment. Passing ships at sea were checked out, as we peered through binoculars to confirm funnel shape and colour. We wanted to know the company; was it one of ours? If so, had they any news? My Merchant Navy Diary had on the inside covers dozens of funnels and badges of every British shipping line. I dipped into it regularly. *Pegu* was a Paddy Henderson ship, part of Alfred Holt's Ocean Steamship Co.

Escaping the clutches of the damaging seamen's strike of 1966, (which had a greater adverse economic impact than the miners' strike of 1984), we sailed, with our Burmese crew, for the Suez Canal. We four cadets worked hard cleaning and painting. I grew—eventually—to appreciate the joys of shining brass and gleaming varnish, though enthusiasm begins to wane after five ships. Today, when I travel to France on scruffy ferries that have let the standard drop I have to resist the urge to scrape off the flaking varnish with a fingernail.

We briefly stopped at Port Said, time enough for the bum boats to come alongside and sell us useless trinkets. I bought a very flexible camel whip made of red plated leather, its business end heavily weighted. But what would I do with a camel whip on board ship? Fellow cadet, Pete Bosanquet and I, also devoured a pineapple—each—with disastrous results.

Tonnage calculation for the Suez Canal differed from the standard net tonnage calculation on which port dues are levied. Therefore all the stores had to be emptied from the lockers kept by the bosun and the lamp trimmer. Piles of rope and paint and thimbles and wire and rags and turps and everything needed to maintain a ship were stacked on the number 1 hatch top. This huge effort was made to create an empty storage space, which were thus zero rated for Suez Canal charges.

Sunset did not stop our transit of the Canal. A powerful flood light was rigged on the fo'c'sle. Controlled by the bosun, its bright beam pierced the black night, to illuminate the way ahead. By day the passage was long and hot. The heat began to play tricks with my eyes. Above the sandy embankments bobbed a disembodied head, swathed in a *keffiyeh*. We sailed on. The missing body emerged from behind the shimmering sand dune, riding a camel.

No air conditioning alleviated the oppressive heat in our cabins. At 88°F (31°C) the skin of my sweaty forearms stuck to the writing paper. Jutting high above the canal banks, two advertisements were mounted on huge frames. An iconic jolly chap dressed in red proclaimed, 'Drink Johnny Walker!' Hardly suitable for a very thirsty cadet. The image of a modern jetliner (busily stealing our passenger trade) filled a billboard, under the banner, 'Next time fly BOAC.' On our slow boat to the Far East, it was a tempting offer.

Little did I know that the Suez Canal would be closed one year later for eight long and damaging years by the Egyptian-Israeli Six Days' War. Two Blue Funnel vessels were trapped in the Great Bitter Lakes. The effect on trade for India and other countries to the east of Suez was devastating. But for Paddy Henderson it was the end of trade with Burma. It was no longer economic; the extra two weeks around the Cape of Good Hope was too long.

A hand roughly shook my shoulder and shouted in my ear, dragging me from a deep sleep.
'On deck! Now! Berthing in thirty minutes! Stations for'ard and aft!'

After only two hours sleep I was not appreciative of the rosy dawn glow suffusing the eastern sky.

'Welcome to Port Sudan, Cadet; the best run ashore on the Red Sea.' The second officer's sarcasm was wasted on me, still unravelling the mysteries of foreign ports. The sun rose higher in the sky, its heat beat hard down.

You could smell Port Sudan from over two miles away, long before you could see it. I wrinkled my nose at the unpleasant odour, particularly sharp on my nostrils after days of breathing in clean fresh sea air. It was compounded of raw sewage and the odours of densely packed humanity. The scorching heat of a relentless sun on open sewers created noxious vapours which rose on the morning air and wafted out to sea.

Pegu nosed alongside the malodorous berth and made fast. It had taken over two weeks and over 4,000 miles to get here. The crew finished stripping off the tarpaulins and hatch boards. Derricks were raised and rigged overside, ready to discharge cargo. Native dockers, chattering and laughing, swarmed up the gangway and surrounded the five hatches, and some scrambled down the hold ladders.

'Batten down all doors except the one next to the gangway entrance,' ordered the chief officer. 'And put a watchman on the gangway. No point in tempting light-fingered natives.'

'Just look at those Fuzzy Wuzzies go!' exclaimed the second officer.

Thin white sticks sticking out at jaunty angles from a high pile of frizzy hair made an arresting sight. Lines of dark-skinned men, clad only in a ragged pair of shorts, snaked into the dark recesses of the hold; boxes were tossed easily back down the line to a rhythmic chant and the tween deck slowly emptied. The Fuzzy Wuzzies worked in bare feet; large misshapen pads without arches, often with one or more toes missing, guillotined by the sharp edge of a dropped packing case.

Two hours later I climbed back into my bunk for a brief kip. I was on night duty 1900 till 0700. Although the blowers were on, the heat in my cabin was stifling. Sweat trickled down my neck and armpits. It was going to be an unpleasant time in port.

By 1500 I gave up the struggle, rose groggily from my bunk and took a tepid shower. I pulled on my shorts and made sure my cadet's epaulettes were in place. I stepped out on deck and tugged my cap over my eyes, glad of its protection against the slamming heat of the sun. Over 39°C and climbing.

I scanned the busy deck. Cargo slings swung ashore; winches screeched, wire runners hummed through the blocks, shackles crashed into hatch coamings, over all the din of shouted calls and commands. Noise and confusion abounded. I retreated to the cool peace of the smoke room.

At 1900 I went out on cargo watch under the sharp eye of the second officer. A desiccated landscape dotted with crumbling houses and slightly larger administrative buildings lay behind the low warehouses. I did not feel tempted to explore the sights. This part of the world was notorious for robbery with violence. A white man ashore was too tempting a target. Even a cheap wristwatch and a pair of sunglasses were valuable to desperate locals.

'Keep away from those thieving A-rabs,' advised the mate. 'Stay on board ship in Port Sudan. There's a good run ashore in Rangoon. Wait until then.'

The casual racism was commonplace. In the 1960s, men of the British Merchant Navy had a very fixed view of their own superiority. Now we are so much more aware of race as an issue and are more careful what we say or permit ourselves to think. Perhaps those days, fifty years ago, were a time of simple honesty of expression, or maybe seamen simply lacked empathy.

The night cargo watch was cooler than the daytime shift but only just. By midnight I had been on duty five hours and although I had had some supper at 1800, I was starving. The ship's routine meant no cook on at night. The second officer and I looked glumly at an unappetising plate of sandwiches grimly imprisoned in greaseproof paper film. My boss had a better idea. Liberating the keys to the galley from a secret location, he applied the largest key to the steel galley door.

'Aha. Good-o. We're in luck!' he exclaimed with a satisfied grin.

There, on the shiny steel preparation surface, lay a dozen eggs, a loaf of sliced bread and the remains of a block of butter on a dish. Very soft. Rattling through the cupboards until he found a large frying pan, the 2/O dropped in a block of butter with a flourish, and, locating the correct burner, turned on a large gas tap. Soon butter was sizzling in the ancient, battered pan. He cracked six eggs and created a scrummy runny mixture. Into this he laid four slices of bread and turned them over constantly until they were soaked through. My stomach rumbled. The eggy aroma whetted my appetite, already sharpened by the illegal activity. In the middle of the night the catering staff were safely tucked up in their bunks, we hoped.

'Eggy bread! Get outside of that,' instructed my nightshift commander. 'Just what hard-working duty mates deserve!'

Relishing the comradely tasty midnight snack, I rapidly devoured my plateful. Sensibly covering our tracks, we washed up all the implements and plates, dried and put the gear carefully away. My partner in crime locked the door behind him, replaced the keys in their hiding place, and returned to the deck. No disasters had befallen the cargo. However, we need not have worried. The dockers had also stopped for their mid-shift break and were catching forty winks in the traditional manner, slumbering in various sheltered alleyways scattered about the ship.

The next morning the cook found the half empty carton of eggs, the depleted ration of butter, and a lingering smell of cooking. The keys were relocated to a better hiding spot and the midnight feast was not repeated. The next night we went hungry until breakfast in the saloon the following morning.

A power shower washed away twelve hours of dust and sweat. Changing into a clean set of whites I felt refreshed and restored, easily put away a large bowl of cereal followed by a full cooked breakfast and toast, washed down by two cups of hot, strong tea. Forty minutes later weariness hit me like a wet sock and I collapsed into bed for six hours of deep sleep.

Each new port was a fresh discovery but I was glad to be leaving behind noisome Port Sudan and escape to the clean open sea, bound for Rangoon.

A short two day passage down the Red Sea brought us to Aden for bunkers. This vital Royal Navy refuelling depot had been a British protectorate since 1839, but in 1966 the natives were getting restless and so the British Army, in the form of the Argyll and Southerland Highlanders, were keeping the peace. A Royal Navy warship lay quietly alongside the berth as we ghosted passed.

'Dip the ensign, Cadet, and be quick about it!' ordered Captain O'Sullivan. I dashed aft and as the *Pegu's* bow came level with the warship's stern I dipped the flag briefly to half-mast. I laughed to see an RN rating running aft to return the compliment before it was too late. It was good to catch the Navy on the hop.

Later that day, bunkering complete, *Pegu* set sail, dipping her ensign as before to a more alert Royal Navy. As the dry, desolate landscape of Aden fell astern, we skirted the island of Socotra, a dangerous coast of jagged rocks, and headed out into the Arabian Sea. Poring over the chart of the coastline I wondered what lay behind its harsh, arid edges. It was a country I would one day like to explore.

The next leg of the voyage took almost two weeks as we crossed the Arabian Sea, the Laccadive Sea, rounding the jewel of Ceylon slung below the neck of India. *Pegu* headed on, up the Bay of Bengal towards Rangoon. Crossing invisible watery borders, we sailed ever closer to the mysterious Far East.

Sundays at sea was Captain's Inspection Day. Captain O'Sullivan was very Old School, a gruff, white haired man with a trim, white goatee beard. He always wore his cap on duty, and set a good example of self- discipline that I was beginning, slowly, to appreciate.

Our cadets' cabin was scrubbed from top to bottom, toilets thoroughly cleaned, all ledges dusted, beds made up with fresh linen. Once the senior cadet was satisfied, we mustered outside our cabins dressed in crisp whites, standing to attention, caps on. It was a nervous moment as the Captain appeared, looking immaculate in whites, wearing his cap with 'scrambled egg' on the peak. More importantly, he wore a pair of white gloves. With his index finger he ran his hand over high, hidden ledges and peered closely at his finger tip. We passed muster. Much relief.

We proceeded on our voyage onwards to Rangoon, across the Bay of Bengal, edging to the north of the Andaman Sea and into the Irrawaddy Delta. The third officer was happy to let me check our position on the chart as well as keep a lookout over the empty ocean.

Did I ever see the Alguada Reef Light when we sailed through the Preparis North Channel? Probably. The jagged rocks of the Alguada Reef lies twenty two miles south of Cape Negrais; a considerable danger to mariners. Fifty years later, an ornate brass container from this famous light is now one of the treasures aboard the *HQS Wellington*. My interest thus piqued, I recently discovered that the genesis of this light lay in the expansionist British Empire and its reach into Burma.

The design of the Alguada Reef Light was based on that at Skerryvore Lighthouse, guarding the rocks of Tyree, in the Outer Hebrides. Its construction had been ordered by the Raj which had incorporated the country into British India during the period of three Anglo-Burmese wars between 1824 and 1886. The British had sent the last king into exile and abolished the monarchy.

In 1853 the Governor of India commissioned Mr Alan Stevenson, (of the famous lighthouse engineers), to produce designs for a series of lighthouses. The actual construction was undertaken by Captain Alan Fraser, Royal Engineers, who insisted that it be made more substantial by using granite. One hundred and one years after it was completed in the teeth of terrible gales, I was another in a long line of navigators grateful for its soaring presence, its white flash every ten seconds at the top of its 161 foot tower, guiding us safely away from the rocks and into the Mouths of the Irrawaddy.

The seeming indestructability of the Alguada Light obscures the awful grind involved in its construction. Lighthouses, with their elegant grace belying their enormous strength, invite mariners and landlubbers alike to pause and reflect upon the sweat and toil that has gone into their construction, and be thankful.

As the distant banks of the Irrawaddy emerged out of the mist so I began to pick out exotic Asian features in the landscape. Rising above thick jungle undergrowth were distinctive golden pagodas, but no sign of roads or villages. I stood lookout on the wing of the bridge as we made our way closer to the capital, Rangoon. It was the time of the wet monsoon. The morning rains fell warmly but relentlessly onto my cap, dribbled down across my face and finding gaps in my collar, soon soaked through to my skin. Distracted from my duties, I watched the rain run off the edge of my yellow oilskins jacket and saturate my thin cotton shorts. I felt its cool fingers crawl down my leg until it reached the tops of my neatly pulled-up long white socks, thence into my Blanco'd canvas shoes, emerging out of my toecaps in a thin white trickle. I followed the thin line wriggling across the teak planking, along a pitch seam and down into the scuppers. I looked up to see a river craft pass down our starboard side. Too late to report it.

The monsoonal downpour dictated the rhythm of the life of we four cadets over the next three weeks, as the deck officers attempted to discharge cargo under the pressure of two conflicting demands; to keep the cargo dry and to unload it it as rapidly as possible. Each hatch needed a temporary cover. A long wire was rigged fore and aft from which was draped a simple triangular tent. Although lashed to the hatch coamings, the sides inevitably sagged under the weight of rainwater. Our job was to bail out these deep pools every half-hour. The pointlessness of the exercise became apparent at the end of the morning downpour. Before we had completed our Sisyphean task, the dockers untied the rope tails along the long edges and released cascades of water down into the hold. Much yelling all round. The mate was not happy and blamed us. If we were unlucky the afternoons were a repeat of the morning. It took three weeks to discharge what had taken a few days to load in Liverpool. Manufactured goods out, raw products home, but of the precise details, this cadet of only three voyages had not a clue.

Leaning over the taffrail we watched the locals commute to work over the watery highway. Crossing the river were small boats overloaded with colourfully dressed commuters. Whizzing up and down the waterway were oversized canoes powered by big, noisy engines. The helmsman, or *sarang*, lowered the balanced propeller shaft into the water and off screamed the canoe at full throttle, fast and dangerous.

On one slightly drier morning, with the sun beating down, the *Pegu* crew battened down the hatches, lowered derricks into their crutches and secured all for sea. We headed across the Indian Ocean to Trincomalee in northwest Ceylon, over one thousand miles and nearly four days away. This vast, natural harbour had been a very useful base for the Royal Navy during the war. My father came here during his war service. And here I was twenty years later.

My fellow cadet, John, arrived in Trinco with pneumonia. He was very ill. The doctor was called out to us whilst at anchor in the bay. As we were to be in port for a week the doctor prescribed a series of penicillin injections which were to be given ashore daily, it being too far for him to come out by boat. Poor John was bundled into a launch, shivering uncontrollably, and taken to a local hospital. I went to visit him and discovered that he had been housed in a damp, grey room—the maternity ward. The women and babies had been unceremoniously moved out and were camped in the corridor. John looked a miserable sight, the tropical humidity causing the walls to sweat with moisture; quite the wrong place for a patient suffering from pneumonia.

When I reported the situation to the Captain on my return I was thankful that he immediately arranged for my friend's transfer back to the ship, ordering the doctor to make the daily voyage out by launch to give his injection. Surrounded by his friends and in the comfort of his own cabin, he soon made a rapid recovery.

In the middle of August *Pegu* set off on the 7,000 mile, twenty four-day return voyage to Liverpool via the Suez Canal, my last opportunity to enjoy that historic seaway. Thence we made our way through the

Mediterranean Sea, passing the ancient Roman city of Cyrene on the Libyan coast, Benghazi just round the headland. Our next landfall was the island of Malta, a blob off the boot of Sicily, before rounding the jutting peninsula of Cape Bon, sheltering the ancient city of Carthage. Onwards we sailed along the mountainous coastline of Morocco, between the Pillars of Hercules, transiting the narrow Strait between Gibraltar and Ceuta, a Spanish enclave on the African mainland. Spain still wants to kick the British out of Gibraltar but refuses to return Ceuta to Morocco. Or even its larger sister-city, Melilla.

The sheer face of the Rock was a grand sight, and as we entered the Atlantic Ocean we could feel our bow lift to a long swell, echoes of a distant storm. Rounding Cape Trafalgar, we headed across to Cabo de Sao Vicente, and rolled northwards in a quartering swell up the Iberian Peninsula to Cabo Finisterre and altered course off Cabo Tourinan, the most westerly promontory of Spain, and headed across the daunting Bay of Biscay.

Ushant, Eusa, Ouessant, marks the north-westernmost point of France. It is the only place in Brittany with a separate name in English. The 'Phare du Creach' marks the southern limit of the Celtic Sea and the southern entrance to the western English Channel, the northern entrance being the Isles of Scilly. Its 180 foot light can be seen for 37 miles, one of the most powerful in the world. The isle of Ushant is also famous for its maritime past, both as a fishing community and as a key landmark in the Channel approaches. It is found in the refrain of the sea shanty, '*Spanish Ladies*:

We'll rant and we'll roar like true British sailors,
We'll rant and we'll roar across the salt seas,
Until we strike soundings in the channel of old England,
From Ushant to Scilly is thirty-five leagues.

I bellowed out this shanty as a schoolboy at Heythrop Primary School. Little did I know that I would alter course off this tall black and white tower countless times over two decades at sea.

Once we had rounded Ushant and started making our way up the English Channel, the whole crew, officers and sailors included, began to suffer that ecstatic feeling of imminent homecoming we called "The Channels".

Someone got out a guitar and over a beer or two we sang the Beach Boys', '*Sloop John B*':

So hoist up the John B's sail
See how the main sail sets

Call for the Captain ashore
Let me go home, let me go home
I want to go home, yeah yeah
Well I feel so broke up
I want to go home.

Memories of home intruded into our waking and sleeping hours as the sights, sounds and smells of the Orient faded into the past. We closed the land off Devon and drank in the vision of the vivid green grass of England. Company policy decreed a Channel Pilot must be embarked off Brixham, because traffic in the shipping lanes in the Channel was unregulated. After several weeks at sea, the salt air had cleansed and sharpened my sailor's nose. I sniffed deeply of that wonderful smell of wet earth. As we sighted the White Cliffs of Dover even hard-bitten sailors became quite emotional.

Up we swept the wide Thames Estuary all the way to the narrow stretch off the King George V docks close to the heart of London. I was coming home. I couldn't wait to be paid off by the Captain. But wait we did. Impatiently.

Having stuffed all my gear into my cabin trunk, I dragged it down long alleys to the top of the gangway. I swung my sailor's kit bag over my shoulder, gripped the trunk handle, bid a quick cheerio to my shipmates and clattered down the gangway into a waiting taxi.

'Paddington Station, please!'

Whist I had been away, the family had moved from sleepy Heythrop to bustling Oxford. I enjoyed getting to know this city, home of dreaming spires. After two weeks of leave and family life, I ran out of money and needed to get back to sea.

I was glad to receive a letter from EDs, enclosing the usual train warrant. I was ordered to return to Liverpool and join *MV Mamfe*, back to West Africa. WAWA!

Chapter 4

LIFE ASHORE I

AFRICA TO THE FAR EAST

My sixties were swung at sea. *Deido* berthed at Casablanca and we went ashore. On entering the first bar we found I had a tot of every spirit I could see on a shelf above the bar. In Freetown on a run ashore we entered a local bar, dim and run down. Basic. Local girls forcefully pressed services which were not appealing; even less so when the dim light revealed what was on offer. A beer and a dance, swaying to the lilt and swing of the West African music which filled the smoky room was enough. Popping out for a pee, I found a handy ditch, but got lost on the way back. I discovered my error only when my foot fell through a space not previously encountered and I nearly followed it into a stinking sewer. The pavement slabs were missing. Not easy to spot on a pitch black night. Carefully retracing my steps I found my companions. They had not missed me.

Going ashore in Nigeria during the Biafran war could be a risky operation. You needed to carry your red Seaman's Identity Card with you at all times because the soldiers guarding the dock gates could be quite awkward. One evening in Lagos in a rush to get ashore I grabbed my ID card and dashed down the gangway. Squelching my way through the crunchy mass of thousands of cockroaches feasting on the scraps of spilled edible cargo I arrived at the dock gate guard post. I was cleared through the security gates with just a cursory glance at my ID. Coming back to my ship after a good night out I opened my folded ID card and to my horror, saw looking back at me a hirsute, square face quite unlike my smooth, long face. I had picked up the card of my cabin mate. I handed over the red pass, fully expecting to be locked up for the night. A quick glance, a casual wave and the guard let me through into the docks. With shaking knees I walked back to the ship, amazed and relieved.

In Takoradi we were taken on a jolly to the Alcan/ Alcoa aluminium works at Accra. This works had been paid for with Canadian and American money to make use of the ample hydroelectric power—and cheap labour—to turn bauxite into aluminium ingots for world export; in our case shipped in the holds of the *Eboe* back to Britain. A vast hangar-like space contained electric arc furnaces out of which flowed hot, molten aluminium, which was poured into moulds and set into solid shiny bars. We tried to lift a single bar and found it surprisingly heavy. Later, these long bars of shiny pure aluminium ingots were loaded on pallets and stacked in our lower hold. We had witnessed their genesis.

Aden. Who could forget such a day in Aden in 1966?

I went ashore on my own soon after berthing. Little did I know what danger I was in from the locals. Grenade Alley was in the news. It was the time when the Yemenis were stirring up trouble, hurling grenades at British troops on patrol. (We seem to have gone full circle and the tribesmen are waging war yet again.) The roots of the unrest then lay in the many attempts to govern this recalcitrant race in the best interests of Britain. The state of Aden set up in 1963 was beginning to fall apart. Keeping Aden as a refuelling depot for the military as well as for merchant fleets was the big idea. Less than a year later a state of emergency was declared which was still ongoing when *Pegu* arrived to take bunkers.

Under a thin blue sky edged with craggy mountain peaks, I walked down the gangway to explore the city. The heat was intense. Barefoot men in skirts pulled between their legs wore an assortment of round hats. They called loudly to each other in Arabic, the sound harsh to my ears. Weaving through the crowd I left the port area, found my way to a street of souvenir shops, and was pulled into a dim interior by clutching hands. I haggled for a Zippo cigarette lighter and brass nick-knacks, and departed.

On my way back to the ship I lost my way among the winding alleyways. Shopkeepers pestered me to buy more brassware. I became very keen to find a way out. A tall white boy walking by himself though an Arab city in turmoil was not in a safe situation. I needed to escape their increasingly persistent demands, bony hands clawing at my clothes. Heart pumping, I hurried down the narrow street and turned into a square overlooked by tall blank-faced buildings. I stopped to get my bearings. On a corner stood a squad of British soldiers. I walked up to one and asked for directions back to the docks. The broad red and white chequered band on his forage cap marked him out as an Argyle and Southerland Highlander. So did his broad Scottish accent as he pointed out the way. I was comforted by the thought that 'our boys' were in charge and quite happy to help. Just over a year later the British withdrew. End of an era.

The southwest monsoon kept us in Rangoon for three whole weeks. It rained every day. After a week Captain O'Sullivan took pity on us and gave us a note (worth ten shilling, I remember).'Take yourself off to the movies for a treat.' he said with a kindly smile. Down the gangway we trotted, free at last. First, we looked around the imposing, golden Shwedagon Pagoda. We took off our shoes and left them at the entrance; I worried that someone would steal them. Needlessly. The impressive one hundred and ten metre stupa in front of us dominated the skyline, shimmering in its thick coat of gold. Sunlight danced on thousands of diamonds and semi-precious gems on a pinnacle high above.

 I gawped at a huge, twenty four foot reclining Buddha, draped in a golden gown, regarding us with a seraphic smile. The hundreds of colourful temples, stupas and statues inspired awe. The atmosphere was strangely calm and peaceful, so different from my experience of European cathedrals and churches.

 Later we queued for tickets and entered a large, comfortable air-conditioned cinema; relief from the humidity and heat outside. The Burmese audience noisily crunched local snacks, releasing strange smells into the air. The film was '633 Squadron'. The tense drama of a dangerous bomber command mission was an engrossing but surreal experience in this calm Asian capital.

 We emerged from our cocoon into the wet black night. Streetlight on shiny tarmac. Under large black umbrellas lungi-clad young men, fingers lightly clasped, melted quietly into the night. Pure Lowry.

 A few days later the agent took the cadets and a few officers to see the War Graves Commission World War II graves just outside Rangoon. I was not prepared for what I saw. The entrance to this vast graveyard seemed like the gateway to a lush city park. An imposing stone archway framed flowerbeds edged with brilliant colour. In amongst the immaculate plantings several gardeners worked diligently to keep up the high standard.

The serried ranks of headstones sparkled white in the hot tropical sun. I leant down to read the inscriptions. Many were about eighteen years old. My age. It was a very sobering sight so early on in my career in the Merchant Navy. Just over twenty years before, these men had fought and died so that I could go freely about my life.

A series of arches over recessed bays contained the names of thousands of men for whom no remains could be found. It was a long list. Picking out their ages carved in stone invoked in me a novel contemplation on the transience of life.

Twenty one years later found me looking at another War Graves Commission Cemetery, this time in Archangel, northern Russia. In contrast, this was an unkempt field without bright flowers to adorn headstones with respect and honour. The Communist authorities appeared ungrateful for the lifeline extended by Britain to their erstwhile wartime ally. But the men who had died on the North Atlantic convoys were also barely out their teens and had hoped for a longer life.

On our voyage home, *Pegu* berthed in Trincomalee, Ceylon. Land of exotic promise. I leapt at the chance to explore it. A £5 taxi ride carried me, three officers and a wife to the ancient Buddhist city of Anuradhapura, a two hour drive inland along rough roads through tropical scenery and scattered rural villages. The taxi deposited us at the entrance to the rambling temple complex. 'Built in 450 BC,' proclaimed the sign by a temple. Quite old, then. Monkeys swarmed over ancient rocks covered in tree roots, topped by a lush green canopy.

Writhing, bangle-covered, semi-naked bodies carved in stone stood under stone arches. A youth wrapped in a clinging wet cloth washed languidly in an ancient, ruined pool. A wall of carved elephants lined an earthen path which led to a large stupa. Here was a sapling of the famous Bo tree, shelter to the Indian prince, Siddhārtha Gautama, whose enlightenment established the Buddhist faith. Planted in 288 BC, it is the oldest living tree in the world. I remember it well because here I lost the lens cap to my trusty Minolta STR 101 camera. The whole day was an extraordinary adventure. I was sorry that my fellow cadet had been too ill to enjoy it.

Bangkok. A city of heat, traffic and golden temples. Pale memories of entering a bar, a friendly welcome, a glass of cold water, moisture beading the outside, a refreshing hot towel and a cold beer. Recovery.

Chapter 5

WEST AFRICA WINS AGAIN

'WAWA!' we said when a cock-up occured. As it often did. This time I blamed the heat. I was the only cadet and I had been given Sunday off at sea to work at my maritime studies, the correspondence course necessary to prepare for the course ashore in Liverpool at the end of the trip. After long days working watches and additional overtime on deck, I was feeling very tired and decided to have a break. Instead of opening my textbooks, I slumped on my day bed and read a good book.

Alas, the grumpy chief officer caught me red-handed.

'What the fuck do you think you are doing, you idle bastard!'

I was hauled before the Captain, standing to attention before his desk as he gave me a thorough dressing down.

'Cadet, I expect you to work on deck, on the Bridge and to do your studies on weekends at sea. You cannot succeed unless you work hard. You are wasting the opportunities the company is giving you. You are a feckless time waster! Now go back to your cabin and knuckle down to your studies!'

'Sir.'

I was now over 18 years old and found it very difficult to accept being spoken to as if I was a schoolboy. I could feel humiliating tears of frustration forming in my eyes and I didn't want the Old Man to see them. I accepted my telling off silently, turned about and went back to my cabin. However, I was not in a studying mood any more.

Thereafter, before I was granted any shore leave, I had to recite by heart one of the thirty one Collision Regulations, the Rules of the Road, the mariners' Highway Code.

West Africa 1, Cadet 0.

Sailing through blue seas south of the Canary Islands, a good breeze soon blew the cobwebs out of my hair. My mood recovered. I went to my favourite place off duty, right for'ard, in the eyes of the fo'c'sle, and leant over the bulwark. I was in luck; there a squad of dolphins was dancing through the bow waves alongside us. Suddenly they dived right underneath the ship, and sprung high out of the water on the other side. It was a wonderful, hypnotic sight.

Mamfe flew the Guinea Gulf house flag from the main cross tree halyards but a large yellow Elder Dempster funnel dominated her profile. She was not as big as some company ships, at 400 feet long and 6,300 dwt, but she had beautiful lines, especially along her midships accommodation. Built in 1947 to carry twelve passengers, we appreciated the legacy of spacious wooden promenades on each accommodation deck. A luxury compared to today's sterile steel boxes.

We called at the usual string of West African ports. I did day work with some watch keeping, mostly keeping lookout. Staying awake was difficult if no ship's navigation lights broke the dark, nor even a lighthouse to blink reassuringly in the night. Any ship that did pass within a mile or two were hailed, 'WHAT SHIP?' on the Aldis lamp. It was good to chat with another cadet across the water—and an opportunity to practice my Morse code skills.

My day was split into two shifts: 8 to 12 and 1 to 5. I was set to work chipping, washing down, greasing and polishing. The mate appreciated a bright and shiny ship. And painting. There was always painting. If at sea I might either be working from a bosun's chair or a long stage. I preferred the latter because it meant working alongside a buddy, giving us time for a bit of chat as we worked. There were no safety harnesses, no goggles and no hardhats. The rule was one hand for yourself and one hand for the ship.

With a bosun's chair and a coil of rope over my shoulder, I scrambled up the mast ladder to the top, fifty feet above the deck. I rigged the rope through the sheaves of a block (attached to a pad eye) and let the tail fall to the deck far below where it was led to a winch drum. Several turns of rope around the drum provided the friction sufficient to prevent a rapid descent. Inserting myself in the chair, a fellow cadet eased the rope over the warp end to lower me down the mast in easy stages as I applied soojee, grease, or paint as required.

In port I assisted the sailors clean out tanks, sweep up empty holds and clear out rubbish. Dunnage was heaved up on deck and stacked neatly for disposal overside once at sea.

Rust is the collateral damage in the chemical warfare between saltwater and steel. A rusty ship was a sign of a badly run ship and rust was to be ruthlessly exterminated. Alongside in port provided the opportunity to rig two or three stages overside, two men to a stage. Sailors and cadets made a grand racket chipping the hull and loudly singing snatches of pop songs. The bosun and his mate kept us supplied with red lead primer, undercoat and topcoat. After several days of hard work a bright shiny black hull emerged. This was very satisfying particularly when a scruffy ship alongside became the butt of our rude remarks.

I stretched up, the heavy weight of the long bamboo dragging at my arms. I pressed the roller loaded with black paint hard against the hull high above, the bobbing raft beneath my feet making it difficult to maintain contact and apply a layer, and move on. A working platform built out of planks lashed to empty oil drums enabled us to reach the flare of the hull for'ard of the rudder. And the cool shade provided by the overhang kept us out of the scorching tropical sun.

It was vital to avoid the thunderbox. The West African dockers were not allowed to use the toilets inside the accommodation for security and hygiene reasons. It was a long walk to the shoreside loos. The solution was for the ship's carpenter to construct a timber framework attached to the steel taffrails and positioned over the water. Privacy was provided by strips of burlap. Voila! A thunderbox. Pollution of the harbour water was not an issue.

After several weeks the trip to the tropics was over and we returned to the cold of England in mid-December. I was still learning my craft and it was time to go to College. What could Liverpool teach me about life?

Chapter 6

NAUTICAL STUDIES I

By order of Captain Smallwood all the cadets were gathered in the recreation room for a good talking to. Rumour had it that some strange misbehaviour had been going on. He swept his ice-blue stare about the room. He had our full attention.

'Some of you young men put your pricks where I wouldn't put my walking stick!' he bellowed, red in the face.

What had been going on? It was a mystery as to who he was talking about. We were not part of the Swinging Sixties and looked at our feet and fidgeted. There followed a lecture about morals and cleanliness which put us off going out for a beer that evening.

After a happy Christmas leave I had reported on Sunday, New Year's Day 1967, to River House at Garston, Liverpool for the start of term on the next day for my first three-month Mid-Apprenticeship Release Scheme. Life after studies sometimes got out of hand but we worked hard in class.

We Elder Dempster cadets enjoyed the luxury of single cabins, unlike the Blue Funnel cadets next door in Aulis House who had to bunk up six to a room. It had been opened five years when I arrived. At the time a total of ninety midshipmen and engineering cadets attended courses at the Riversdale Technical College just across the road. Elder Dempster was keen to ensure that their midshipmen had a thorough grounding in theory to match the practical training at sea.

Nautical Studies I

After sharing cabins at sea with up to four cadets we much appreciated having our own single cabins. We enjoyed meals together in the dining room, relaxed in the recreation room and hobbies room, and played games at least weekly on the large sports field.

Silence reigned. Someone had thrown a huge stack of old Beano comics into the rec. We relished a little schoolboy nostalgia as we chuckled over familiar stories. After three months away the music charts were filled with strange names and new songs. Top of the Pops got us back in touch, as did the antics of 'The Monkees' TV show. *'I'm A Believer!'* we shouted at the telly in the corner of in the crowded room.

A welcome break from the classroom was preparing for our EDH tickets (Efficient Deckhands). I well remember how fiendishly difficult it was to splice an eye in stiff unyielding wire. In Lifeboat School we attempted to row—in unison—a large ship's lifeboat. This was difficult even in the calm of a sheltered dock. Far out at sea exposed to the elements and a lumpy swell it would have been extremely challenging. Luckily I never had to try.

Learning to sail was a testing experience in the midst of winter on the saltwater lake overlooking the Mersey. Being approached at ramming speed by kamikaze cadets required an instant response. Tiller up too hard and the result was capsize. Legs went totally numb in the time it took to wade back to the dinghy through three foot of freezing water, re-right her, clamber aboard and bail out. Useful skills had been acquired by the time we had sailed triumphantly back to base. Terry Beggs was an inspiring instructor and the only tutor's name I remember during my whole time at college. With such generous and committed training facilities we felt assured us of a career for decades to come. Soon exams were over and my end of term report was posted home. The initially intimidating figure of Captain J Smallwood R.N. wrote encouragingly to my long suffering mother: *"Your boy has worked well,"* which must have cheered her up no end. My English grade in my last term at school had been E5. Whereas the English teacher thought that my work was *'slapdash and lacking evidence of solid learning and serious thought'*, I had now, according to my college tutor, scaled the heights of 81 percent, *'able, thoughtful and original.'* It was nice to be appreciated at last. Working in the vacuum of school was meaningless and without motivation for your average pupil. Applying learning in a useful, relevant and interesting environment helped me shine. My college report was encouraging: *'Worked conscientiously throughout. Results quite pleasing.'* I might have found the work difficult but the stimulating environment made a huge difference. For the first time in my life I felt that, academically, I was going somewhere.

I would put all that theory into practice at sea aboard the company's training ship. But first we had to be kitted out. We were taken to Greenberg's, the famous Merchant Navy outfitters which occupied an ornate four-storey building on Park Street (which has since been demolished to make way for an ugly housing block). The staff took us down long dark corridors stacked high with cardboard boxes. We were issued with denim jackets, work trousers, T-shirts with sleeves edged in blue, and a leather pouch containing a sharp Green River knife, with its companion marlin spike, strapped to the waist with a leather belt. Now we were properly equipped to work on deck.

Commercial pressures led to the merger of our various companies into Ocean Fleets in 1968. This meant the abandonment of our Elder Dempster cap and blazer badges, symbols of our loyalty to the company. There was much resistance among the cadets and officers to the change. I appreciated how merged army regiments must feel on the demise of their beloved regiments with all their traditions.

By 1975 River House and Aulis housed 280 cadets. It spoke volumes for the rapid decline of the Merchant Navy that these wonderful training facilities fell empty only a few years later. Future officers were no longer being recruited and trained by the company. Contraction not expansion was now company policy. River House finally closed in 1986.

Chapter 7

CADET SHIP

'Very proud of this,' the bosun boasted, patting his beer belly happily. 'Cost me a lot of money!' On thin legs, a pot-belly clearing deck space before him like the prow of an old sailing ship, he moved with surprising speed, especially when preventing imminent disaster. He ran a crew of twenty cadets—all EDHs—with a firm hand, aboard *MV Fourah Bay*, the company training ship. But she had to pay her way, on the run between the UK and the usual West African ports from Freetown to Lagos.

The Master was the white-bearded Captain O' Sullivan from the *Pegu*, the stickler for discipline and cleanliness. In this he was ably supported by the chief officer, who briefed the bosun daily; under him the cadets were managed on deck day-to-day by a leadership team of three. On my second voyage the headman was Alan Provan, an affable, sharp-witted Scot. (I met him 50 years later at an FB reunion in Liverpool, where I soon discovered that *Fourah Bay* had been the excellent training ground for an extraordinary range of careers.)

On my final voyage the headman was 'Pop' Hawke, a tall, slim chap with sleepy eyes and a hook nose; Noddy Holdsworth was second headman. (So-called some said after Noddy Holder, a guitarist in the 'N'Betweens', forerunner of the glam rock band, 'Slade'.) Rory was lampy, the store keeper. He would not allow us to pour tea from the pot at smoko for at least five minutes after it had been made. 'Leave the pot,' he would drawl in a broad Irish brogue. 'Let it draw, let it draw.' He was a fount of tall stories that kept us all laughing.

We were kept busy; cleaning out the holds between cargoes, maintaining the running gear of the derricks, including the heavy lift, all the various blocks, running tackle, wires, winches and anchor cables. We chipped the hull from stages rigged overside. We shimmied up main masts to wash and paint the steelwork from bosun's chairs. Dressed only in a pair of shorts, I acquired a deep tan under the tropical sun; no sun cream was applied, just a spot of cooling Calamine lotion. After a winter at home, I burned easily. The deceitfully cool sea breezes only added to the damage. I pulled festoons of skin from my back. It made a strange, soft unzipping sound as it peeled away. Only after removing the second or third layer would a really good suntan get a grip by the time we returned home to the cool climes of England. I was proud of having one of the best tans aboard.

I thrived in this practical environment. I learned to steer a deep-sea ship, allowing for the heavy ocean swell without overcompensating. A wandering wake and the mate's shouted, 'Keep her steady on course!' kept me focused on the task.

After a trick on the wheel at night I went lookout for an hour. In the English Channel navigating through busy shipping lanes there were always plenty of vessels to report. Standing out on the wing of the bridge, wearing shirt and shorts on a warm, balmy night in tropical waters, the stars shining on smooth seas, felt good. Butting up the English Channel in a north-east gale, the bitter wind laden with snow, was grim. After an hour of that, going down for our watch below—the 'farmer' slot—to enjoy a strong cuppa and a doorstep sandwich, was a relief.

Lookout was not kept during the day. Instead the watch-keeping cadet was employed on duties in the vicinity of the bridge such as the eternal scraping of taffrails and applying of varnish, polishing brass, repairing ropework on pilot ladders and checking the lifeboats. Those cadets not on watch-keeping duties were employed on day work. I preferred turning-to at 0600 and working through till 1600, with 'smokos' for tea and lunch to break up the day.

Work started on holystoning the promenade decks before breakfast. A holystone was a large stone block held within a wire frame, attached to the end of a mop pole. Three men vigorously scrubbed their stone 'mops' along the grain of the wooden decks. Another man hosed down with seawater, until the deck gleamed white in the morning sun. Very Royal Navy.

Sea salt on white paintwork was removed daily with a soojee wash-down. I heaved myself up onto a metal taffrail to reach higher up the accommodation housing. I groped up to find a rail. No handhold. My foot slipped and my body lurched towards the edge. A hand pulled me back. Heart thumping, I dropped back down to the deck. Looking over side I watched the deep ocean slide by. 'Nearly a goner.' I thought. Man overboard at sea is not good. A Williamson Turn takes time. Steering the ship back down on a reciprocal course with the crew searching for a bobbing head in a mass of white wave caps does not often result in success. Almost too late I remembered the Golden Rule at sea: 'One hand for the ship and one hand for yourself.'

In port it was 'show time'. Stages were rigged to deploy the assault team. Battle was permanently waged against the Demon Rust. Three long planks were hung over the front of the accommodation housing bridge front. We scrambled on, checked friction lines, (three turns of the rope tail over the end of the plank, a catch turn over the horns) gear was handed over the bridge dodger and hung on hooks: buckets for washing down, chipping hammers, scrapers and tins of red lead. Thus well-armed, battle commenced.

The hatches below us yawned wide open from the top deck through the tween decks, right to the bottom of the palm oil storage tanks whose lids had been lifted up to allow for tank cleaning. Sitting on my little plank, I could see down to the very bottom of the ship, and thought, 'Ummm. That's quite a distance!' Checking my grip on the down hauls I added an extra turn of the tail rope and carried on working. Carefully.

Cleaning out palm oil tanks ready for loading the next day could mean very late nights—a 'field day'. The Mate revived our drooping energies by sweeting our midnight tea with a drop of whisky.

The cargo that filled the cavernous holds was loaded via the hatches. These openings in the main deck were strengthened by strong coamings. They were made watertight with a complex rig of beams, king beams, hatch boards and tarpaulins. On completion of loading the ship was prepared for sea. Our lives depended on doing a good job. Derricks swung the heavy metal beams athwart-ships into place. Two cadets shuffled out along the king beam over the hold like circus performers, holding an end of a 6 ft. x 2 ft. hatch board and slotted it up tight against its neighbour. Next three tarpaulins were pulled over the hatch boards and secured with three long, flat locking bars. Flat steel bars were dropped into place around the edge of the tarps, like an elastic band round a jam jar lid. Finally, wedges were driven tight round all sides of the hatch coaming to ensure that no angry sea could pick up the edges of the tarpaulins and rip them away, and allow a solid wall of 'green' water to penetrate the hold and flood the ship.

The sobering truth is that in a violent storm the might of the sea quickly finds out shoddy workmanship. Over the centuries many ships have been lost with all hands, especially in areas of confused seas and currents such as off South Africa, where the powerful Aghulas Current meets huge swells piled up by westerly storms. Three of the thirty seven vessels in which I served later sank, one with all hands.

Having secured the hatches the next job was the well-practised drill of lowering the derricks into their crutches, four to each hatch, and securing them tightly for sea. We raced to be the first team to have their hatch ready. Three turns of the lowering wire were wrapped around a winch warp end, the slack fed to guide the derrick down into its crutch, assisted by a man on each stay. To prepare all five hatches ready for sea, running gear, stays and downhauls for twenty derricks and two heavy lifts would take at least half a day.

In the 1980s my ships routinely left the berth and proceeded downriver with hatches open. The bosun pulled a lever controlling big electric motors which dragged strong chains linked to clunking heavy steel hatch lids. Flicking on the securing cleats made three hatches watertight in ten minutes. This mechanisation resulted in rapid reduction in manning levels. An 8,000 dwt break bulk ship in 1966 carried forty or fifty crew. By 1988 this had been reduced on my gearless bulk carrier to fifteen and still falling.

Obuasi was the first cadet ship from 1953 until 1961, when *Fourah Bay* took over. But after eight years her role as a cadet ship ceased. Manpower and the related training schemes had been dramatically pruned.

Life was not all deck work. Study periods were built into the week. Sundays at sea was split into study watches and sea watches. We carried an extra second officer who was our instructor. I needed to brush up on my Morse code, always a problem with me when 78 percent was a fail.

We completed correspondence course work in the floating classroom under the beady eye of the training officer in all maritime subjects such as navigation, naval architecture, seamanship, meteorology as well as mathematics, English and a smattering of engineering. I didn't like study and found it a real chore; it was even worse when on some ships I was the only cadet.

Sailing into Lagos one voyage we berthed behind a long row of distinctive yellow funnels; nine company ships Apapa-side. With several days spent at this our turnaround port, we had time to go down to Lagos Yacht Club and twice I was allowed to take out the company Tarpon class 17 foot dinghy. I had two hairy experiences trying to sail by myself as I wasn't too sure what I was doing. On one occasion a fellow cadet and I sailed the few miles down Lagos harbour to Tarkwa Beach, situated just inside the West Mole by the harbour entrance. Just beyond lay the Gulf of Guinea and the relentless rollers crashing onto nearby Lighthouse Beach.

We anchored just offshore and had a great time diving into the warm waters. We swam ashore, skipping over the hot, fine sand to buy an ice cream before swimming back. Unfortunately we had miss-timed the sail home and the afternoon breeze died away as the tropical night rapidly closed in. We suffered the ignominy of being towed home by a passing motor launch. We handed over the dinghy to an African Yacht Club boatman who was not at all happy about our very late return. On a later trip I made up for my error by spending many hours stripping down and applying marine varnish to the dinghy hull. It was good to get away and do something on solid land for a change.

A wall of scorching hot, oily flame roared towards us and I ducked, directing a powerful spray of water from my fire hose tightly gripped in both hands, my number two backing me up, the fat canvas tube bucking like a python. Edging slowly forwards, we beat back the hydra-headed beast until the searing red flames collapsed into the steel trays from whence they had sprung.

I had re-joined *Fourah Bay* for my last voyage, in Liverpool, in late October. All cadets had been sent on a fire-fighting course at the Fire Brigade Training Centre. Squatting in the middle of a large open space was a fire-burned shell—a steel mock-up of a ship's accommodation. Fires aboard ship in the middle of the ocean cannot be fought from outside, so we were learning to fight fires from the inside. Dressed in fire suits and fireman's helmets with full-face visors, we had far more kit than we would ever have had at sea. But it provided us with a very real, and alarming, experience. One big cadet with a fine bushy beard failed to obey the order to duck when entering the fire space, and emerged from the exercise with only half a beard. He took a trip the barber who shaved off the burnt remains. Lesson learned.

Mike's raddled face betrayed his addiction to drink. He downed a bottle of whisky in one after a dare. And was ill in his bunk for two days. No-one checked him out other than to open the cabin door an inch to see if he was still breathing. The smell of stale booze and vomit put us off. We callous cadets left him to get on with it. He looked in a mess when he emerged. But he was expected to turn-to on time. Do your work and keep up with your studies, or leave, was the expectation. I was more restrained in matters of drink and drugs; a few beers were fine but drinking to excess gave me such terrible hangovers that I did not repeat the experience too often. Cadets were allowed two beers a day, though obviously some found ways round this limit. A can of beer cost less than two shillings but running up a large monthly bar bill was out of the question. In my first year I earned £243 per year, £4.67 a week.

Ginger was my cabin mate on one trip. I had got to know him when at Riversdale House. Returning from a night out in downtown Liverpool on the 82C bus he could be quite rowdy, and on board he was very entertaining. He acquired an African grey parrot when in Warri, up the creeks. It roamed free in our cabin and chewed chunks out of the corner of my picture frame with his sharp beak. The parrot had a reputation as a good mimic, but try as we might, we failed to get it to speak a word. To avoid the Liverpool customs search gangs on their regular visits, Ginger smuggled the parrot off the ship when we docked. How? I have no idea but he had the makings of a successful importer.

Leaning over the taffrail shortly before sailing from Sapele, we saw Steve haggling in the gloom, making an illegal grass deal from a man on the quay. Clutching his plastic bag, he climbed the gangway and returned to the privacy of his cabin. 'It enhances life's experiences,' he muttered to this naïve cadet. 'It makes you let go of your inhibitions.' I left him to it.

After three voyages totalling nine months full of rich experiences, I finally paid off *Fourah Bay* on 18 December 1967. I hauled my gear down the gangway one more time and proceeded home to Oxford on Christmas leave.

Chapter 8

USE NO HOOKS

I ran with a light step over the hot sand, dived into the boiling surf and struck blithely through the sparkling sea. Beneath my innocently kicking feet the beach shelved steeply into the deeps. The ocean swelled like a giant's barrel-chest drawing breath. Heaving Atlantic rollers gathered me up, rolled me over and dumped me heavily on the hard shingle. The beast had not done with me yet. A watery coil held me fast and rolled my battered body back down the slope like a sausage. Fighting for breath, lungs bursting, I began to panic. A huge wave flung me beyond the reach of the foaming fingers and I staggered up the beach, freed at last from the grip of the wild waters.

A few days before I had carelessly poured a kettle full of boiling water on to my leg. I had not been paying attention during a slow cargo watch. The second officer had slapped on a pat of butter to cool it. It had sizzled nicely. And soon smelled awful. The crazy rolling in the rough sand had painlessly scoured my healing wound of peeling flesh, a saline rinse which swept the muck away.

Egori was berthed at Lagos, the officers and cadets on a jolly, enjoying the challenges of Lighthouse Beach on the Atlantic coast. Tarkwa Beach next door was considered rather tame...

I had joined my sixth ED ship in Liverpool on New Year's Day 1968, a good start to the year. Bigger than my last vessel, she too was built in the classic British style. Towering above the curved lines of the midships accommodation, her massive yellow funnel imparted a feeling of strength and power. Cabins, even for cadets, were fitted out with solid wood furniture. She proudly carried on her stem post the Elder Dempster Line company badge of red cross on a white background, Royal Mail crown in the centre. I was set to paint the details, seated on a bosun's chair, pots and paints swinging from hooks fixed to the seat. Far from the clatter of cargo work, I savoured my solo task.

After a voyage to West Africa of just over two months I arrived back in England in March. I needed to gain more sea time before going on in my second MAR course, so ED's Personnel Department posted me to the *Fian* for two weeks coasting round the UK whilst she discharged her cargo of West African timber and logs in Tilbury before back loading with manufactured goods.

I was sent home for two weeks leave then on to a Blue Funnel ship, the *Aeneas*, also discharging cargo in London. My duty as night watchman was to patrol the various parts of the ship, checking all was safe during the night when no cargo was being worked, machinery unattended and the crew fast asleep. All was silent in the docks.

I had been issued with a rickety clockwork check-in system that failed to rotate and so all the letter punch keys printed uselessly one atop the other. Quietly padding around the accommodation decks, the hum of a generator the only sound, I paused to locate the source of a strange muffled, rumbling sound coming from behind a cabin door. Very carefully, I turned the handle, and gently pushed. Loud snores emerged from a large, fat figure, fully dressed, flat out on a bunk. I had found the shoreside security guard. There he remained every night.

Sleep during the day was elusive. Roughly handled electric winches howled and juddered to a stop; slack wire whined loudly through metal sheaves; heavy crates hauled out of the tween decks crashed against the hatch coamings. Men bawled out warnings. Heavy crates were dropped. No matter, just personal effects. The injunction USE NO HOOKS, clearly stencilled on each hessian sack, was ignored. Each docker clutched a vicious curved spike, a piratical extension of their fist. These they plunged into the swollen sacks and dragged them into the stow, corners ripped, contents spilled.

One afternoon before going on duty I observed this organised mayhem with tired, somewhat bemused eyes. A two ton sling of sacks, bulging with costly pepper grains, rose swiftly from the hold. A fat sack caught against a sharp steel corner. The air rent with the harsh sound of ripping hessian as a cascade of black pellets rattled like coins onto the steel deck below. I reflected upon the price of a handful of pepper sold in the shops. It gave new meaning to the term 'cash flow'.

After this short but enlightening coasting experience it was time to return to nautical college.

Chapter 9

NAUTICAL STUDIES II

'It is my considered opinion that this student did not really endeavour to do more than necessary minimal work and is his own worst enemy.'

I did not agree with Head of College, Captain Rutherford's end of term report. I think he had the wrong man. I found my studies demanding, but I thought I was doing well and I was depressed by his words. There was little knowledge of dyslexia in those days. I wanted to make a success of my career so I knew that I had to make a bigger effort. But it was a struggle.

My final three month stint at Riversdale Road College had started at the end of April. I continued to find signals and navigation a challenge. I took comfort in the more positive comments in Seamanship, Naval Architecture, Meteorology, Engineering, English and Sailing. This was to be was my last training session until I crewed a much faster Dragon class yacht out of Royal Hong Kong Yacht Club two years later.

Study pressures were relieved in the pub. The 82C bus set us down outside the Seamen's Mission by the Pier Head. Here we downed a few pints over several cigarettes. We finished off the night at the seedy 43 Club in Catherine Street, where we danced with mini-skirted girls who had no small talk and left no lasting memories. I met a pretty girl at a party organised between us cadets and the local nurses' home and took her back to my cabin. My fumbling naiveté failed to prolong the relationship before I returned to sea, and left behind yet another girl.

Another missed opportunity was a visit to the Cavern Club, old haunt of the Beatles, who had long moved on. It was just not on our radar.

My time at college was mostly a productive, formative experience. The company brochure expressed the hope that *'by living together as a purposeful community, our midshipman and engineering cadets will acquire deep appreciation of their future careers as maritime officers and develop that esprit de corps which will stand the officers concerned and the company in good stead in the years to come.*

Lofty language indeed. I did not at the time appreciate my good fortune in receiving training from a company who believed in its future, and which was prepared to invest the time and money needed to inculcate strong company loyalty. It certainly shaped my attitudes to work and a commitment to the greater good. When I finally came ashore these values were not prevalent and I missed them.

I was glad when, at the end of July, our time at college was over and I went on home leave. After a week or so I became restless so was pleased when my joining orders came through. I was sent to *MV Glenorchy*, a beautiful but elderly vessel. On long voyages across the South Atlantic and Indian Oceans the complexities of astro navigation would begin to make sense as I applied theory to practice.

Chapter 10

TO JAPAN WITH AN OLD LADY

Lugging my seagoing kit to the bottom of the gangway, I paused for breath. Large white letters proudly proclaimed *GLENORCHY* along a flaring bow. A mass of derricks bristled along the foredeck, her wooden bridge front topped by a huge red funnel. She looked a very big ship to me.

This posting was my first indication that the separate manning of Elder Dempster, Glen Line and Blue Funnel ships had now been amalgamated under Ocean Fleets.

The most obvious difference to my previous ships was that the paint scheme was not yellow; the derricks and masts were a strange reddish colour and a hull black with pink boot topping. Pink!

Decades later I learned something of her past. Built in 1941 in Dundee, she was by now an old lady with a chequered history. Initially named *Priam*, she had carried explosives during the war. Bad weather on the voyage had caused this hazardous cargo to become very damp and so she was refused permission to transit the Suez Canal until it was unloaded. The subsequent arguments between the owners and insurers set an important legal precedent for future cases.

After a post-war refit in 1948 she was transferred to the Glen Line and renamed *Glenorchy*. The officers' saloon was still beautifully kitted out with comfortable chairs and mahogany fittings. There had been a piano in the days when she had carried passengers but it had been removed as being unsuitable for mere officers to enjoy. The wooden promenade decks surrounding our accommodation offered a cool space to stroll at the end of a hot tropical day; no air conditioning of course.

In due course we sailed from the King George V Docks, London bound for the Far East: Singapore, Hong Kong, Shanghai and Yokohama. I was looking forward to sailing to these exotic ports of call. We kept sea watches down the Channel and across the Bay of Biscay and as the weather improved off Portugal we cadets were set to day-work; the eternal round of cleaning, greasing and painting.

In about latitude 30° the northeast trades created following seas and heralded even warmer days. After two weeks running down the West African coast and across the South Atlantic, we closed the land off the Cape of Good Hope. A launch puttered out to us, cutting through the steep swells just off Cape Town, to exchange company and personal mails, our life line to family and friends.

In previous voyages I had gone as far as Lobito, 12° south. I was now venturing into new territory. On rounding disappointingly low Cape Agulhas, the most southerly point of Africa, we struck a terrible storm and simultaneously one of our two engines broke down. Immediately our speed was reduced to a few knots. The engineers worked with manic fury amid much cursing to restore us to full power.

Opening the access door to the engine room, a blast of heat and sound hit my senses. The door banged behind me as I gripped the handrails, shiny with constant use, and I descended to the main engine control deck.

The Chief Engineer, a worried frown on a face smeared with grease, stood watching his team hard at work.

'Captain's compliments, but the weather is getting worse and do you have any hopes of completing repairs in the next few hours?' I asked the Chief nervously.

'No way, laddie! Just look there and just you tell the Captain what you see!'

I gawped at the astonishing sight of a junior engineer actually working inside one of the giant piston casings, reinserting fresh piston rings.

'Aye Aye sir!' I shouted above the din of generators, pumps and the one good engine thumping away. This would be a long job, it seemed. Later that night the engine was repaired and we resumed normal speed. At eighteen knots it took twelve more days to reach Penang.

Marine diesel engines of the 1980s produce a screaming 500 revolutions of the prop shaft per minute. *Glenorchy's* much larger double-opposed, heavy oil engines (Burmeister and Wain) thumped along at a stately 112 rpm. A low, vibration-free rumble powered us onwards.

I was back on sea watches, doing some time on the wheel to improve my indifferent steering skills. It was very difficult keeping the ship's head on course, eyes glued to the gyrocompass compass card, the tell-tale click informing the officer of the watch of the steadiness— or otherwise—of the course followed. Gentle ticking indicates a steady course. A rapid surge of ticking indicates an erratic course, the helmsman not in control. Wishing to avoid a shout from the mate, 'Keep to the course, Cadet!' kept me focussed my hour's trick on the wheel. The helmsman had to apply sufficient helm to allow for the effect of wind, waves and swell which took a ship's bow off course, but to be aware of the natural movement of these forces to bring her back without overcompensating. The skilled helmsman could feel the movement of the ship through his body. He would know when she was going too far to port or starboard and when to ease corrective rudder.

After a spell on the wheel, at night we went lookout on the bridge wing, and then below for a welcome cup of tea; or, during the day, we were set-to on ship maintenance tasks. Sundays were a break with routine, when we were required to keep up with the MAR Correspondence Course-work, polishing my cargo work and navigation knowledge.

There were sufficient sextants on board for the cadets to take morning and noon sights. When on the 8 to 12 watch the third officer taught me how to take a morning sight of the sun. Five figure logs were used to resolve a complex formula involving spherical trigonometry, to convert the observed altitude to a longitude position line. This would be run up to the noon position by dead reckoning, drawn on the plotting chart and crossed with our latitude obtained from the observed noon altitude.

The captain, chief, second and third officers, and the two cadets, gathered on the wing of the bridge for the daily ritual. Being under the close scrutiny of so many professionals was unnerving. The second officer had pre-calculated the time of noon and we set the sextant index bar to the pre-calculated, but approximate, altitude. As the sun's zenith approached we took up position on the crowded bridge wing and raised our sextants, making sure that we had adjusted the shades on the sextant to protect our eyesight. Remembering also that now we were in the southern hemisphere, we looked to the north as the sun climbed to its maximum. I struggled valiantly to rotate the index bar so as to bring the bright orb down onto the distant sea horizon, fine tuning with the micrometer screw. We waited for that moment of hover which announced, (to the skilled practitioner anyway), that the sun was no longer ascending into the sky and within seconds would begin its descent to the western horizon.

At that point the second officer shouted 'STOP!' It was his privilege as navigator to make that decision—having pre-calculated the time of noon—and at that moment we carefully noted the sun's altitude, read off from the micrometer screw dial and figures compared. My big worry was that I would be several seconds of arc adrift from the mean. If so, the Captain might well say witheringly, 'We will ignore the cadet's observation today.'

Not good for morale.

'Fog on deck!'

I had done it yet again. Condensation was streaming down the inside of the bridge window, the air clammy with excess warm moisture. I had let the kettle boil away until the air was filled with man-made fog.

'Make the coffee, Cadet! Keep your wits about you!'

I switched off the kettle, in the doghouse again. Time for a treat: cappuccino coffee. Take one teaspoon of instant coffee, two teaspoons of sugar, one glug of condensed milk. Mix vigorously. Add boiling water, stir briskly. One coffee with a frothy top. Drink quickly before the froth disappears. Mild redemption. I brought through the sandwiches from the back of the chart room; bloater paste and sweaty cheese, curling in the heat. Mild disappointment.

Not only were cadets instructed in seamanship and navigation but also in good table manners. The long-suffering radio officer had the misfortune to be in charge of a table of cadets. He had a round, red face, framed by a deeply receding hairline. His poppy eyes were framed by thick tortoiseshell spectacles. We were inclined to avoid upsetting him. His somewhat choleric disposition was not improved by our casual attitude to eating 'properly'. He was very exercised by the proper use of The Butter Knife. The dining saloon was equipped to restaurant standards, with white linen tablecloths, white linen napkins, silver napkin rings. Full silver service, all polished and gleaming. This included The Butter Dish. Dining in sweltering tropical heat without the benefit of air conditioning was, to put it simply, sweaty work. However, the niceties were still observed. The butter dish had a lower compartment filled with ice which kept the butter quite firm, for the first part of the meal at least. I leant forward with my large, dirty main course knife to spear a curl. I was halted mid-spike by a red-faced Sparky:

'Use the butter knife, Cadet!' he thundered. 'Didn't your mother teach you anything?'

Thus thoroughly shamed, reprimanded and educated, the experience etched its lesson into my brain for evermore. I am impelled to use a butter knife to this day.

As soon as we were comfortably berthed in Penang, the third officer and I went ashore for a beer at a roadside eating house. We ordered a simple dish. I unpeeled thin green palm leaves to reveal the appetizing rice within. No plates to wash. I bought a colourful umbrella made of split cane and tar paper; useful in tropical downpours but now gone solid in my attic, repository of other marine memories.

We discharged our cargo of manufactured goods and loaded local products for return to UK: bales of rubber, sacks of nutmeg, coconuts, rice, and tanks filled with palm oil.

After a week at sea we arrived in Japan, calling at Kobe and Yokohama. We were collected by the Missions to Seafarers Padre who took us on runs ashore to explore temples and dine out, Japanese style.

The radio officer doubled as the purser. In port he busily produced loading plans for a multiport discharging the UK and on the continent. On a table top was spread a large plan of the ship showing a cross-section of the holds, tween decks and lockers. Each space was scribed with colour-coded labels for port of discharge, cargo and tonnage. Cargo parcels had to be accessible in each port. If a part-discharge of cargo left a free face it had to be tommed off with a timber wall.

The stowage plan was vital information which had to be posted on from the last port of discharge to the arrival ports. Was it necessary to make a dozen copies free hand? No. Bring forward the large wood-framed sun-powered document copier. In a darkroom lit only by a red bulb, a large sheet of copy-film was inserted into the frame with the cargo plan. Sparky and I carefully lifted the prepared frame into a sunny patch and laid it down on the deck. After a count of ten seconds or so we carried the frame back in for processing. Repeat. The six copies so made were posted on to the discharge port agents.

From Japan we returned home via the Cape of Good Hope, picking up mails on the way past Cape Town as usual. We floated alone in our watery world and letters from home were always deeply appreciated by all on board.

I pushed open the storm door and closed it behind me, knocking up a couple of dogs. Sliding down the smooth handrails of the accommodation ladder, I jumped the last step and landed easily on the main deck. I looked over the side and saw a mother and baby hammerhead shark swimming very close by, their distinctive features clearly visible. Bright sun sparkled on silver wings as a shoal of flying fish burst from the sea and cut a glittering trail across our track until, after several suspended seconds, they smacked into the blue like bullets and disappeared.

I gazed over the wide ocean, a rippled tablecloth swept clean of ships and land. I carried on up the hot steel deck and climbed the fo'c'sle ladder, weaved between the bitts and windlass, leant my elbows on the warm bulwark, and soaked up the sun. Flecks of foam broke along the edge of a perfect, never ending bow wave. Mesmerising. A squadron of dolphins broke the surface and flew alongside me, playing chase, their sleek bodies slicing effortlessly through the waves until, bored with the game, they slipped away. I felt a sense of loss as I turned to walk aft to the mess for a quick cup of tea before I went on watch.

I slid the slim yellow sea thermometer into its black rubber bucket, coiled up the attached rope and made my way down to the main deck. Checking I was clear of any water outfalls being pumped overboard, I lowered the bucket into the sea racing by, checking the pull on the madly jerking rope. Hauling the bucking bucket through the water, I drew the precious sea water sample safely back aboard. Carefully withdrawing the yellow glass tube, I noted the temperature before the mercury fell. A constricted neck, as used in a medical thermometer, would have been a great help. Back on the bridge, I opened the Metrological Office Ship Reporting Log and entered the sea temperature for the 1200 observation. Next I noted the direction of sea and swell, estimated its height and entered the data. Ditto for presence of cirrus, alto and stratus clouds, if any, in fractions of eighths, called oktars. Nipping up to the Monkey Island I opened the Stevenson Screen door and read off the temperatures for the wet and dry bulbs, and calculated the dew point. I took the barometric pressure and tendency from the barograph. I logged our noon position, course and speed. Finally the entire weather report was coded up for transmission by the radio officer.

'Here you are, Sparky,' I said. 'Weather report for you.'

'Ooo thanks. What a treat!' he said, and got it off smartly by Morse code to Portishead Radio. In the days before weather satellites, the Met Office relied on a fleet of Volunteer Reporting Ships to plot the network of marine observations sent in from every ocean.

Wearing dark glasses on night watch was an occasional novelty. In the still tropical air, the restless, oily sea reflected painful shards of starlight off its mirrored surface.

Long weeks later, flying up the English Channel close to Christmas, we were desperate to catch the tide for King George V Docks. Would we make it? As we made our way towards the Thames Estuary our hopes rose higher the closer we got to home. Starved of hard information, anxious eyes scanned the horizon towards the coast. The sight of the pilot boat speeding out to us confirmed the good news.

Tugs made fast fore and aft and manoeuvred us through the lock system towards our berth. A welcome sight on the quay was the minibus with the relieving crew. Very soon after they had trudged up the gangway, poor things on duty over Christmas, we happily clattered down back into the minibus. I caught the last train home from Paddington to Oxford.

I listened on my transistor radio as the chimes of Big Ben struck midnight and announced Christmas Day. I'd been away for over four months and shouted out my delight of coming home to my fellow passengers.

'Happy Christmas everybody!'

Those miserable folk turned round to see what the noise was about and stared at me with silent distaste.

I was met by my family at Oxford Station, swept up in the excitement of the moment. When I woke the next morning I felt completely disorientated by my change of circumstances. I had the usual seafarer's problem of relating to a landlubber's narrow concerns. They had no concept of the adventures I had experienced and it was difficult to explain.

Christmas at home was fun but the cold was not. I missed the warm benediction of a tropical climate.

Chapter 11

MAO'S LITTLE RED BOOK

```
QUOTATIONS
FROM
CHAIRMAN
MAO TSE-TUNG
```

After nearly a month on leave I was stony broke. The post arrived on a cold winter's morning. Good news.

'21 January 1969.

'You are ordered to proceed to King George V Dock, London to join *MV Glenfalloch*. Your Travel Warrant is enclosed'.

Thus began my last year at sea as an apprentice. I was now a Senior Cadet and proudly wore a thin gold braid on my sleeve.

Built on the Clyde, *Glenfalloch* was only six years old when I joined her, much younger than the twenty seven-year-old *Glenorchy* and the difference was marked. There was less wood in the cabins and accommodation, with modern equipment on the bridge and on deck. She looked smart and was well run, and our Captain was very proud of her. Not that we knew it then, but she was to be the last Glen Line ship.

As we sailed down the Western Approaches the QE2 went by on her second maiden voyage after emergency repairs at Brown's Shipyard on the Clyde. The Captain sent her message by VHF radio: 'Good luck on your voyage' and was rather put out by her supercilious, rather curt acknowledgement: 'Message received.'

Glenfalloch sailed with a cargo full of manufactured goods for Malaysia, Singapore, Japan, and with some high-tech equipment for China. I particularly noted one crate which held a delicate piece of engineering suspended on four springs. It was carefully loaded into a secure tween-deck locker.

It was to be an eventful voyage.

We proceeded as normal down the English Channel, across the Bay of Biscay, round the bump of Africa, swapped correspondence with a mail launch at Cape Town, continuing on at twenty knots across the Indian Ocean. The Suez Canal was still closed; rounding the Cape added an extra seven days to our voyage. Twenty four days out from London and 11,714 miles later we arrived at Singapore. I had hoped to try a Singapore Sling at the famous Raffles Hotel but I was too broke to go into the bar. In company with the third mate, we wandered around the streets, absorbing the oriental feel and tropical warmth of this crowded city-state.

After two days, with a liner schedule to keep, we sailed the three-day passage to Hong Kong. Our course took us several miles off the Vietnamese coast, to avoid any encounter with the ongoing Vietnam War. And also to avoid payment of a War Bonus. Nevertheless, we were challenged by a bright signal light cutting the black night; an American warship demanding: 'WHAT SHIP?' There were the usual stroppy remarks; 'Who do these Americans think they are, challenging British ships!' Nevertheless, we cadets signalled our name in Morse via the Aldis lamp, giving port of origin and port of destination. Good practice. I could see faint flashes on the distant horizon which looked less like lightning and more like bombing. I felt sorry for the people on the receiving end.

In Hong Kong we enjoyed a few hours ashore, climbed the Peak and drank beer with pretty hostesses in the bars of Wanchai. Before we set off on a further two-day voyage to Shanghai, some of our Chinese crew decided to leave the ship because they had relatives in China and they were frightened of the undue political pressure which might be applied to the detriment of their families

On route to China, cadets were warned by the chief officer to cover up the word *Formosa* on world maps pinned to our cabin bulkheads. To the Chinese government that name was a political red rag to their Communist bull. As far as they were concerned, Taiwan was part of the Chinese mainland and the Nationalist government was not regarded as its legitimate rulers. As ever, still.

We were also warned not to take any photographs or appear to be recording information as we headed up the Yangtze River into Shanghai. I noticed that we were proceeding at such a speed that we set up a strong stern wave and the ship began to bottom, that is, dipped her stern towards the river bed in the increasingly shallow waters. The Captain tried to remonstrate with the pilot but it was very difficult politically to interfere. A grim faced Political Commissar stood next to the Pilot.

As we approach the inner port, I saw several low, grey warships, including a submarine. A launch whizzed past us at speed, the Chinese sailor on the foredeck signalling furiously in semaphore. I was impressed by his speed. What alphabet did they use?

On reading Richard Woodman's history of the Merchant Navy much later I discovered that by this time *Glenfalloch* was one of only a few British cargo liners to call regularly at Chinese ports. The Communists were very touchy about security and the year before my trip, Captain Richards and Second Officer Peter Crouch of the *Demodocus* had been arrested for 'spying'; only doing what second officers do—plot the course on the chart by taking bearings of features on the shore. Ocean Fleets policy said after that incident only one ship could be in Chinese waters any one time—and we were it.

When we berthed, the Political Commissars herded the officers into the saloon and the crew into their mess room. We were harangued with the thoughts of Chairman Mao. Each of us was given a copy of the famous Little Red Book, 'Quotations from Chairman Mao Tse-Tung', with its distinctive red plastic cover, smooth to the touch. Turning its thin pages, I read Mao's exhortations:

'We must have faith in the masses and we must have faith in the party. These are two cardinal principles. We doubt these principles, we shall accomplish nothing.' (p3)

'People of the world, unite and defeat the US aggressors and all their running dogs!' (p 82)

I have it still. My fellow cadet made sycophantic noises about how impressed he was with communism and was rewarded by being given half a dozen hardback books on More Thoughts of Chairman Mao, and other books on communism. Up to that time my only exposure to what went on in China was through the magazine, China Pictorial. It was full of propaganda pictures of brawny factory workers and farmers, happily praising Mao and their leaders.

Liverpool and London dockers worked in gangs of eight men. In Shanghai sixty dockers swarmed over each hatch, all dressed in blue padded jackets and trousers. The pungent reek of garlic emanated from clothing and bodies. I was sent down the hold to keep an eye on loading and unloading of cargo. The Chinese were fascinated by this tall, thin white boy and pressed close. A youth was pushed to the front of the crowd and he spoke to me in broken English.

'I am student, from university. The Party send me here. To work, not study.'

He was to experience how dockers lived and worked; the programme to re-educate the intelligentsia.

I was on cargo watch in the hold, loitering without any serious intent. A two ton pallet of frozen rabbit was lowered too quickly into the hold and swung out of control deep under the hatch coaming. The pallet edge clipped the back of my head and flung me forward. I was knocked out cold.

Standing alone in the officers' pantry, I stirred a spoon round and round a mug. Tink clink. 'What am I doing here?' I thought to myself. 'Why am I making tea? How did I get here?'

The fourth mate bustled by.

'What's going on?' I asked, bewildered.

'What's going on, what's going on?' he responded irritably. 'I'll tell you what's going on. I've been dragged from my bed at six in the morning because the stupid cadet wasn't looking and got himself knocked out, that's what's going on. An ambulance is coming for you to take you to the hospital so you had better wait here until it arrives.'

When the ambulance pulled up at the ship I walked down the gangway, climbed aboard and lay down as directed on the stretcher. After a journey of some twenty minutes we arrived outside a grey hospital building. I stepped out of the ambulance, climbed the steps and walked through the main doors. Before me was a long corridor lined with grey, silent people. I was shown into a side room. Lowering myself carefully into a low 1930s style club armchair, I awaited the translator. The doctors ignored me. I couldn't explain why I was there, or my medical condition, my Chinese not being up to much.

In due course the translator arrived. Not permitted to travel with me in the ambulance, he had cycled over to the hospital. He explained what had happened. I wasn't sure myself so I'm not sure how he knew. The doctor in a white coat examined my head, presumably for concussion. I returned to the ship the way I had come; walking, lying, walking. I was given a week off to recuperate which I was meant to spend in bed. I became very bored, and the chief steward was very cross at having to bring me my meals to my cabin.

'What do you think this is? A bloody hotel!' he complained.

Of course everybody else thought I was skiving and so I was glad to recover rapidly and return to duty.

Reading Richard Woodman's book, 'Fiddlers' Green', I learned that the following year *Glenfalloch* would be placed under arrest. Chief Officer Brian Hood was taken off the ship. He was interrogated for three days and returned on board as the ship was about to sail. Second Officer Patrick Duff was taken off and left behind and *Glenfalloch* was forced to sail without him. The second officer arrested from the *Demodocus* and taken ashore two years before had still not been released.

As a result of this political turmoil in which Shanghai was trying to prove itself more Maoist than Beijing, the Ocean Steamship board decided to cancel all further trade with China and ships in transit were diverted to other ports. This did the trick and the detained officers were released. However these incidences brought an end to a very long trading relationship between England and China and further services were discontinued.

In early April we sailed from Shanghai for London. The voyage of 14,000 miles took almost a month. That would have been an interesting passage to plan but this was not in a cadet's remit. I worked on deck, sometimes aloft or on deck or keeping watch on the bridge, as *Glenfalloch* sailed south through the East China Sea, through the Formosa Strait and the South China Sea, passing between Malaysia and Sumatra along the infamous Straits of Malacca. Here we were concerned about pirates but none challenged our fast vessel. We sailed across the watery wastes of the Indian Ocean, past Rodriguez Island, Reunion and Mauritius.

One bright starry night our wake boiled bright green. Pulsating bands of bioluminescence stretched from horizon to horizon and cast an eerie glow. Phosphorescent arms rotating around a central luminous hub shimmered in the black night. Oddities of the ocean.

Rounding the southern coast of Africa off Cape Agulhas, we made our way northwards across the South Atlantic, safely through the doldrums having paid our dues to Neptune, till just north of the Canary Islands we put away our tropical whites and added more layers of winter gear as we pitched into steeper seas, lifted by crisp north-easterly winds.

Approaching the Bay of Biscay, we began to run into the southwesterly weather systems moving in from the North Atlantic Ocean which blew us up the English Channel. By this time we were all suffering from The Channels yet again; the seafarer's longing for home sharpened by the sight of white cliffs off the Isle of Wight, Eastbourne and of course, Dover.

A downside of transiting the English Channel was, once we had picked up the Channel Pilot off Brixham, doubled up watches, four on four off, so that there were always two officers and two cadets on watch. Company regulations in Glen Line, unlike in Elder Dempster, demanded this extra vigilance in busy waterways. This was of course before the introduction of the Traffic Separation Scheme made shipping lanes in the channel so much safer. But with less than four sleep at a time, I was often more dozy than usual.

Normally cadets disembark on arrival UK and proceed on leave. I was looking forward to celebrating my twenty first birthday at home. However, Head Office in Liverpool had other ideas, saying that I needed drydock experience. *Glenfalloch* spent several days back at King George V docks unloading those cartons of frozen rabbits, bags of rice, and 'cotton piece goods'. Then we sailed for Rotterdam. The Dutch dock masters wanted our draft in feet, not metres, a surprising revelation of the historic connection between English and Dutch shipbuilders and repairers.

We warped into the dry dock, the lock gates closed and the water was pumped out. It was fascinating to walk beneath the ship its whole length, 12,000 tons of steel towering over me. Now I could see for myself that the massive structure was strong enough to keep its shape out of water. It made me more confident of a ship's strength and integrity when being tossed about in the violence of a hurricane.

On the *Glenfalloch's return* to London's King George V dock I was released for an extra-long 25 days leave. There is not a lot a one can do on £6 a week. I explored the Cotswold countryside and prepared for my last few months as a cadet.

These two voyages over nine months had given me a taste of the Far East and I wanted more. I was determined to press for a Blue Funnel or Glen Line ship after I had qualified as Second Mate at the end of the year. But first I had two more voyages to West Africa.

Chapter 12

LIFE ASHORE II

FAR EASTERN ADVENTURES

The stinging rain lashed down on our bare skin. A grey blanket obliterated the skyline. Huge droplets dashed violently into the flat surface. We jumped in the warm water, laughing at the elements. Hunkering low in the pool we escaped the pain. September in Penang provided a tropical welcome to escapees from a northern autumn. Penang's main attraction for us was a welcoming Seamen's Mission. The wharves where *Glenorchy* had berthed were close to the town centre so we cadets walked ashore to the clubhouse for relaxation, fellowship, a drink—and a swim in the pool.

Just a short voyage 190 miles south lay Port Swettenham, the port to Kuala Lumpur. The colonial name had stuck, preferred to the modern 'Port Klang'. It was the British administration in the 1880s that had transformed it from a malaria infested region to a very busy port.

Immersed in the bubble of our traditional break bulk ship I was unaware of the massive changes in cargo operations taking place. By the end of the decade container ships operated out of this port. Too old to change, *Glenorchy* was broken up just three years after I left her, in 1971. She was thirty years old. By 2007 Port Klang was the sixteenth busiest container port in the world. It is no longer a sleepy port of call where vessels like mine spent several days discharging cargo in the old-fashioned style, using derricks to swing out two-ton sack-loads lifted in rope slings.

Hong Kong a few days later was a different proposition altogether. Here the crowds I encountered on a walk ashore along the main street were so thick that I dived into the nearest shop to regain my equilibrium. I found the persistent battling against the crowds after weeks at sea quite daunting, much worse than Oxford Street.

I enjoyed travelling on the Star Ferry to the mainland from our berth on Hong Kong Island, absorbing the harbour scene of modern shipping interspersed with warships and traditional junks, both sail and motor powered.

Next came my first trip to Japan. We called both at Kobe and Yokohama. I had a day ashore in Yokohama courtesy of the Mission to Seafarers chaplain who took a group of us out to the ancient Buddhist temple of Kamakura, 30 miles south-west of Tokyo. We enjoyed the novelty of a train journey across the Japanese landscape to the famous 700-year-old bronze statue of the Great Buddha of Kamakura. I climbed an internal staircase and looked out of the Great Buddha's eyes, eleven metres above the surrounding landscape. A sweeping view of temples amid the hills lay before me.

On returning to Tokyo we were taken out to a traditional Japanese meal. I was grateful for the pit beneath the table under which I could stretch my long legs. I drank deeply of a cold lager during the long wait before we were served with a tasty meal; my first with chopsticks.

In the crowded streets outside I was struck by the contrast between the modern neon-lit skyscrapers, ladies in colourful traditional kimonos, wearing one-toed socks thrust into what looked like flip-flops on platforms. The pavements were crowded with people, some wearing white surgical masks, which looked very odd to me.

I went into a large store and bought a souvenir—a vase for the family. Its clean green curves were plain but perfect. Packaging was an art form. The vase was placed in a light wooden box and then enclosed in precisely folded quality paper. Discovering the vase within made the gift even more appreciated.

In Kobe I visited the Sumadera temple sited high up on a hill. My eyes were immediately drawn to the deep, curving roofs held up by intricately carved pillars. A tall, three story pagoda stood centre-stage, its many roofs deeply set back and the whole structure embellished with detailed carvings. The beat of a base gong filled the air with deep peace.

I stood at the top of a steep flight of steps and looked down. This would take a while, I thought, and set off. Two students ahead of me were soon overhauled, and with a friendly, 'Hello', we fell into conversation. They were from Tokyo University, on a visit with their little sister. At my suggestion we found a local restaurant to enjoy a coffee together. We were busy talking when I belatedly realised that my companions were waiting for me to start my coffee first. I slurped my drink noisily, whereupon came appreciative sighs and nodding of heads, and then they also drank. We parted with much bowing, and shaking of hands. I returned to my ship, content with my stimulating run ashore.

Arriving in Shanghai on *Glenfalloch* at the height of the Cultural Revolution, we discovered a city thronging with people on bicycles and little motor traffic. An armed guard was permanently stationed at the foot of the gangway.

'Don't worry about locking your cabin door when you go ashore,' the helpful official informed us when we went ashore on a trip. 'It will be perfectly safe. The guard will shoot any thief!'

Heavily escorted by the Chinese authorities, we were taken to two factories in a coach. Our first trip was to an old British built and operated cigarette factory. First we were taken to a large room and sat around a huge conference table. In front of us were placed a lidded pot of tea, a packet of cigarettes and a box of matches. How I wish that I had kept them; they would have made an interesting souvenir of our visit. I tried the cigarettes later. They were many times worse than Gauloise. We sipped our tea as we were harangued for ages in Chinese but without the benefit of translation. Then we were taken onto the factory floor. The air was filled with the hum of belt-driven 1950s machinery, which corralled thousands of spinning little white tubes, and fed them into soft cigarette packaging.

Driving through the streets of Shanghai I saw very little traffic, just a few coaches, taxis and army lorries, and masses of people on bicycles. An open top army truck loaded with soldiers banging large drums made its noisy way through the throng. A great press of the people pushed close against large poster-clad walls, exhorting the people to higher productivity, praising Mao Tse-Tung, and the glory of China.

Most folk wore the faded padded blue trousers and jackets topped with a blue cap, a red star above the peak. The patterned blouse of a woman stood out against a sea faded of blue, as she walked along the pavement, holding a child by the hand.

On another visit we were taken to a poster printing factory where they showed us how they produced their propaganda posters. Even to my untutored eye there was something very primitive about the whole process.

One day we were taken to the large Friendship Store on the Bund. After perusing displays of china and a strange mix of souvenirs, I purchased a set of smoker's requisites in blue chinaware. The pots were covered in a pewter filigree of swirling dragons and flowers. There was a lidded pot to hold cigarettes, a matchstick container and a little pot for the dead matches, all set on a little blue tray. I have it still. Years later I read the bestselling book 'Wild Swans' by Jung Chang. The author had been a Red Guard who had learned sufficient English to work behind the counter in this Friendship Store. Who knows, she could have served me. Reading that book gave me a fascinating insight into what people were suffering when I, a curious but ignorant 20-year-old, came shopping in her store, only seeing the surface of Shanghai life.

Later on we were taken to the International Seamen's Club to enjoy a beer at the famed Long Bar, longest in the world. Built in 1910, it replaced the 1864 building, once the Correspondent's Club. It became the Shanghai Club, used by white male elites, such as Noel Coward who sang, played and drank here. Old hands who had been here before the 1956 revolution said Shanghai was one of the best runs ashore in the world, a place of wild entertainment of every kind. But now, just over a decade later, we were instructed to sit down, corralled at a table, and I was served my first Tsingtao beer. Today I can buy it in any supermarket. Imported by container ship. Forty two years later this Baroque building opened as the Waldorf Astoria Shanghai on the Bund, a luxury hotel.

I missed the grand opening by a year, when I returned to a dramatically altered city. Twenty million people now live in this vibrant modern city given over to capitalism. Skyscrapers, futuristic television station towers and hotels dominate the skyline. Motorcycles, cars and coaches full of foreign and local tourists clog multiple ring roads, flyovers and a triple spiral overpass. The views from Floor 88 of an hotel revealed far, far below cavalcades of boats and barges crawling along the wide meanders of the brown Hwang Po River. Down there was the famous European Bund, close to where I docked four decades before. The city was proudly preparing for the World Expo and all was change and bustle.

It was my twenty first birthday. I was not celebrating at home but in Rotterdam, when *Glenfalloch* was in dry dock. I was given the day off, so I took my self out to lunch at a pleasant restaurant at the base of Rotterdam's landmark Euromat Tower. I sipped at a glass of sherry whilst awaiting the main course; chicken in a rich cheese sauce, accompanied by half a bottle of white wine. Later a coach trip took me to the Delft Pottery works, (blue ashtray souvenir still in my possession), and the miniature Madurodam model 'city', replete with scale models of Rotterdam cathedral, ships floating in the docks, moving railways, road and rail traffic, streets of Dutch houses. It was named after George Maduro, a WWII Dutch Resistance fighter who had died in Dachau concentration camp. I strolled slowly along the long sandy beach at Scheveningen, wishing that I could share this landmark birthday with somebody, preferably female, young and pretty. Decades later I returned to this beach with my wife, on a windy walk amongst stunning sand sculptures.

On my way back to the *Glenfalloch* I fell into bad company in the shape of junior officers, free at last to come ashore, and we repaired to a local bar near the docks in time honoured fashion. I was bought too many beers and gins, far too much alcohol—I did not have a good head for booze—and to the amusement of my shipmates had to be poured into a taxi and shipped back. I did not feel at all well in the morning.

Chapter 13

CARRYING THE ROYAL MAIL

The trick with supping a bowl of soup in a storm at sea is learning to sway. Spillage is failure. Preparation is key. The saloon table is firmly anchored by two central pillars. The white linen tablecloth is soaked with water by the steward. Thus the cutlery and crockery are firmly anchored. I drag my chair, secured by short chains to the deck, closer to the table. The steward places the soup before me and I deftly grasp the edge in one hand, and roll the bowl in an impromptu dance against the surges of the sea, supping from the edge of the spoon. The fiddle round the edge of the table provides a handhold during especially violent lurches. This vital seagoing skill had taken much practice over many months at sea as a deck apprentice. Now I was coming to the end of my time and this last voyage was to be a special one.

I had joined *MV Aureol* at the north Liverpool docks where she was discharging her cargo from West Africa. She was a complete contrast to my previous general cargo vessels. Built in 1951, *Aureol* was part of Elder Dempster's shipbuilding program to replace losses of the Second World War. A fleet of three had offered a fortnightly passenger service between Liverpool and Lagos. Unknown to me, winds of change were blowing through the passenger fleet and her sister ships *Accra* (1947) and *Apapa* (1948) had already been sold.

Aureol carried 451 passengers and 145 crew. And I was one of them. It was easy to get lost along its labyrinthine alleys but I soon settled down to the routine of watches and cargo work. This elegant vessel with its yacht-like lines carried the Royal Mail from Liverpool to Lagos via Freetown, Monrovia, Tema (southbound) and Takoradi (northbound). Therefore she ran to a strict timetable, compared with the sailing times of a general tramp ship which traded where and when the freight market demanded. Reliability and punctuality were the watchwords.

Just as when on other ships in the fleet, a cadet's regular job in port was to tally the Royal Mail bags into, and out of, the lock-up store. This was a vital duty, but it was a mind-numbing task—scratching four lines, crossed with a fifth, in neat little rows, keeping an accurate tally of this valuable cargo; business and personal mail, parcels for Christmas, samples for the office—all important. But sometimes my numbers did not tally with the shoreside tally clerks. Very disheartening and a cause a grief and conflict.

The major difference to my previous vessels was that deck officers on passenger liners wore smart uniform and caps at all times, even on night watches, and certainly during the day on cargo watch. Allowing greasy block and tackle to foul the holystoned teak decks was a crime against which we had to guard during loading and discharging of often dirty cargoes. An almost impossible and largely unsuccessful endeavour.

On arrival off the coast of West Africa at Freetown we picked up deck passengers for the coast-wise journey down to Lagos. They occupied various spaces, mostly in the fo'c'sle, which offered some shelter against the weather. As dawn broke on a hot tropical morning the chief officer sent me for'ard.

'Go and check on the deck passengers in the fo'c'sle, Cadet,' he ordered. 'Make sure all is well.' Whatever that meant.

Picking my way through the tangle of black limbs dimly revealed in the gloaming, the oppressive heat and powerful smell of hundreds of sleeping natives powerfully assailed my nostrils. As I carefully placed a clean Blanco-ed uniform shoe into a gap between close-pressed bodies, my eye caught a large expanse of flesh; no, not a thigh but a vast mammary gland flowing down into the darkness. In all my life my sheltered eyes had never been exposed to such a sight; I tore away my gaze and moved on through the sleeping bodies. The sound of quiet breathing filled the enclosed space as, bent low, I navigated myself clear of packed humanity, stepped over the coaming and gratefully breathed cool, fresh night air.

'Now that was an experience to remember,' I said to myself. 'Not quite what I had expected.'

A cadet has many duties. Some were more fraught than others. One was to lower President Tubman of Liberia's Presidential flag from the cross-trees each sunset, carefully roll it up and restore it to the flag locker. On my first nervous attempt, the presidential flag nearly touched the deck and a sharp-eyed soldier moved forward to reprimand me. But with a quick movement I scooped the errant tail up and saved it from disgrace. I got better at this tricky flag duty over the long days at sea from Liverpool to Liberia, where we would deliver our special cargo.

Well drilled, smartly turned out troops lined up at Freetown quay. Large field guns executed a loud and impressive 21 gun salute in welcome to President Tubman as he arrived on a short stop-over in this former British colony. He had been in England for medical treatment and was now returning home. Leaning over the taffrail from the upper decks, we cadets had a grandstand view and were moderately impressed.

Arrival in Monrovia was a different story. Liberia, 'Land of the Free,' had been established by a penitent America to provide a home for those freed slaves who wished to return to the Africa from whence they had been ripped centuries before. The influence of casual American training was only too apparent. A squad in crumpled sailor suits sauntered along the quay and shuffled into line. A sailor bent down and pulled the lanyard of a two foot long starting cannon and popped a jaunty 'Welcome Home' to their President. We heartless cadets could not help laughing.

The second officer was a short, mousy little man with grey, thinning hair, a wispy grey moustache pinned under a large nose, set in a pallid face. He was very neat in his habits, his uniform always crisply pressed and his chart work exact. The day we sailed from Liverpool he felt torn away from hearth and home. He longed for the moment when he walked back up the garden path.

'I know exactly what day and time I shall return,' he explained. 'The predictability of our schedule makes time away from home bearable for me'.

This officer's attitude was very different from those free spirited men with whom I had sailed on previous Elder Dempster ships. They lived for the moment and took life as it came. On a scheduled run a cargo liner could allow the timetable to slip a little according to cargo pressures. Ports of call could be varied in order to load unexpected cargoes as head office responded to last-minute requests. Not so on a passenger liner. Sticking resolutely to the timetable was essential.

The *Aureol* was my last ship before my Second Mate's ticket, the navigating officer's exam which would allow me to get one foot on the professional ladder, leading all the way up to my Master Mariner's

Certificate. However, the last ship before the vital, in-depth oral examination was the basis of detailed examination of knowledge of the regulations. A passenger ship in this context was deeply undesirable because of the wealth of regulation candidates needed to memorise. However, professional exams and the career of a junior deck officer lay far ahead of me on my final voyage and I was able to enjoy myself as a senior cadet. At long last, I was able to ship the coveted half-diamond Forth Mate's stripes, a privilege not granted by Glen Line.

Aureol was a beautiful ship, popular with expats returning home on leave or going back to duty. Decades later I met some of these colonial types who had sailed on this fine vessel, now in retirement in a gracious Elizabethan stately home divided up into apartments. Here ex-colonial administrators reflected on their lives serving Queen and country in remote lands. *Aureol* was the link with Home. Representing Civilisation, she played host to the local white community.

On one occasion I took my usual post at the top of the gangway, smartly dressed in starched Number Tens. My sleeves had been so stiffly starched that I had to punch my fist into the arm hole before I could do up the row of 'Royal Mail' brass buttons on my white tunic, half diamond gold braid epaulettes proudly borne on my shoulders. I saluted a 'Welcome aboard *Aureol*, Sir and Madam!' to each guest as they climbed the gangway. My constricted arm swished like a sharp white blade, more threat than welcome. I was not pleased with the overzealous dhobi man. I came to miss those days when dirty laundry was taken away and brought back clean and pressed, epaulettes inserted. By the end of my career twenty years later the laundry men and personal stewards who had looked after me so well were no more.

The Master was the Commodore of the Fleet and was retiring at the end of this trip. Though this rank had been formally abolished three years before, he liked to feel that he, as Senior Master in Elder Dempster, continued in that tradition. And he was very keen to be dressed in his favourite Number Tens for his final dinner aboard. In spite of heading into much cooler weather, the 'Rig of the Day' order remained: tropical whites. However, bad weather ruined his party. As we made our way up the Western Approaches it was freezing cold, fog set in and the Captain was called to the bridge. I was miserably cold in my long white trousers and tunic, even wearing my duffle coat. I don't think the Captain was much happier. He was even less so when he put his head beyond the bridge dodger to better observe the rough weather and the wind whipped away his cap. He had to borrow a junior officer's cap for his final berthing at Pier Head, Liverpool; no gold braid on the peak.

Aureol berthed at the Princes Landing Stage, under the blessing of the Three Graces, dropped off her passengers and then shifted to her berth in Brocklebank Dock. Six years later jet travel superseded those leisurely days at sea and she was sold on to be an accommodation vessel in Jeddah.

I was taken by Elders' Marine Superintendent, Mr R.E. Hutson, to the Mercantile Marine Office at Cornhill for a very important occasion: the cancellation of my Indentures as an Apprentice, authorised by the MMO Official Stamp, dated 22 September 1969.

On the back of my Indenture was typed the following:

'We, Elder Dempster lines Ltd, agree to the cancellation of this Indenture, with all its covenants and engagements, to enable Midshipman STD Quail to study for his Second Mates examination. He has completed a continuous period of training with this company of a standard not lower than that of the Merchant Navy Training Board. His service has been to our satisfaction and during this time he was reported upon by the Masters under whom he served as being honest, sober and attentive to his duties at all times.'

And duly witnessed by all parties to the Indenture. The name of each vessel on which I had sailed was typed below this paragraph, with dates of sea time served. I had completed the necessary sea time and I was now ready to study for and sit my Second Mate's Certificate of Competency exam.

I paid off the *Aureol* the next day, no longer an Apprentice, and walked down the gangway into the next stage of life. I caught the train home for a couple of weeks leave before commencing my final term at Riversdale Road Technical College.

Chapter 14

TICKET TO THE FAR EAST

It was time. Time to obtain that precious Second Mate's Ticket, the focus of all my hopes for so long. After three and a half years of correspondence courses at sea plus two periods of three months ashore at college, I now had to face the examiners. I had six weeks of cramming to get up to speed. This was to be my last opportunity to enjoy the comforts of River House and the comradeship of my fellow cadets. Then I would have to get a post.

The classes in navigation, ship stability, cargo work and meteorology and periods of private study went by very quickly as we forced fed our tired brains with reams of practice papers. In the final week we sat for long hours in the exam room. I was very pleased to pass all my papers first time except the wretched signals exam. Though I was longing to go home I was forced to spend an extra month living at River House until the next timetabled exam.

Every day I caught the 82C bus down into Liverpool and pushed open a heavy door in the side of the magnificent Liver Building. Clattering down concrete steps to the basement I entered a dark, airless room. Here I sat for an hour, twice a day, every day, practising my Morse code. Candidates paired up; one focused intently on the little dot of light and whispered hoarsely, mouth close to ear, each block of letters and simple sentences to his scribe, before swapping roles. Those long hours in that dark and confined room have left an indelible memory. How the yeoman signaller put up with the monotony of it I never understood.

At last, on 14 November 1969, I was notified that I had duly passed my signals exam and with great relief went down to the Merchant Marine Office, Cornhill—the London Dock Office. I was given a green slip of paper signifying that I was now the proud possessor of a Board of Trade Second Mate's Certificate of Competency (Foreign Going). I would pick up the smart black folded cardboard certificate months later after my first trip to sea as a junior deck navigating officer.

    I realise now that it was extremely generous of the Elder Dempster to pay and feed me during this time, when I had resigned to fulfil my dream of sailing out of Hong Kong. I had enjoyed the Far East and wanted to see more of it. Elders were unable to offer me a berth on a ship trading to Australia, so with little consideration of my options, I left. Looking back to the freedom of employment opportunities enjoyed fifty years ago it seems amazing now that I should so easily move from one shipping line to another or think so casually about exploring the world. As a callow youth I certainly didn't examine possible difficulties in any depth. I did not properly value the high training standards experienced. I was a selfish youth with itchy feet. I wanted to sail in Far Eastern waters. I was hungry for experience and free to go. So goodbye Elder Dempster and West Africa. Hello Hong Kong.

    But first I needed to earn some Christmas cash.

The Cadet Years

*The Niger Creeks.
On route to Sapele
Little children in big canoes*

*Passing Ships
on the
Niger Creeks*

Boxes ashore

*'The Dockers Statue'
at the Royal Victoria
Dock by Les Johnson.
Dedicated to all
dockworkers from
1800-1988*

*Aboard MV Mamfe
approaching the
Devil's Cauldron,
Matadi*

*MV Pegu
Fellow cadet
John recovering
from pneumonia*

Fourah Bay: Cadet at the wheel

FB Headman 'Pop', relaxing before arrival in port; and below, centre

Off duty cadets by the pool. Spot the author, back row

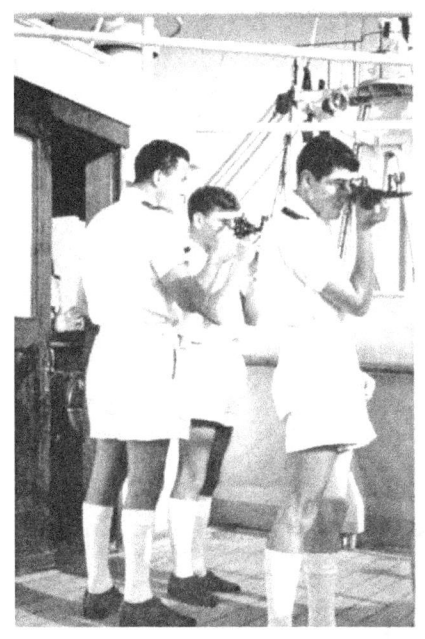

Cadets learning to take horizontal sextant angles

Chris on standby in clean T shirt

G17

The Captain of the Fourah Bay commanded our utmost respect

West Africa. A cadet takes away the jolly boat

Company ships Apapa-side

Stoppering-off.

Glenorchy. Morning coffee in the Smoke Room with the Third Officer

Sunset in the Indian Ocean

Chapter 15

SPANISH WINE

I proudly waved my piece of green paper at the Marine Superintendent in the Mercantile Marine Office close to Tower Bridge and he signed me on the Ship's Articles; my first time as a third officer. I had obtained the post via the officers' London Pool. In those days companies were frequently short of officers and made regular use of this marine industry employment agency.

I had taken just one week's leave at home in Maidenhead before, on the 21 November 1969, I shipped out of London on *MV Vargas*, 2,053 grt, a McAndrews Line ship engaged on the traditional trade between Spain and the UK carrying foodstuffs out to Gibraltar and bringing home oranges and wine. I kept the 8-12 watch at sea and, under the close direction of the mate, supervised cargo operations in port.

The shore gangs had carried on quite happily without me.

A three day passage took us down the Thames, down the English Channel, across the Bay of Biscay, closely hugging the coast of Portugal until we came to the picturesque port of Lisbon. I took the opportunity to explore ashore. In the main square I discovered an unusual lift that took pedestrians from one street level to another. High on the cliffs above the town the castle and a great church that had survived the earthquake of 1755 still dominated the skyline.

A day's voyage further south took us to Gibraltar. We berthed under the shadow of the sheer face of massive rock which I had seen from sea when on the *Pegu* three years before. After the population of the fabled apes fell to seven, Sir Winston Churchill gave orders in 1942 to rebuild the numbers of Barbary apes, or more correctly, macaques, to ensure that, keeping faith with an old legend, Gibraltar remained under British rule. I climbed the Rock but do not remember seeing any macaques. Are the Empire days of Gibraltar numbered?

Our cargo consisted of basics; boxes of yo-yos, household supplies and shoes, left-footed shoes in one crate and right-footed in another, in an attempt to reduce pilfering. What could a thief do with two left shoes?

Evenings were a welcome opportunity for a run ashore, visiting the various bars on Main Street patrolled by Bobbies in British uniforms. Red telephone boxes and red pillar boxes stood sentry by walls and byways. At home abroad.

We met a bunch of US Navy sailors on R&R. The saddest guy was the sailor, called the Father, who was not allowed to drink, but was responsible for his men, keeping them out of the clutches of the military police we could see patrolling the streets and get them safely back to their ship.

The officers of *Vargas* enjoyed a glass of wine at lunch, a first for me. The large wicker demijohn was routinely refilled for five shillings a time. Followed by a glass of plum brandy, sleep was inevitable. I woke from an illicit slumber, dashed out on deck and the chief officer discovered me on duty… just.

Next stop was a day's voyage to Valencia to fill our wine tanks. Then just three hours on to Burriana, a 'one mule' port where we loaded boxes of oranges from a broken down jetty. There were no tugs to pull us off and space was tight. Although we completed loading during the morning we had to wait for the evening offshore breeze to build up. Springing off, *Vargas* turned about and headed out to sea.

On our return voyage we sailed right up the Thames and docked at Butler's Wharf, in the shadow of Tower Bridge. This was a Friday night and no cargo was to be worked until Monday. I was granted weekend leave. It was a novelty to walk down the gangway, along the quay, climb the stairs to the pavement level of Tower Bridge, walk across to the tube station and catch the train from Paddington to Maidenhead. On Monday morning I reversed the journey. It felt so strange to join the throng of commuters, destination not an office but my ship. I paid off and received my first 'Very Good' conduct and character report in my Seamen's Record and Discharge Book. This Report of Character, (Very Good (or VG) for ability and general conduct), was vital, for without it no officer or seaman could gain further employment. A 'Decline To Report' in each column (a double DR) spelt unemployment.

Whenever we joined a ship, officers and crew signed a legal document called Articles of Agreement. These laid out under Board of Trade Regulations the conditions of feeding, (victuals) we were allowed by statute and regulations which bound us to the ship under the command of the Master. We could not take shore leave at any time without his permission. Paying off the ship was the moment when we were legally freed from our Agreements, and when we would receive wages in cash for the voyage less any allotments made for parents or wives at home, less any bar bills or other sundry expenses loaned against our final payoff day. Some men would pay off with virtually nothing in their pockets having spent all their wages on beer and women.

McAndrews has survived as shipping agents for a modern container line. It survives because it modernised and diversified. Diversify or die. The truth of that epigram is proved in the graveyards of the many once great British Shipping Companies.

After an excellent Christmas leave I went up for an interview with Butterfield and Swire in Fenchurch Street, London. This long-established company which had traded for many years within China now traded between Hong Kong and Oceania. I wanted to sail in the South China Sea, through the myriad islands of the Philippines, to the distant shores discovered by Captain Cook. I wanted to encounter new cultures, embark on new adventures.

Second Life

Junior Navigating Officer

in

China Navigation

Hong Kong to Oceania

Hong Kong to Oceania Routes

Chapter 16

HONG KONG

I stood outside Swire House on Fenchurch Street, headquarters of John Swire and Sons. Nervously adjusting the knot of my tie I swept a hand through my hair and pushed open the door that led to my future.

'Good morning,' I addressed the city-groomed receptionist. 'I have an appointment for a post on the sea staff.'

'Good morning. Do take a seat and I will tell Personnel Manager that you are here.'

Anxious minutes ticked on. I had at last been called in for interview and I badly wanted it to be successful.

'Mr Quail. Welcome. Do come in,' invited a tall urbane man with slightly too-long hair, flecked with grey. He waved me politely though the big brown door and I entered a large office, a map of the world adorning one wall. He indicated an office chair and I sat bolt upright, opposite an imposing desk. Urbane Man slipped easily into his chair.

Hong Kong

'Now tell me, Mr Quail, why you want to work for us?' he smoothly enquired.

I launched into an account of my adventures in China, Hong Kong and Japan and spoke passionately of my desire to see the Far East, of developing my craft, operating between the South China Sea and Oceania. And emphasised my excellent training in Ocean Fleets.

Urbane Man—I was too nervous to remember his name—was sufficiently impressed with my tale, and also needing deck officers for their large fleet, to offer me the position of junior navigating officer with their deep sea trading arm, China Navigation, based in Hong Kong. I was delighted.

China Navigation founded in 1876 in London, initially to trade up the Yangtze River from their Shanghai base with passengers and cargo, expanded operations in 1883 and set up a service to Australia. I was joining a well-established company.

A couple of weeks later I bid a fond farewell to my mother and my brothers and took a train to Heathrow for the long flight to Hong Kong.

After checking my baggage, I waited for my flight departure. Quietly drinking a cup of coffee and reading the paper, an insistent tannoy announcement finally registered in my brain.

'This is the final call for flight BOAC 0031 to Hong Kong. Would all passengers make their way to the boarding gate immediately! I repeat, immediately!'

'That's my flight!' I yelped. I zipped through customs, (no security check in 1970) sped down unending corridors, arriving very puffed at the Boeing 707, last man on. The stewardess smiled a welcome and carefully closed the door behind me.

A long letter home written a few days later from Hong Kong described the flight and my early days in Hong Kong. I settled into my window seat and we took off with a surge of power that pressed me against my seat. Thirty seconds later I looked down on a Lego city, as we climbed on through the clouds to 30,000 feet. One and a half uneventful hours later we landed at a snowy Frankfurt for a thirty minute stopover, during which time I stretched my legs in the transit lounge. I enquired about making a phone call but it would have taken over an hour to make a connection. Ninety minutes later I was chatting up Italian girls at Rome airport. Enjoyment of food was an important element on my first international flight. Lunch was smoked salmon, pate, cheese and biscuits, enjoyed with a large glass of wine. The afternoon tea fruitcake was a little dry...

Peering through the porthole as we flew over India, I saw occasional pinpricks of light which pierced the darkness, indicating small towns. No lights relieved the gloom in the rural villages. No electricity. Delhi, even in the middle of the night, provided a welcome opportunity to walk about in the airport transit lounge, after six and a half hours cooped up in my seat. Magnificently turbaned Indians in bright uniforms and sporting marvellous beards and moustaches offered trays of coke and orange juice. There was barely time to down our refreshments before we took off for Bangkok on the next three and half hour leg. The stewardess offered orange juice, the Delhi water heavily tainted with chlorine. It tasted awful. I stretched my long legs across the three seats that I had to myself for the entire flight and dozed for a couple of hours.

On arrival in Hong Kong I was met by a CNCo office 'boy' who handed me HK$50. This was not a gift. My first pay slip revealed that this was only an advance on my meagre salary.

Happily there was no room in the junior officers' wing at the China Navigation Officer's Mess in Quarry Road, so I was given a Captain's cabin. Very nice. I had a view of Taikoo Dockyard, with the mountains of Hong Kong rising behind it. It was rather dull and misty, the temperature a cool 57°F. In front of my window was a full-sized bowling green. A Chinese gardener languidly swept worm casts off the lawn with a long, curving bamboo pole. The perfect grass is now the base of yet another skyscraper.

One evening I visited a Glen Line ship at the Blue Funnel Wharf and met the third mate with whom I had sailed on *MV Aureol*.

'There are many of us ex Blue Funnel and Elder Dempster men in China Navigation,' he said, passing on fleet news. 'There is now a shortage of officers in Ocean Fleets and promotions have been speeded up to encourage more people to stay.'

Too late for me.

I sent a telegram home announcing my arrival and continued to explore Hong Kong. A 23-year-old chief officer and I went to see *'Carry on Doctor'*. Silly, but entertaining. Promotion is very fast here, I noted. After a quick game of snooker in the Mess, I retired to bed.

In the morning I saw Mr Havilland, the Hong Kong office Personnel Manager. 'Nice chap,' I laconically noted in my letter home. 'In a couple of days he will let me know to which ship I am to be posted.' In the meantime, I spent a week or so idling around, getting to know more people, visiting company ships and finding my way round the bars, churches and cinemas. I took the tram up the Peak and enjoyed the view of the modern city spread before me, skyscrapers shooting up everywhere.

I read an interesting magazine article about China's trade with the world via Hong Kong. 'In one month China gets US $30 million in exports so Hong Kong is safe for ever'. An interesting viewpoint twenty-seven years before we lost Hong Kong.

I met an attractive girl, June Billimore, who gave me the address of her great friend in Melbourne. Friendly introductions would be useful when there on shore leave. I was really looking forward to exploring Australia's famous cities.

I was taken to a local nautical instrument supplier and acquired a solid, black Canadian-built 1946 micrometer-screw sextant. This was my faithful companion on every ship on which I served, and I used it to find my way about the oceans of the world for the next eighteen years.

At the end of January I received orders to fly the next day to Sydney to join *MV Taiyuan* at Wooloomooloo.

Unfortunately my fellow officers were determined to send me off in style. I drank far too much whisky in the airport bar and was very unwell on the flight.

I cleared Sydney customs in a haze and weakly climbed in a taxi. Stomach churning, I urgently requested the driver to stop at a local pub. I jumped out and rushed through to the door. The barman was hosing down the tile walls with generous gouts of water. I did not need a shower; I needed to talk to God on the great white telephone. I just made it. Welcome to Sydney.

The hot morning sun blazed down as I dragged myself up the gangway, lugging heavy suitcase, sextant, nearly dropping the office post for the Captain, and staggered straight to bed. I slept like one dead. Apparently I was duty officer and all the other fellow officers went ashore leaving me in charge. It was Saturday and no cargo was being worked until Monday.

Later that afternoon Captain Cunningham signed me on Articles as fourth mate. By the evening I had recovered sufficiently to enjoy a good dinner served by Chinese stewards, in the recently re-fitted dining saloon.

We enjoyed the same food as the passengers but had to behave ourselves on our separate table. Later I joined the junior officers and ambled ashore down the long wharf of Wooloomooloo to the pub near the gate. I nursed a cold and refreshing soft drink.

Sunday morning opened fine and sunny so I walked down the gangway and across the inviting green space of the Domain, past the imposing red sandstone of the art gallery (must visit that later, I thought) to St Mary's Cathedral. Taking a pew under soaring Gothic columns I was comforted by the familiar liturgy. Physically and spiritually refreshed I took a long walk back through the Domain and across the tree-covered space of the Royal Botanic Gardens to Mrs Macquarie's Chair. Here I sat on a bench and contemplated the sailboats on the sparkling waters; a chance to breathe and to be…

A letter home written on 11 February tells of the marvellous week I had enjoyed in Melbourne. June Bullimore's great friend Lynn made me very welcome and so did all her flatmates. We four deck officers shared cargo work duties between us and so I enjoyed several days off. Over the weekend I met a lively bunch of people. On a blazing hot Sunday (97°F) I spent a day at the beach with them. After a long dinner I brought them back to the ship at 1 a.m., gave them a drink and a lightning tour before they went home amid warm expressions of friendship. As I put it, Melbourne was well set up for friends and indeed I did meet up with them on the next call.

We departed Melbourne, down the Yarra River and across the wide Port Philip Bay and rounded the tall stone tower of the lighthouse on Wilson Promontory, the most southerly point of Australia. From there we shaped course 1735 miles across the Tasman Sea, leaving the long finger of New Caledonia to port, on out into the South Pacific Ocean, and after five sunny days arrived at Suva, Fiji. On a quick sortie ashore I discovered a long, palm tree-lined main street with simple shops selling souvenirs, watches and expensive camera equipment. A parallel narrow-gauge rail track carried big diesel-powered engines which pulled a string of little sugar-cane wagons. Most of the mills and tracks had been built by the Colonial Sugar Refining Company in the late 1800s. By a twist of fate I would return to these islands two years later, on a chemical tanker loading thick brown molasses for Australia.

Our next port of call was Hong Kong, a voyage of almost two weeks and 4,507 miles. We left Vanuatu to port, the scattered British Solomon

Islands to starboard, and sailed between the islands of New Britain and Papua New Guinea. After an early breakfast I was on the bridge by 0750, in good time to get my bearings before taking over the watch. At sea I took my evening meal at 1830 with the duty engineer and returned to the bridge to relieve the chief officer. He had passengers at his table that he was required to entertain. As ever, food dominated our days.

I stood on the bridge wing, checking the horizon for shipping, coastlines and seagulls, breathing in the warm tropical air. *Taiyuan* pitched her bows softly into a low swell. Bright diamond lights of the first evening stars pinged into focus as the red glow on the horizon faded to pale orange. The passengers below enjoyed their meal as we threaded through the scattered Santa Cruz Islands.

Before the Master retired for the night he always wrote up his Captain's Night Orders. My duties were carefully listed and courses of action limited. The officer of the watch was required to maintain a steady course and keep a good lookout; to call the Captain before any alter course was made, either at the expected alter course position, or to avoid potential collision. Watch keepers were given very little latitude to alter the track of the ship, compared to my final years at sea in the 1980s when, as second or chief mate, I was expected to adjust courses to keep the ship on her track. And we certainly manoeuvred as necessary to avoid collision when transiting busy European waters. But now I signed the Orders and settled down to my clearly stated duties.

Keeping a good lookout was vital, as was a clear knowledge of the Rules of The Road, the highway code of the sea. The black tropical night was pierced by white, red and green navigation lights of passing and crossing vessels. Sharp eyes and a good pair of binoculars were essential. Estimating from the bearing and pattern of navigation lights the course and closest point of approach (CPA) was a prime duty. If less than a mile, then call the Master. One hundred passengers and sixty crew slept safely in their beds, trusting in the junior officer of the watch. Me! Those first watches made me nervous. Was the Captain watching though his for'ard porthole, fretting about his very junior deck officer? How well did he sleep at night?

Built in 1949 the ship's radar, basic by modern standards, was only switched on when in close inshore waters or when landfall was expected. The rhythmic sweep of the radar beam revealed a fuzzy orange outline of the land. In busy shipping areas I plotted the glowing orange blobs, each target manually tracked in white chinagraph pencil, checked CPA, and thus collision risk.

'Wouldn't it be wonderful if we could identify each target on our radars, to see in figures actually on the screen, to be able to read off its CPA, course and speed,' was an oft expressed opinion between officers on the bridge. 'It would make collision avoidance decisions easier to make, and thus shipping lanes safer.' Like the system air traffic controllers use. How long would it take to get that technology fitted on ships? Over thirty years. Automatic Identification System (AIS) became mandatory in 2002 and has led to a reduction in collisions. AIS has been effective in managing traffic flows in shipping lanes, maritime security, search and rescue, and fleet tracking for owners and shippers. All impossible to imagine in 1970.

Landfall off a well-defined headland was confirmed by comparing the fuzzy orange outline to the chart. One dark night we were due alter course off an island headland, so I switched on the radar well ahead of expected landfall time. The radar trace painted a solid horseshoe shaped landmass just five miles away, dead ahead. Horrified, I phoned the Captain.

'Fourth Mate here, Captain. Unexpected radar echo, dead ahead. Five miles away.'

'Right,' he said, 'I'm coming up'.

He calmly checked our position. He had been here before. An unexpected current had set us a few miles off course. Rapidly rotating the course control knob on 'George', the auto pilot, he altered direction, taking us back to our plotted track. Much relief felt by this junior navigator.

On sunny days at sea, of which there were many, passengers lay on the sunbeds getting a tan. If a distant rain cloud was spotted, watch-keepers were under standing orders to plot its track and if on a 'collision course', alter our heading to pass well clear upwind. Keeping our one hundred passengers dry and happy was the priority.

The swimming pool was made of canvas and temporarily rigged in the hatch coaming of Number 4 hatch once we had cleared harbour and were out at sea. One day I decided to join two girls swimming in the pool but had not taken into account the rather choppy sea causing the water to slop about heavily. I jumped into the pool to give them a mighty splash but the water sloshed away and I landed on my bottom in two feet of water.

Luckily it was just enough to break my fall but give me a very sore coccyx. The girls were oblivious to my antics.

After lunch at sea I carried out various deck duties, making sure that the lifeboats, life-saving appliances such as life rafts and life buoys and fire extinguishers were kept up-to-date. Metal storage compartments were bolted under the lifeboats thwarts. Every tin of condensed milk and every tin of emergency biscuits was scraped through the access porthole the size of my fist. After checking for soundness, rust and quantity, they were repacked and the numerous fiddly butterfly nuts secured. Tedious work. Water was checked for cleanliness, rust and signs of little wriggly beasties. Every few months tanks were drained out and refilled. Letting off fire extinguishers to test their effectiveness was fun but refilling with water, chemicals and sulphuric acid glass vials, time consuming and risky. Acid burns are painful, I discovered many years later.

I paid courteous attention to the too few luscious female passengers. Coming off watch at midnight was rather late to meet one girl as her parents kept a very close eye. I persuaded her to come to a furtive meeting under the lifeboats. She satisfied my desperate need for a kiss from her soft, yielding lips but she refused my attempts to stroke her glorious breasts. Sex was forever on the mind of this junior officer; being so close but not being allowed even to touch was deeply frustrating. However, one passenger did become a girlfriend for a time. She and her friends introduced me to Sydney life; parties, swimming off Balmoral Beach, BBQs, movies, sport. I loved it all; so much so that a few months later I made Sydney my home for four years.

Later on in my seagoing career I missed those days of meals served by a steward, followed by coffee and liqueurs in one of the bars. Even as a lowly forth officer I could press the bell in my cabin and a steward would bring me my afternoon tea on a tray containing a yellow teapot, yellow cup and saucer and a plate of cakes. He would take my laundry away and bring it back starched, pressed and with epaulettes attached. One day I called the Chinese steward over to take my order but made the cultural error of using an overhand action. He complained to the Captain and I was called before him for a dressing down.

'You've only been here a few weeks and you are already upsetting my stewards!' he sternly admonished me. 'Let me give you some advice. As a junior officer you must learn to be culturally sensitive. When requesting a steward's assistance, beckon with an under hand motion. Politeness is everything and don't you forget it.'

It was a useful lesson but the telling off was hard to take.

Saturdays at sea were special. At lunchtime the stewards set up tables on the officers' promenade deck, laden with lashings of meat, salad and cold cans of beer and tonic. And gin. And ice. The sailors set up the half oil drum barbecue on its stand and lit the fire. The chief engineer and captain donned aprons and got busy barbecuing masses of steaks and sausages. The officers gathered round on the sunny deck, dressed in tropical whites, chatting and enjoying a cold beer or a glass of gin and tonic, to the satisfying sound of clinking ice. My plateful of meat devoured, I retreated to my cabin for a much appreciated two hour kip on the day bed.

Hong Kong harbour was impressive, filled with numerous motorised junks; some with iconic sails; countless freighters were on the move and dotted about the anchorage. A huge aircraft carrier, attended by two warships, lay quietly but menacingly centre stage. The whole maritime scene was framed by green mountains, their flanks clad in soaring skyscrapers and vast white cliffs of residential blocks; cities in the sky. A few verdant slopes had, so far, escaped being clad in concrete.

We berthed at Ocean Terminal. After the bustle of mooring, we gathered at the gangway to bid goodbye to the passengers, including the shapely but shy teenager. Time to explore the bars of Hong Kong.

Cargo loading was still a mystery to me. I watched the chief officer, Dudley Groves, open the wooden lid of the Ralston Stability Indicator and reveal an engraved plate of a cross section of the ship. Stability tables were pasted to the inside. He flicked over the weights fixed to pivots representing fuel and water; then he placed in each space metal blocks, representing the weight of the cargo. He cranked the lever to float the whole device in the gimbals, and it balanced. So he was happy. But I was still not much the wiser. I met Dudley over thirty years later at a lunch on HQS *Wellington*. Much water had passed under the hull of our lives over the years.

Soon after clearing the junks and crowded shipping channels we sailed through the South China Sea on route to Sydney, Manila to port. Sailing on, we traversed many seas and narrow straits on the two week, 4,500 mile voyage. On through the Mindoro Strait, avoiding the many islands of the Sulu Sea, the narrow Basilan Strait hard by the resoundingly named Zamboanga; on through the Molucca Sea, the Seram Sea, and the Arafura

Sea bounded by the coast of Australia. After a week of weaving through these tropical seas we arrived off Thursday Island where we picked up the pilot. We relied on his expertise to guide us through the tortuous but beautiful channels of the Great Barrier Reef.

Over five wonderful days of cruise-like conditions, we raised headlands named by Lieutenant Cook nearly 200 years before. I possess a facsimile copy of the chart that he drew in 1770 of the East Coast New South Wales, or New Holland as it was then also known. Named after English places, high-ranking members of English life or events on the voyage, the headlands and rivers tell the story of exploration and discovery; Endeavour River, Cape Tribulation, Whitsunday Passage—the sea painted an astonishingly vibrant ultra-marine blue, mixed with soft, milky swirls, like a cappuccino for a goddess. We checked off more significant landmarks: Cape Palmerston, Sandy Cape, the Glasshouse Mountains, Point Danger, Smoky Cape and Sugarloaf Point, until we entered the stunning natural harbour of Port Jackson. Lieutenant Cook never investigated this glorious setting, merely noted the potential opening in the forbidding cliffs. Hence Botany Bay was the inappropriate landing of the First Fleet in 1788.

Taiyuan berthed at Walsh Bay, immediately to port after passing under Sydney Harbour Bridge. I was soon down the gangway, out the dock gates, up the grassy bank and strolling through The Rocks. I was energised by the sweeping cityscape. A line of old houses sheltered under the looming Bridge. A green and pleasant park was set with inviting benches. Ships lay snug at their berths below, mine included. George Street, Pitt Street and the surrounding streets were all within easy walking distance. Over the next few days—when released from cargo working duties—I explored the vibrant harbour by ferry from Circular Quay, discovering little jetties jutting out from beaches and promontories along the North Shore. I opened an account at David Jones, ate at local restaurants, drank in the city pubs and walked the spacious city parks. After just two calls at this wonderful port city, I began to feel that Sydney was my city.

I grew to love the *Taiyuan* and my four months on board were all too short. After only two voyages, the Hong Kong office decided that it was time to move me to another ship for further experience of their fleet. I really did not want to leave.

Back in Hong Kong by May 1970, a few days after my twenty second birthday, I regretfully signed off the *Taiyuan*. It had been a great experience. After a night in the China Navigation hostel I was flown down to Sydney to join the *Marsina*.

Chapter 17

SAILING THE CORAL SEA

'Take care with that f'ing bike!' the Second Engineer roundly cursed the dockers as they nearly damaged his beloved motorbike being swung ashore on the stores davit. Fury was swiftly followed by freedom, as with a cheery, 'Let's go!' we roared off down the quay to explore upcountry Rabaul, with me perched precariously on the pillion. Along a winding road we discovered a line of gloomy but enticing cave mouths. Brushing away hanging tendrils of encroaching jungle we discovered cavernous but empty storage areas, once used by the Japanese during the Second World War to hide their munitions. Driving on round the harbour it was difficult to visualise that this was a flooded volcanic caldera, till I picked out the high mountains of the caldera rim curving round us on two sides.

I had joined the *Marsina* in Sydney, signed on by Captain (call-me-Cyril) Cocksedge. He was a short man, with thick black hair above an open, pleasant face. His white uniform was always immaculate. *Marsina* was a happy little ship, on a run between Sydney, Brisbane, Port Moresby, Rabaul, Kavieng and Honiara. She was in effect a grocery and hardware supply ship. We filled up in Sydney and Brisbane with general supplies and other needs for the far-flung communities living in the British Solomon Islands, Papua New Guinea, New Britain and New Ireland. Berthing at these simple little ports on the edge of the South Pacific was a revelation. Life was slower, simpler. We had time in port to explore. I vowed to return one day.

The acrid stench that assailed my nostrils told me that this was definitely not the correct path through the jungle. Right before me was a dark, gaping hole. It was a rancid cesspit. Carefully retracing my footsteps I peered through an open doorway into the gloom of a native hut.

Stretched out upon a simple wooden bed, one leg up, one leg stretched out flat, a Solomon Islander slumbered away the afternoon heat. Not wishing to disturb his dreams, I moved quietly along a muddy path that led across open ground.

Ahead lay a dark, narrow opening in the encroaching jungle canopy. Distant snapping of dry branches echoed through the undergrowth. A large shadowy figure emerged into bright sunlight and blocked the narrow path ahead. What was in the large sack over his shoulder? He drew closer. I held my breath. A wide, white-toothed grin spread across his friendly, black face. 'Good day!' he cried cheerfully. It is only our fears that stop us exploring the world and meeting new people. And here I was in Honiara, taking an afternoon walk.

Others had been here before me. Stepping free of the encroaching jungle I found myself on a narrow ridge with expansive views to distant rolling hills. A peeling, hand-painted, wooden board proclaimed that at this point a U.S. Army division had defended the ridge against a Japanese attack in 1942. We were enjoined not to forget those who had fallen in defense of freedom.

My maritime travels had taken me to the other side of the globe, sailing between Hong Kong, Sydney, New Zealand. Now I, the third officer on board *MV Marsina*, was sailing around the islands in the northern sector of the Pacific Ocean known as Melanesia. We had berthed in the capital Honiara, on the main island of Guadalcanal, still, in 1970, in the *British Solomon Islands*.

When I was a boy growing up in the Cotswolds I read an extraordinary tale called the *Pattern of Islands* by Arthur Grimble. From 1912 to 1932 he was Our Man in the Gilbert and Ellice Islands, rising from cadet to Resident Commissioner, later a Governor. My time sailing the Coral Sea gave me a thirst that is yet to be assuaged. I want to discover yet more about the geography and culture of these scattered island communities.

I had just obtained my driving licence after only four days of driving lessons when in Brisbane dry dock for two weeks. We moseyed over to the Kavieng Agent's Office. 'May I borrow a car, please? I've passed my driving test. It would be good to explore a bit.'

'OK Mate. No Worries,' the Australian agent kindly but unwisely acceded to my request. I was keen to go for a drive and show off to my fellow officers. However my driving skills were rudimentary to say the least. I found it difficult to coordinate the foot pedals between changing gears and making efficient use of clutch, brake and accelerator. The car went kangarooing down the main street, almost out of control, my shipmates laughing their heads off at me. To add insult to injury when I returned the car to the parking lot, I failed to apply the brake in time, and crashed into the bollard marking the agent's parking slot. He was not amused and Head Office deducted wages from my salary over a period of a few months to pay for the damage.

'Pack your swimmers. We are going to the beach for a swim and a snorkel.' The harbour pilot drove a group of us out for a welcome jolly. Hanging head down in the warm water, kicking my flippers against the current, I spent a happy time observing a reef alive with colourful fish and amazing coral. A BBQ lunch on the beach followed, with a cold beer from the esky. Life was good.

Midday was gin and tonic time. The gin was a generous measure, up to the CNCo oval logo (halfway up the glass), topped up with tonic. Two of those before lunch were rapidly followed by a two hour zizz on the day bed, resting from the tropical heat. Air conditioning was not installed.

China Navigation had bought the *Papuan Chief* in 1966 and converted her in Hong Kong to side port loading for the East Australia-New Guinea service. Big holes were cut into the hull in the way of the tween deck, huge doors fitted and made watertight. In 1969, renamed *Marsina*, she was chartered by a shipping agency which operated throughout the South Pacific islands, the famous Burns Philp Co Ltd. (Burns Philp operated the first tourist trip in 1884 from Thursday Island to New Guinea.)

On the multiport Pacific Island run, turn-round time had to be reduced. Time was money. For hundreds of years ships had been loaded and discharged using the break bulk method. Teams of men stacked boxes one by one onto a flat tray. Four men attached the corner strops onto a crane hook. The crane driver swung the two ton load up from the dock high over the hull and down into the hold. If derricks were used, two winch drivers were needed. A man directed the crane driver or winchmen to slow, stop, heave or slack the load. A hatch gang of eight or more men manhandled boxes into a new stack in the hold, building a safe and secure stow, box by box, crate by crate, sack by sack. This took time, lots of time. And manpower. And money, lots of money.

The answer was palletisation. Boxes or whatever were pre-loaded in a distant warehouse and secured to the pallet by steel strapping. A dockside forklift delivered this straight to the side port cut into the hull, where it was met by the ship's forklift and rapidly manoeuvred into position. Or delivered to a crane hook and lowered into the hold. Pilfering, the bane of break bulk stowage, was hugely reduced. Dock labour requirements were drastically cut. Not popular with the unions. But palletisation was fast and efficient. Containerisation was being developed in a parallel universe, but that is not my story.

On completion of loading in Sydney and Brisbane, the ship's forklifts were tightly boxed-in at the centre of each hatch and secured for the voyage with final pallets slotted carefully into position. In the island, shore-side fork lifts rapidly removed the cargo from the newly fitted side ports, fed by the ship's forklifts as space was created. When all pallets had been lifted ashore I drove the forklift across the empty hold and parked it close up to the spar ceiling, (horizontal battens securely attached to the hull framing which kept cargo away from the damp ship sides), where it was securely lashed in place. It was a complete contrast to my experiences on the UK/West Africa trade.

Sailing southeast down the tropical coastline of Papua New Guinea, we entered the Solomon Sea, keeping clear of the many islands dotted about, hugging the south coast of New Britain and headed north into the St Georges Channel, the green clad mountains of New Ireland to starboard. After a comfortable three day passage we anchored off Rabaul to await our berth. Time for a swim. Willing hands un-dogged and opened the side port cut into the hull and I dived into the cool, clear, fish-filled tropical waters. Bliss.

Exploring ashore later on the motorbike, we stopped on a sandy promontory high above the natural harbour, formed by a volcanic lake crater, sat on rusting Japanese gun emplacements and admired the view. Decades later, in 1994, the volcano erupted and buried Old Rabaul under several feet of ash. What I saw then has now vanished. But New Rabaul has risen from the ruins.

Half a day north, skirting the edge of the Bismarck Sea, we followed a lush and mountainous coastline until we berthed at Kavieng. This sleepy backwater with somewhat basic infrastructure facilities was the administrative centre of the Papuan New Guinean province of New Ireland. Within an hour of arrival, the cargo was rapidly discharged by our efficient forklifts and lifted into utility trucks lined up on the land side of the narrow quay. Easy. A simple, slick operation compared to the usual bustle of cargo worked by noisy gangs of dockers controlling a forest of derricks.

I repeated the circuit twice over four months and was beginning to get to know the locals in each port. I had made friends in Sydney, and enjoyed the camaraderie of my shipmates. I wanted to stay but orders came through posting me to yet another ship.

I paid off *Marsina* at the beginning of September, nine months after coming out from England. I was in desperate need of a break from the routine and so was very happy to get three weeks local leave. Ralph from Cheam had dark slicked-back hair, a wide smile and a diffident, somewhat shy air. We had sailed together and had arranged to meet up in Sydney. He very generously allowed me to kip on his sofa and we spent most the time supping amber nectar in Sydney's bars, meeting up with other CNCo colleagues. A great adventure was planned: a drive up to Brisbane but it was cancelled. Too far. It was over 600 miles after all. It was a time of aimless drift and nothing exciting happened. I did not feel refreshed by the time I got ticket and instructions to join my next ship.

The Sydney Office sent a telegram warning of my impending arrival.

To: CAPTAIN STAGG, *MV TSINGTAO*. AUCKLAND.

QUAIL FLIES OUT SYDNEY 24 SEPTEMBER TO RELIEVE THIRD OFFICER DOVE WHO FLIES BACK THE SAME DAY.

I arrived quite exhausted.

Chapter 18

MOMENTOUS DECISIONS

Breathing hard, heart pounding, I halted to catch my breath. 760 feet below me was a sweeping beach vista, my ship just out of sight. I had climbed the steep, winding path to the top of Mount Maunganui, an extinct volcanic cone. A profusion of seashells were scattered in the soft soil. Shell middens I later learned, evidence of Maori occupation over many centuries. Not a huge rise in the sea bed after all.

Soon after returning aboard *MV Tsingtao,* we completed discharge of cargo and prepared the ship for sea—dropping derricks into their crutches and sealing the hatches with boards, tarps and locking bars— and I took my third officer's station on the bridge. I stood by the engine telegraphs and meticulously entered the times of Captain Stagg's orders in the Movement Book, as usual. We came off the berth easily, dropped off the pilot, and headed north along the Coromandel Peninsula, weaving through the many islands of the Hauraki Gulf. After a short twelve hours passage we came to the pleasant port city of Auckland, to back load for Hong Kong.

On Sunday, with no cargo being worked, I went for my usual walk and found my way to the local park. Families played games together, kicking a ball, throwing a Frisbee. Couples chatted happily as they ambled along the paths, enjoying close companionship. A pretty girl walked by at speed. She at least had a clear destination in mind. I was overwhelmed by the need to talk to her, get to know her. I desperately desired female company. I was going stir crazy—it's time to take drastic action and sort out my future.

I reflected on my career at sea so far. What had I achieved? How was I going to meet a girl if I stayed at sea? Did I really want promotion to Second Officer? If I stayed with China Nav, I would have to serve two and a half years before being granted home leave. Officers below the rank of chief officer were not allowed to get married. That was the old colonial rule.

More time ashore in Sydney would be good. It was time to settle down, cease sailing away. I could think about my future while living in the city I had grown to love. I would study for my Mate's ticket there. Much better than grinding through college in winter-grey England. I would speak to the personnel manager in the Hong Kong office about taking ticket leave in Sydney, or even leaving the company. This decision filled me with a renewed sense of purpose; a positive step, re-gaining control of my seemingly empty future.

On completion of cargo loading, a two day voyage south along the coast brought us to Wellington, known as the Chicago of the South, for it too is a very windy city. I walked to the top of Mount Victoria and drank in the windswept views overlooking the city. Forty three years later I explored the same city parks and historic streets with my wife and second child, now in her mid-thirties. I wish I had known then that such family happiness would indeed come to me.

We crossed the Cook Strait and headed south along the edge of the Pacific Ocean to Port Lyttelton, tucked under the southern flanks of the Port Hills. Down the gangway and away into the mountains I went. I pressed on up the settler track through farm gates, hemmed in by barbed wire fences till I reached to the top. I gazed down across the sweep of blue waters edged by the distant peaks and even higher mountain ranges. The view was breathtaking. Up this steep and unforgiving path had pushed the early settlers, their goods piled high on ox carts, as they made their way to Christchurch and a new life on the Canterbury Plains, far below.

The next day three junior officers took a taxi to Canterbury, driving via twin tunnels bored through the hillside and arrived at a non-descript suburban house. Someone had found girls and set up a party. It made a change but failed to ignite my interest.

Sauntering around later on a shopping trip I was surprised by the tall elegant spire of a very English Cathedral—now shaken down in the 2011 earthquake. I saw it again in 2013 with my family. Visitors walked by slowly and spoke in low muted tones, as if mourning an old friend; a reminder of the fragility of life.

From Port Lyttelton *Tsingtao* sailed to Hong Kong, a 5,400 miles voyage through some of the most fascinating waters of the western Pacific Ocean; great training for a deck officer, navigating with sextant and ancient radar through seas sprinkled with numberless isles.

We left Lord Howe Island to port, Norfolk Island well away to starboard. Keeping clear of dangerous reefs and scattered islets, we headed up the Coral Sea through the Luisiade Archipelago, Woodlark Island and on through the Solomon Sea. I was in the same waters through which I had sailed on the *Marsina* a few months before; Honiara to starboard, Port Moresby to port. The Vitiaz Strait separated the eastern nose of Papua New Guinea from the long tongue of land that was New Britain. Like a stray slick splattered on the chart, the island of New Ireland slid away to the northwest, separated from Rabaul by the St Georges Channel; the chart makers of long ago spreading the influence of *Pax Britannica* in this remote part of the globe. We entered the Bismarck Sea, its northern limits bounded by the Bismarck Archipelago. German cartographers had left their mark here too. The Great Powers fighting proxy battles with paper charts.

Sailing close to the West coast of Papua New Guinea, just south of Madang, I noted ahead of our course a sharp change in the colour of the sea. Intrigued, I swept a magnifying glass over the chart and made a detailed inspection of the cartography. A swirling mass of black contour lines provided an explanation. The vast swathe of muddy water that had cascaded down steep valleys from deep inland was swept miles out to sea by the powerful flow of the Gogol River. The rich soil of the forested highlands over which had sounded the exotic calls of Birds of Paradise now punched a russet fist into the crystal-clear aquamarine waters of the Bismarck Sea.

We sailed on between the Palau Islands and their off-lying reefs towards the myriad islands of the Philippines. On through the Philippines Sea, and the Luzon Strait, sprinkled with many islands, and entered the northern limits of the South China Sea. Finally, after eighteen days of expert navigation, we made safe harbour in Hong Kong.

On Christmas Day 1970, *Tsingtao* was alongside Ocean Terminal, and I the lone duty officer. All the officers had managed to find themselves a shore billet for the night. Sitting in the saloon by myself I was served a fine steak lunch by the Chinese steward. As he stood watching me chew it belatedly dawned on me that he was desperate to go home.

'Just put my pudding and cheese on the side table where I can help myself and go home to your family!'

'Are you sure?'

'Of course! Off you go.'

'Thank you, Sir, thank you.'

Christmas is a notoriously difficult time to be far from those we love. To be on my own on this day of family and community celebration rather sealed my fate.

A few days later, after an interview with the Personnel Manager at the offices of China Navigation, I made the worst decision of my life. Extreme boredom, lack of a love life and lack of leave had distorted my view of the opportunities before me. I resigned, free to set up home in Sydney. I would find employment in the Australian Merchant Navy for three times the pay. Would the money be worth the pain of loss of the benefits of being part of a professional team of British officers, on a well-run ship, staffed with attentive stewards? Time would tell.

I was about to change direction yet again and seek life in Australia. Would I find that which I sought? What *was* I seeking?

Third Life

Sydney

Home Leave

Australian Coasters

Chapter 19

UNSETTLED IN SYDNEY

Tsingtao returned to Auckland from Hong Kong on a final South Seas sail. My febrile mind retained few memories of that voyage, a privileged moment in time. What do I recall of tropical islands, narrow passages, blue waters, hot balmy days cruising south? Not a lot.

Captain Stagg paid me off on 29 January and wished me good luck. I dragged my trunk and kit bag down the gangway in search of a better life in Sydney. The New Zealand Airways lunch of lamb cutlets in aspic was delicious. Would my new life taste as good?

I arrived at Sydney on Friday night and phoned the CNCo Office. They didn't know what to do with me so Christine agreed to put me in the Australia Hotel. Thus I enjoyed a final weekend of luxury whilst I sorted out my own accommodation. I particularly remember the tinkling of piano and fountain during long meals in the elaborate dining room. Now destroyed. The fatal attraction of development.

Because I had worked for CNCo for a year I was entitled to three months' leave to study for and sit my Chief Mate's Certificate of Competence. Through an advert in the local paper I found a flat-share at Cremorne Point overlooking Sydney Harbour. Its great attraction was the wonderful view of yachts of all sizes racing across the shimmering waters.

I was happily surprised to receive $17 a week in subsistence money to top up my low salary. I popped into the office regularly to pick up the cash—and chat up the lovely Christine. (I fancied Christine. We all did.)

Each morning I strolled in warm sunshine from my flat to Cremorne Point wharf and boarded the ferry, mingling with summer-clad commuters. The harbour was alive with craft cutting white wakes. As we swung away from the jetty, three icons hove into view: Fort Denison, the Opera House, and the Bridge. Spindly cranes scored the sky over Utzon's emerging sails as we approached Circular Quay, the busy waterfront framed by a cityscape of towering office blocks. We came alongside with a creak of strained headrope and gangway clatter. I joined the surging throng pressing to reach the upper level train platform. Less than two years later I would be working on these ferries as a ferry hand.

Ultimo Technical College was my destination, to study for my Mate's Ticket. Unfortunately I had not learned the value of hard study. The lunchtime beer didn't help either. I sat my exam three months later and unsurprisingly failed to pass.

During my four months in Sydney I had become very attached to the life of sunshine and barbecues on the beach. I decided that I would indeed stay here and try my luck in the Australian Merchant Navy. A colleague passed on the news that there might be a job going with the Colonial Sugar Refining Company. They were looking for a deck officer for their chemical tanker fleet. I made an appointment and went along for an interview. The magnetic attraction was money, up from £1,800 to over £5,000 a year. I was easily seduced by the cash and did not think about what life aboard might be like. I was very pleased to be given the job. The only condition was that I became a permanent resident of Australia. I went to the Passport Office to find out how I did that. Arriving just before the Office closed for lunch the cheerful official behind the counter said,

'Just pick up your passport after lunch. She'll be right, mate, no worries.'

I did. It was. My passport proudly bore the stamp:

> DEPARTMENT of IMMIGRATION, SYDNEY.
> Permitted 19 May 1971 to Remain in Australia.

I was in.

The very next day I signed on board MV *Silverhawk*, 6,770 gross tonnage of low-tech chemical tanker. I was the third officer, working eight hours on sea watches but twelve hour shifts in port, day or night, in rotation with the second mate. The way of life compared to China Navigation was completely different. Gone were the smart, efficient Chinese stewards, replaced by a couple of charming gay Australians. The radio officers were ocker Australians, called Bruce or Bluey. This was going to be a new experience.

We carried sulphuric acid, hydrochloric acid, xylene, toluene, molasses and occasionally heavy oil. Cleaning the tanks after carrying heavy oil or molasses to back load pure chemicals required a harsh industrial cleaning process, using Matrax. The resultant filthy mix of oil, chemicals and water was pumped over the side into the clean blue ocean. I was ashamed of our brown wake. Once in international waters it wasn't against the law. The ocean was seen as a universal dump. Out of sight, out of mind.

We had a good variety of runs. We sailed from Bernie on the north coast of Tasmania to Melbourne, Sydney, up to Brisbane, Bundaberg (famous for its rum), Gladstone, Rockhampton, Mackay, Townsville, Cairns and little Lucinda. This bijou port boasted a street of bungalows and a basic telephone exchange. To make a phone call to my girlfriend skiing in Thredbo I stood outside in the street whilst the operator pushed plugs into sockets. Very basic. Like the ship.

The ship's equipment was somewhat creaky at the seams and the hydraulically operated valves from the control room often failed. Manual operation of the valves in the pump room below decks became necessary. However, when loading toxic chemicals such Xylene or Toluene, the air in the lower pump rooms was unbreathable, due to leaky joints. I donned a bright yellow plastic protective suit, strapped on the compressed air breathing apparatus and struggled awkwardly down several flights of ladders to find the relevant valve and open or close it as required. It was sweaty, unpleasant work in the heat of the tropics.

I was walking the deck, on cargo watch, checking the tanks, when crash! I was sent tumbling on to the hard steel deck.

'Ow! Who did that!?'

'Me! Saved your life, you bozo. You were headed towards a cloud of ammonia gas drifting out of that open hatch lid. Keep alert!'

I was in great danger of corrosive injury to the eyes, lungs and guts. Very painful.

The flight from Sydney to Thredbo only took a couple of hours, but the transition from subtropical Sydney to the Snowy Mountains was sharp. I was courting Carol on a brief 24-hour respite from cargo work. The fresh air of the mountains, white snow, blue sky and new-found love conspired against me and I missed my return flight. The second mate was a big, balding man with an oval face, and hard grey eyes. He was not happy when I eventually got back to the ship twelve hours late.

'Right, mate, glad to see you back. You owe me. See you in 24 hours,' he said and stomped off. And I did. I worked a double shift as a suitable punishment for my transgression.

The concentrated hydrochloric acid gurgled thickly and I watched it warily from the open tank lids. It sounded and looked evil, the swirling surface rising higher and higher. I measured the ullage (the space from the top of the liquid cargo to the height of the tank top) with a tape measure nailed to a wooden float. Very high tech. The remotely operated monitoring equipment had failed. Again. Time to stop loading. I rewound the tape and a drop of acid flicked off my glove and into my eye. Horrendous stinging pain. Scrabble with glove. Get it off. Pain. Panic.

A helping hand, water poured on my face, pouring down everywhere.

'What happened, mate?'

Garbled answer.

'Ambulance somebody, quick. Maybe acid in the eye.'

Crew members coming up the gangway after a run ashore had found me struggling by myself. I was whisked off to hospital to have my eye irrigated with pure water for an hour, courtesy of a very pretty nurse. Nice.

I spent that night in a hotel and flew down to re-join my ship in Hobart, Tasmania. My eye had fully recovered. The Captain was not pleased with me but could say nothing because loading concentrated acid with open lids was a dangerous procedure that should not have been permitted.

Silverhawk was tied up in a remote, silent chemical terminal. No sign of life. Just the rumble of cargo pumps grinding the sulphuric acid ashore.

The pumps would not balance equally to get an even flow. Ullage readouts remained constant.

'No cargo is actually flowing ashore,' I reported to the mate.

'Really? Unlikely,' he grumbled, disturbed from his crossword. 'Go and check the dials again.'

I checked. Again.

'Nope, nothing moving, Chief.' I was bored, tired and wanted to go to bed. This all seems so pointless.

Irritated, the chief officer lifted the shore phone and called the sleepy shore operator in his little cabin. Ages later he answered:

'Yeah. What?'

'The third mate here seems to think no cargo is being pumped ashore. Unlikely, but could you check the acid is actually coming ashore?'

'OK. Wait a mo.'

The operator ambled off to check, leaving us alone in the industrial gloom as the pumps growled away, getting nowhere.

'Yeah, mate, you're right!' the bemused stevedore reported half an hour later. 'The shoreside valve has been closed all night!'

'What!' yelled the mate, fully awake now. 'I don't believe it!'

'Open now, though,' the Aussie operator continued laconically.

I was glad to be proved right. Ullage readings were now increasing nicely as acid flowed ashore. Glug glug.

I was missing the busy dockside scene of shore cranes and ship's derricks loading and discharging a variety of break bulk cargoes—bags of powdered milk, bales of rubber, boxes of apples. I was missing knocking off in the evenings and going ashore for the night from a berth close to the city. I was finding the process of pumping liquid ashore from a distant jetty hidden away in the middle of an industrial setting, with just me on duty and no sign of anybody ashore, extremely dull and boring. This career move for the sake of money was definitely a mistake. I had had a couple of leaves at a generous rate almost equal to two months on and two months off. But was it worth it?

At last, in mid-November, I paid off *Silverhawk* in Brisbane and flew down to Sydney. I went into the offices of CSR and confirmed with the personnel manager 'on the handshake of a gentleman' that my job would be available on my return from extra unpaid leave in a couple months' time.

Secure in the knowledge of a job, a few days later I made use of the free air ticket that I still had courtesy of China Navigation and went home to England on long leave.

Chapter 20

HOME LEAVE

I stopped over in Rome for a few days to see Elvira Matzetti, an old friend of the family who gave me a generous Italian welcome. We were the same height last time I saw her.

After a nap to recover from jetlag followed by a late supper, we strolled round to look at an exhibition at an art gallery; very Italian. A day at the beach was another treat. Scrabbling my toes in the cool sand, I began to unwind, re-adjusting to the welcome cooler northern climate after the almost continuous tropical heat of the last two years.

I went to Mass at St Peter's Basilica, overwhelmed by its astonishing scale. Every pillar sheltered a statue to a past pope. And St Peter. And the fabulous Pieta, so perfect before a crazed Australian smashed off her nose. The high domed ceiling was lost in shadow. Hidden mystery.

Next stop was Paris to see my brother, who was a student at the Sorbonne. I slept on his heated tiled floor. Hard and hot. We journeyed by train out to the Palace of Versailles. I was impressed by its mirrored hallways and vast rooms but was surprised by its total lack of furnishings. Vast gardens. But I didn't take it in. I looked but I did not comprehend.

On a warm afternoon in a French garden forty years later I observed with intense delight a single red poppy bright against tall green grasses dancing gracefully in light airs. The hard midday shadows softened as they slowly laid a long velvet caress over the garden. Four decades earlier I had merely looked at the world about me and moved on.

I arrived back in England to a happy reunion. Stories were told, relationships restored. But I was an angry man not at peace with myself nor certain of my future. I mooched about, using my camera bought in Fiji the year before, my trusty Minolta SR-T 101. I liked its slim, sturdy metal case. Snapping away, I was puzzled by the reading of the light meter. Why was a 1.8 f-stop needed to get a decently exposed image? No, the camera was not broken. England in winter, like my mood, was wrapped in deep gloom.

I decided to attend the Board of Trade examination centre in London and retake my Chief Mate's Certificate of Competency. No fees then. Now it costs hundreds of pounds. A new examination syllabus was being introduced so I was allowed to re-sit the old exam three times. Three times I failed. This depressing result left me very confused. I did not know where my future lay; was it either in England in the hateful cold, or back in sunny Australia where I had a job waiting for me? But I had failed to pass my Mate's Ticket four times and prospects in my chosen seafaring career looked bleak. Keep moving onwards, I thought. 'Do something with your life!' remonstrated Mother.

I went to see my bank manager in Chipping Norton and on the strength of a personal interview was able to borrow the £400 needed to buy my single fare back to Australia. I had a visa that permitted me to remain. Getting back in would be no problem.

'FLYING BACK 1 FEBRUARY READY TO RETURN TO SEA' I cabled the CSR Personnel Manager.

And set off once more to try my luck in Australia.

Chapter 21

RETURN TO OZ

My first job was to clean the toilets. Next I cleaned the jetty, strewing wet sand over the deck using the 'plough the fields and scatter' technique. Sand, cigarette butts and matchsticks are nudged into the mouth of a long handled metal dustpan with the short edge of a wide broom. Tricky manoeuvre. Bending down to use fingers was not permitted. To this day I feel a real empathy with road sweepers each time I pass one leaning on his broom or pushing his trolley.

I had landed back in Sydney via Singapore. I was relieved to be back in the heat of an Australian summer but at a loose end; where to stay? I called up an old friend and invited myself over. I stood in the doorway of the North Shore flat and watched the torrential rain cast a grey sheet across the harbour, obscuring the South Shore from my view. What was next in my life?

On yet another bright sunny morning in February 1972 I presented myself, full of optimism, at the offices of CSR to reclaim the promised job.

'What job? Sorry can't help you,' said the personnel manager with a mildly apologetic lift of an eyebrow. 'Didn't think you'd come back. Job's gone. I'll let you know if another comes up.'

I was gutted. So much for the word of a gentleman. Well he was Australian, I reasoned. What more could you expect? Now what? I couldn't stay with my friend forever. I answered an advert in the newspaper and found new flatmates in Lane Cove. In a clean, modern flat

Gangway

I met an Englishman, an American and an Australian. I needed a joke right now to raise my spirits.

Searching for a vacancy down at the job centre I was glad to see a job for a ferry hand on the Sydney Harbour Ferries. I applied and got it. I cleaned the loos. Just like being a cadet back at sea.

Unfortunately with a 6 o' clock start I had to pay for a taxi to get to work on time—a Mr Micawber finance gap; income after paying rent was negative. I realised that this couldn't last but rather than draw dole I was determined to make use of the experience until I could get a ship back at sea. Once dressed in my uniform I felt very much the ferry hand, working on the run from Circular Quay over to Neutral Bay, Mosman Harbour and Cremorne. I had a little routine on arrival. My job was to bring the ferry safely alongside by slipping a mooring rope onto the jetty bollard in the approved manner and ship the short gangway aboard for the passengers. After letting go the rope and pulling back the gangway, I stayed ashore at each jetty. At Cremorne I retired to my little cubbyhole and brewed a cup of tea. There was a handy shop at the head of the wharf where I bought my pint of milk and a snack. Shaking open my paper and settling down for my smoko, I felt like a real local citizen.

Sydney Harbour is beautiful. No, more than that. It is sublime, stunning, spacious. I had sailed these expansive waters the previous year, docking at Woolloomooloo, and at Walsh Bay just under the Harbour Bridge. Criss-crossing the spangled blue waters in the yellow and green liveried Harbour Ferries I felt part of the scene.

I watched the Captain and his Mate on their nice clean bridge, in control, dressed in their smart white uniforms topped with gold braid and thought, that's where I should be. I should go for my Sydney Harbour Master's ticket. A four year apprenticeship as a ferry hand was my route to the top. I could manage four years, I thought. I had not managed my foreign-going tickets but home waters sailing should be easy. Life ashore in Sydney, home every night. Great. And so I went down to the Maritime Offices.

'I'd like a copy of the book and charts needed to study for my Harbourmaster's Ticket,' I confidently asked the friendly man on the desk.

'No worries. One chart of Port Jackson. One Harbourmaster's Book of Lights, Headlands and Waterways. Learn that by heart and comeback in four years. Good luck, mate.'

I turned the pages crammed with the numberless, numbing details of lights, headlands and waterways. Ohhh dear. Four years of sailing around this harbour as a ferry hand and working my way to the top seemed like at least two lifetimes and I quailed at the thought of the effort required.

I was beginning to realise that making big life-changing decisions by myself did not always produce the best results. But I had nobody but myself to consult. The family 13,000 miles away in England was too far away from the reality that confronted me. No mobile phones then.

I began to look around at other opportunities at a more realistic salary. I turned my back on a career on the ferries when, at the beginning of April, I was offered a job as third mate with Union Bulkships. I would have another go at life on the Aussie coast with a different shipping outfit. It was a career in which I had trained long and hard and I set my face to the future, more in hope than with any real confidence of success.

I bid au revoir to my faithful flatmates in Lane Cove and took a taxi down to Darling Harbour.

Chapter 22

DISCOVERING TASMANIA

Smoke from the Pyrmont coal-fired power station chimneys drew charcoal smears over the clear blue sky. My next ship, the *Poolta*, lay quietly alongside. She was short and compact; three hatches, two cranes, green hull above red boot topping, bright white accommodation. She looked well cared for. I trod up the short gangway. Trip trap. Captain Duff welcomed me aboard and signed me on articles. Third Mate again.

Our berth at Cockle Bay Wharf just inside the swing bridge at Darling Harbour was just a few minutes' walk from Hyde Park. The flaring spray of Archibald Fountain catching the bright Sydney sun, framing fabled creatures was a favourite site of mine. Here I sat in the cool green shade of stately trees; relaxing, off watch.

On a fine late April day the Pyrmont Bridge swung open and the *Poolta* glided through. I looked at the traffic held up on each side and wondered what busy daily journeys we had interrupted as we headed out to sea, leaving behind impatient commuters. Round Barangoo Reserve, Goat Island to port, Walsh Bay to starboard. It hardly seemed two years since I had berthed there on the *Taiyuan*. I remembered those days with regret but I had burned my boats and could not go back.

We sailed under the great arch of the Sydney Harbour Bridge, into the dramatic space dominated by the perfect sails of the Sydney Opera House. It was still under construction, giant cranes scoring the skyline, like Thomas Hardy's tangled bine-stems. Leaving Fort Denison to starboard, we held on, whistle blowing frequently, through the colourful harbour traffic of merchant ships, ferries, pleasure boats and myriad brightly coloured spinnakers; Taronga Zoo to port, millionaires' houses of

Vaucluse and Watsons Bay to starboard. *Poolta* sailed between the magnificent vertical cliffs of Sydney Heads, rounding Hornby Light to starboard, and shaped course for Hobart. Ringing down for full speed ahead we soon shook off the flotilla of yachts as our bows lifted to the southwesterly swell. The 638 nautical miles would take us just under three days at ten knots. The smoking chimneys of industrial Wollongong and Port Kembla poured their filthy black smoke into the evening sky as the sun set redly over the mountains through a haze of forest-fire smoke.

At Cape Howe we lost the comforting radar contact off the coastline of Australia and made our way across the edge of the Tasman Sea, the eastern entrance of the stormy Bass Strait. Squads of seabirds escorted us along the rocky coastline of the granite mountains of the Freycinet Peninsula to starboard (Named after the nineteenth century French navigator who circumnavigated the earth, and in 1811 published the first map to show a full outline of the coastline of Australia. France challenging Britain for the supremacy of the seas of the unexplored 'new' world).

Rounding the dramatic flat topped one thousand foot high Tasman Island, its 85 foot light created a stark silhouette, excellent for taking check bearings as we navigated our way round the coast.

We left North and South Bruny Islands to port as we crossed Storm Bay—calm for once—which gave way to the mouth of the River Derwent. Just short of the modern Tasman Bridge we berthed alongside the docks close by Hunter Street. Beyond the city rose the mighty Mount Wellington, 4,165 feet, capped in winter snow. Later one spring after the snow had melted, I ascended to its rocky windblown summit and surveyed all that lay before me, a shrunken *Poolta* far below. On another jaunt ashore I found my way to Battery Point, where the solid Victorian houses reminded me of the Cotswold stone Heythrop Lodge of my youth.

I hired a large Holden car and drove over Richmond Bridge just south of Hobart. Built in 1823-5 it is the oldest bridge in Australia. I liked its simple symmetry. I had only just learned to drive the year before and found taking this large car down narrow lanes quite difficult. I had to really concentrate. However, I successfully navigated along the thin ribbon that squeezes through sheer cliffs either side of the road at Eagles Neck, to the old penal settlement at Port Arthur. I loved the wild, wide open landscape that unfolded before me as I drove the Arthur Highway through the high bluffs of the Forrestier Peninsula.

I parked in front of bleak sandstone ruins. Entering the old jail block I tried but failed to re-capture the atmosphere when the convicts were imprisoned here back in the 1880s. They were hardened, difficult men sent here when all other attempts at correction and incarceration failed. It was a hard, depressing life. Though we sailed on a steel box miles from land, friends and family, life was never this bad.

The seas off southeast Australia can be enormous. On the return voyage to Sydney I stood on *Poolta's* poop as she rose up on a forty foot swell, then plummeted down into the next trough; up and down we went over several days. I was pleased that I had kept my sea legs.

Those wanderers of the Southern Ocean, the albatross, followed in our wake, their six-foot wingspan enabling them to float effortlessly alongside, awaiting food scraps from the cook as he flung the slop bucket over the bulwark after meals. They were our aerial companions for days on end. What thoughts lay behind their black beady eyes, what oceans had they crossed, what storms had they had endured? I tried to snatch a photograph as they slid by but failed to capture a focused image.

With three Mates working four hours on and eight off, the hours were civilised, with time ashore and good leave. Our three cranes were much quieter and more efficient than derricks for discharging the cargo of bulk paper pellets. However, working with bulk cargoes was a monotonous business.

After six weeks aboard I went on five weeks' leave, relaxing with new-found friends, playing squash, enjoying barbecues and swimming in the sometimes battering surf off Bondi and Manly. Life was good—ashore. Life at sea was much more challenging to morale, as I was to discover, yet again.

Chapter 23

AUSSIE COASTER

An incredible rust bucket lay alongside the berth, her streaky hull an effective camouflage against the background office buildings. *Kootara*. This was to be my next ship. Captain Ferguson signed me on for the voyage as third mate.

Leaving Cockle Bay we made our way with care though the ever engaging Port Jackson, passed lively yachts and green hulled ferries. Leaving the security of that vast harbour, and my friends back in Longueville, *Kootara* headed out to sea, the towering cliffs of Sydney Heads to starboard and butted into the incoming south east swell, puttering passed the headlands of the east coast of New South Wales and Victoria. It was a comfortingly familiar coastline. We rounded the high bulk of Tasman Island. Not stopping at Hobart on this voyage, we pressed on up the calm reaches of the Huon River till we arrived at our destination deep in the countryside, a paper mill jetty. We were to load 3,000 tonnes of bulk paper pellets.

I trudged down the gangway for a walk ashore. Friesian cows morosely chewed the cud and stared with blank eyes. Blank and empty headed. Like me. I met no one on the deserted road until a passing car stopped to offer me a lift. 'No thanks,' I declined, wallowing in my loneliness.

On Sunday morning I took a taxi to the nearest church and was surprised by guitars and folk songs. It was a refreshing change from traditional organ and hymns. The brief contact with Christian fellowship only highlighted my deep spiritual malaise. Dissatisfaction with life at sea set in deeply. I was filled with a great sense of ennui. The empty narrow lanes amidst lush green pastures dotted with black and white cows reminded me so much of growing up in the Cotswolds that I felt quite homesick. I missed intelligent conversation. I missed any conversation. The crew was a monosyllabic lot with little more to discuss than the weather, women (lack of) and going for a beer.

Cargo operations in Sydney used an ancient inefficient crane which could take ten days to discharge our cargo. Weekends were off for Sydney dockers and therefore for us too. I went home each night that we were in port, which on top of my leave gave me plenty of time ashore. I just wished the cargo run wasn't so boring! Listlessly watching pellets of cardboard the size of cattle cake being grabbed out of the ship by the tonne load and dropped into a waiting truck just highlighted the pointlessness of it all.

The crew were paid in cash on a Friday when in port. The second mate was the paymaster and walked into town to the bank and drew out thousands of dollars which were duly paid over to the officers and sailors lined up outside the box-like office on the boat deck. We were then given a half day's leave to go ashore to pay it back in the bank. Talk about antiquated management practices. The office was also the officers' television room. It was accessed across the open boat deck. Three chairs and an old television filled the space. Standing room only at news time. In port only; very poor signal when at sea.

Kootara oozed rust from every surface. Big flakes erupted like carbuncles from the hull. Orange streaks dribbled down the white accommodation block and winch housing. Rust sprouted round the base of the bitts and leached through the white painted bitt tops like an adolescent with frightful acne. The masts were held up by stays rusted solid. Dark scale blisters scattered like cornflakes over the teak decking around the hatches. The inside of each hold glowered with a dirty brown blush. Rust leached from every crevice. *Kootara* was so rusty I created a photographic study to exorcise its depressing grip on me. Rustic Art. I yearned to grab a chipping hammer and knock her back into tiptop condition, apply several glossy paint coats to return the hull to the original shiny livery. Not allowed. Union work. And as a junior officer not my responsibility. And the Union Bulkships did not want to spend the money.

After trotting up the coast for over a month between the Huon River and Sydney I earned five weeks' leave. A time to enjoy playing squash, BBQs, bush walks in the Blue Mountains, relaxing. All too soon I was called back to *Kootara* where I signed back on for another voyage.

Imagine turning up to the office for work and not being able to start work until a legal document had been signed, binding you over to work, live and sleep in the building for a period of time. Also, that the canteen would only fill your plate to a legally agreed minimum level, and no more. That's what it meant for mariners when they signed Articles of Agreement each time they boarded a vessel for work.

In 1937 a shipping line issued rations once per week; 1 lb of bread or biscuit, 1 ½ lbs salt beef, ¼ lb salt pork, 1/8th oz. tea, ½ oz. coffee, 2 oz. sugar, jam, butter; 3 quarts of water, and of course Nestlés condensed milk. One tin per fortnight. There was little fruit or veg on the ration. In sailing ships, and until a few decades ago, also in steam and motor ships, these rations were taken to the cook for individual preparation in the galley. How did they manage to keep each man's ration separate? 'The Last Grain Race' by Eric Newby describes these challenges as experienced by the cook on sailing ships in 1939. I have seen the galley on the Cutty Sark. It is a remarkably confined space in which to produce a meal for a crew of twenty six.

The shore-side office-wallah might successfully improve his victualling, but not the mariner. Over the horizon and out of sight, who cared what the sailor ate? We did better than the official ration (also known as the Wack) in the shipping companies of my experience, but the regulations were always hung, framed, in an alleyway. A warning not to complain.

And if you wanted to go home early? The penalty for leaving the ship without permission was an automatic DR or in other words, the sack. Leave was granted by arrangement with the management. Up to the 1950s two years away at sea was the norm. (And this can be the case for many Third World crews today who come from Russia, Eastern Europe, India and the Philippines.) China Navigation in 1971 was still expecting officers to serve two and a half years before being granted leave. Hence the appeal of working out of Sydney.

After five weeks sampling the pleasures of Sydney I returned to the *Poolta*. I had decided that this was to be my last voyage, after which I would seek a new life in Sydney. It was the same old battle: boredom versus employment, fear versus opportunity. No life at sea versus a stimulating life ashore. I was still seeking love and companionship: a wife. I was longing for a wife. My longing was so deep it was carving a hole in me. I am a social animal. I thrive in the company of an intelligent, stimulating and lively bunch of people. I like playing squash with my mates, going for long weekend walks in the Australian Bush, exploring old towns, learning new things. Not a lot of that at sea.

After six weeks on the run between Tasmania and Sydney, *Poolta* sailed between the imposing bulk of the Sydney Heads, up the magnificent harbour of Port Jackson busy with ships, ferries and yachts; Fort Denison then the Opera House, under the Coathanger, the many fingers of Walsh Bay Wharves filled with busy ships, through the Swing Bridge and into the berth at Cockle Bay.

On 8 January 1973 Captain Bordern signed me off. With my Seamen's Certificate of Discharge in my hand, I walked down the gangway with great relief. I had left the sea at last. Like the Little Billy Goat Gruff, I sought fresh green grass.

But trolls were lurking.

Chapter 24

IF AT FIRST

A fragrant frangipani tree smothered the large window to the right of the front door. My window. My home. The classic porch-fronted bungalow situated in the leafy suburb of Longueville sat foursquare. The home of an Australian, an American, and two Englishmen. We became good friends. The Australian later became my best man. BBQs, squash, bushwalks, shared meals, lazy evenings listening to music, theatre and jazz outings with girlfriends framed a good life.

Just a short walk down the street took me to a neat park by the waterfront. Mature trees offered relief from the hot sun. Burnt grass fringed an ancient stone outcrop. Squatting down close, I traced my finger along faint lines scored in the rock, a powerful link to an ancient civilisation. A kangaroo. By 2014 wooden railings protected the site, but by then the carved markings had grown very faint. Across shimmering waters of the Lane Cove river skyscrapers sparkled in bright sunshine under an eternal blue sky. I was looking forward to living and working in this vibrant city. I was twenty five years old and hope surged.

Scanning the classified ads in the Sydney Morning Herald, I read that Park Developments wanted a salesman. Good money, good prospects. I can do that, I said, applied for the job and got it. Commission only. The developer allowed us ten days in which to complete the sale of a flat, from first viewing to exchange of contracts. We were required to generate our own appointments with potential customers. Given a desk with a telephone in a side office we responded to callers enticed by glossy adverts for our smart apartments which were shooting up in the suburbs. Working under an assumed name, I arranged for them to meet my 'contact' with the builders, (me) who would show the potential client around but would not be allowed to arrange finance. 'Dermot Cunningham' my 'finance man' alter ego, would do that. All highly illegal and only netted me two appointments to view in two months and so I was let go.

What next? I still wanted to see the world and travel by air was better than by sea. So I got a job in a downtown travel agent. Booking travel arrangements under the watchful eye of an acerbic female boss, coping with telexes, juggling two phones and a fax machine proved too stressful for the harmony of the otherwise all-female office and I was let go.

If I couldn't see the world I would see Australia. By truck. A heavy goods vehicle driving licence would allow me to haul road trains across Australia. Three days of instruction in a large flatbed truck and an examiner wishing to finish early on a Friday afternoon and I acquired the necessary licence. 'Experience Required,' all job adverts demanded, even to make sandwiches. So I started off in a parcels delivery outfit, loading trucks and taking parcels round Sydney until I accidentally dropped a crate of champagne in the mayhem and rush of delivery under pressure. A puddle spread expensively over the dirty floor. The boss took the breakage cost out of my meagre pay packet and stuffed the change into my top pocket. 'Now leave!' he breathed menacingly into my face. I left.

My next truck job was driving a boxy white van for the rag trade. I discovered hidden parts of industrial Sydney, delivering huge rolls of cloth to warehouse workshops which always seemed to be at the top of long flights of stairs. Out at Parramatta I picked up piecework from homeworking migrants. I got to know the western suburbs, parking up in a handy layby for smoko, with my thermos of tea and a Big Ben meat pie oozing hot gravy. Keeping to the schedule in heavy Sydney traffic was a goal I constantly missed, to the chagrin of my Eastern European depot boss.

At the end of another long day I gratefully climbed into my borrowed car to go home. Ignition on, engage gear, press accelerator. No movement. Strange. More accelerator. Lots of engine noise. Still no movement. A kindly passer-by discerning my trouble put his head through my window and said, 'Try releasing the handbrake, mate!' So I did and hurtled across the street under full throttle, across the pavement, between the parked cars and buried my bonnet in a factory wall. Not good. An expensive bill, no transport to work and so it was time to move on. The dream of a road-train career remained a shimmering mirage.

I stood on a dark street corner in the rocky North Shore suburbs just before midnight.

'Hop on, mate!' a big bloke invited me from the cab of a huge truck.

I was on my first night shift as a garbage truck driver. Local bylaws decreed that 'garbos' had to be off the streets by sun up. At 8 o'clock in the morning I was still at it. So much for regulations.

Handed a hessian sack I ran down long steps to houses hidden a great distance from the road. Upending the contents of the stinking bin into my leaky sack, I swung it over my shoulders and ran back up the steps. Tipping the gooey mess into the open topped truck, I was sent up to tromp it down with my booted feet. The driving part of the job was another chimera.

I lasted three nights.

A groundsman/driver job at a government package testing station was a more cushy number. For six weeks I turned up at 8 o'clock in the morning and turned on the sprinklers outside the boss's office, signalling that I had arrived at work. Thereafter I repaired to my little shack for tea and biscuits before emerging to mow the lawn, burn rubbish and hoe a few weeds. No thought processes required. Occasionally, I would share with my flat mates the jars of coffee that had survived the shaking machine. The driving part of the job never materialised.

There are times in life when the door opens and you stumble through it without being aware that something momentous has just happened.

Richard, Charles and I were enjoying the peace of Longueville after supper, relaxing in the living room, reading and listening to music when in walked Robert, our resident Australian.

'OK guys, next weekend we're going for a walk in the Blue Mountains. We're meeting up with mates from Hélène's flat. How does that sound?'

'Sounds good to me', I said. I'd always wanted to get out and explore the bush.

So on a fine Saturday in late July we travelled west in three cars.

I leant on the rail guarding the deep drop overlooking Govetts Leap, mesmerised by a silver thread of water plunging off the cliff edge to vanish into the forest below. I drank in the sweeping slopes and deep fissures of the mighty wilderness of the Grose Valley and marvelled at the huge cliffs of warm sandstone marching across the blue hazed vista. We set off on foot from the lookout point, ducking under hanging swamps which dripped diamonds as we descended, our footing tested on steep steps cut into the rock. Sweeping views drew our gaze left and out to the far horizon. Our friendly chatter was interrupted by periods of concentrated silence as we negotiated slippery slabs. Reaching a clearing in the canopy we sat on rocks, ate our sandwiches, and drank in the deep peace.

We gathered together at the end of a stimulating but tiring day's walk, chatting over tea and cake. Among the group was a pretty girl with blue eyes who wanted to drive across the Nullarbor desert.

'Would anyone like to drive to Perth with me in three weeks' time? I am meeting up with my mother who is flying out from England. We plan to explore southwestern Australia, and see the fabulous desert wildflowers. I need a co-driver on the long trip.'

I thought very carefully about my options and decided to grab at this last opportunity to explore Australia. The idea appealed to me enormously. I was beginning to feel that the adventure in Australia was coming to an end. Life at sea did not appeal. Getting a job ashore without qualifications was proving impossible. It was time to return to England and take stock. Again. The good life that I sought kept slipping through my fingers. Although I picked myself up after each stumble, each blind alley, each wrong turn, it was becoming increasingly difficult to remain optimistic.

I rang Marilyn a few days later. 'Is the offer still open?' It was. I chucked in my groundsman's job and accepted her offer of co-driver. I took Marilyn out to dinner during which we concluded that we would rub along together just fine on our extended trip to Perth. I sold my car and bought an airline ticket to the UK via the US. (I was planning to meet up with an old friend in America on the way.) This took far longer than expected and threw out my trip preparations. I pushed my few possessions into a cupboard in a corner of the house.

The evening before the big trip Marilyn looked resplendent in ball gown and black velvet choker at my flatmate Richard Parker's wedding. I recorded in my diary; 'Marilyn's company was most enjoyable. She is a very attractive girl.'

Marilyn dropped me back at Stuart Street at 2 o'clock Saturday morning. Not the best preparation for a long journey.

Chapter 25

NEEDS MUST

After an amazing outback adventure lasting five weeks and 5,000 miles to Perth and back, I returned an engaged man with responsibilities. Marilyn had—amazingly—accepted my proposal of marriage. The drive had yielded far more than I could ever have expected or hoped for, and my life would now take a new direction. The details of this story are material for another book. Another day.

The morning after our return I immediately went flat hunting and was delighted to find the perfect marital home in Badham Avenue, Mosman. The top right hand side of a block of four flats had a view of the Coathanger with glimpses of distant water across a wooded suburb. It was a short walk to the Mosman Ferry jetty. My prospective in-laws moved in to reduce their living costs. M.I.L-elect generously contributed by scrubbing the 'Early Kooka' stove of its years of neglected filth.

As decided back in Western Australia, I would have a second stab at passing my Chief Mate's certificate and so went back to nautical college. I relaxed on the morning ferry ride across the busy, deep blue harbour, so familiar from my recent transits, berthing at Circular Quay and on by train to Ultimo Tech, sited at the end of Pitt Street just south of the city centre. I made the tactical error of not attending a revision class. I trusted my ability to study at home but was badly distracted by the surrounding construction boom.

17 November 1973 was one of the few sunny weekends that southern spring. I stood at the chancel steps of the sandstone Victorian-Gothic Villa Maria Church, Hunters Hill and nervously awaited my bride. The wedding ceremony was emotional, uplifting and life changing. We walked out into the sunshine, and stood amongst our family and good friends, a delighted couple grinning happily at each other. Going on honeymoon, (a twenty five foot cabin cruiser on the Hawksbury River), was not conducive to serious study.

I sat my Chief Mate exams two weeks later. Failed again, unsurprisingly. Success was to elude me for nine more years. Though bitterly disappointed, it was time to return to work. I was a married man with responsibilities, out of work and needed to earn some money. What my father-in-law thought of his daughter marrying a penniless, unemployed seafarer he was too polite to say. I don't think that I would be quite so reserved with my own daughters.

I stared sightlessly out of the window. The train from Sydney was taking me south, further and further away from my wife of just three weeks. I had broken my promise to Marilyn that I would be home for Christmas. But it was a job and a husband needs a job. But two weeks before Christmas is not a good time to leave a new marital home.

I found the *Silverharrier* on the chemical berth amongst the plumes of dark smoke soiling the bright blue sky.

A tall, wiry man in a crisp white shirt and shipping four stripes stood up from his desk and shook my hand.

'Welcome aboard, Simon. Captain Willard. Good journey I hope? Sign here and the mate will fill you in on your duties. Have you been on a chemical tanker?'

'Yes,' I replied, scribbling my signature on the Articles. 'I was third mate on the *Silverhawk* for six months, two years ago.'

'That's fine, but we are smaller and less specialised, but the run is similar; sulphuric acid from Tasmania to Brisbane and Cairns, and out to Fiji to pick up molasses for Melbourne.'

Yes, and less pay too, I reflected as I threw my gear into my cabin. My mood was as dark as industrial Port Kembla. How long would I survive this time?

The cargo was hidden from sight, carried in stainless steel tanks, all controlled from a pump room. Arrival in port was the usual quiet affair. After making fast to a jetty in the middle of nowhere a hose was connected to the main outlet to pump ashore whatever liquid cargo we carried. Very soon the low howl of pumps indicated that cargo operations were under way and all I had to do was watch the dials to check pressures and take ullages to monitor the rate of loading or discharge. When the tanks were empty they were carefully cleaned with a semi-automatic process. Sailors donned their waterproof suits and with powerful hoses squirted hot water and chemical cleaning solution over the tank walls. No excitement at all really.

A month later we were back in Port Kembla with time for just one night ashore in Sydney. Three of us travelled north by train. I was so looking forward to meeting up with my new wife. Because it was Sunday we arranged to meet up at St Patrick's Catholic Church on Grosvenor Street, just off George Street. She said later that she was not too sure if she would recognise me. Such short meetings are not good for emotional stability.

Although we enjoyed living in Sydney, being apart half the time was not conducive to marital bliss. Therefore we began to make plans for developing a career ashore. Another two months went by, carrying sulphuric or hydrochloric acid between Brisbane and Melbourne with the occasional foray to Fiji for a cargo of sticky brown molasses.

One particular night on duty in Lautoka, miles from nowhere, did it for me. During a long twelve hours shift spent pacing between the pump room and the open tank lids to make visual checks, the growl of pumps grinding the minutes away, as the brown sludge of molasses glugged on board, I wondered what on earth I was doing, allowing myself to become brain dead.

At last the stars were washed away in a Fijian pale pink dawn, and I collapsed exhausted into my bunk. The pumps grumbled through the hull, inducing grim dreams.

A few days later on arrival in Melbourne I paid off. 8 May 1974. My birthday. Not a memorable day. I had resigned from the company—again. Rather annoyingly CSR paid me off in cash rather than through my account as usual. I walked up the road to find a bank with a $1,000 wad bulging conspicuously in my pocket. It is a vulnerable feeling.

I had lasted five months back at sea. Now I had to find a new shore career. I would have to go to College or University and re-train from scratch. A big ask for my new wife. But what I had failed to do on my own I now felt much more confident to do in partnership with one whom I loved. And who loved me. That was empowering and releasing. But I was responsible for making it work. We had learned over the last five months that marriage and the Merchant Navy did not mix. Together we would find a way forward; together we would carve out a future. Ashore.

Another Billy Goat trudge down the gangplank, seeking green grass. Were there any more trolls lurking out there?

Australia 1970–1973

In Port Moresby with Captain Cyril Cocksedge

Kavieng, New Britain

SS Himalaya passing Sydney Opera House

At Port Kembla, aboard Silverharrier, off-loading acid

Fourth Life

Return to England

Summers at sea

Chapter 26

SUMMERS AT SEA

I haunted the halls of the Education Department in Chifley Square seeking a place at teacher training college but to no avail. My Second Mate's Certificate of Competency was not recognised as a sufficient qualification to get me on the course. I had reasoned that a job in teaching would give me a worthwhile career—and long holidays. That rejection added to my despondency after eight 'lost' years at sea. It made me feel quite homesick. What to do?

I looked to England and successfully applied to study for a Certificate in Education at a teacher training college in Nottingham. The English education authorities were more open to the experience of 'mature' students. Being regarded as mature at the age of twenty six was an interesting concept. I persuaded Marilyn to support me in this next venture. After three years at college I promised to bring her home, back to Sydney, to continue our most enjoyable life here, working as a schoolmaster. Her career as a physiotherapist in the North Shore Hospital had been very successful and could be resumed. We had a wide group of good friends. But being apart from each other for prolonged periods was extremely painful. Therefore we thought the sacrifice of a return home to UK worth the effort.

We would take one more adventurous swing through Australia. In May we booked our coach trip through to Darwin via Adelaide, Alice Springs, Darwin, where we would fly on Bali, thence overland through Java to Jakarta for our onward flight home via Singapore.

The month long trip assuaged our appetite for travel for a while and it was with relief that we flew into London 1 August 1974, right in the middle of the three-day week and power black outs. Friends said that we were mad to be back, but I was glad. It was home.

During the summer I had a successful interview with Mary Ward College, Nottingham. We rented my brother's house in Hempshill Vale, near Nuttall. And so began my four years of study for a Bachelor of Education degree.

As a mature student my Local Education Authority gave me a grant of about £1800 a year. Plus transport costs. Marilyn earned a fair salary as a physiotherapist but I needed to make up a budget shortfall by working in the summer holidays. I did not have to work in a bar or in a shop. I had a profession on which I could rely to provide the extra cash.

The British Merchant Navy was sailing away to foreign shores by the mid-1970s. Flagging out. The traditional break-bulk general cargo ship manned by British officers and crew would, by the end of the 1980s, be a sunset industry, replaced by internationally crewed container giants, specialist tankers and cruise ships, very few of which would be manned by British officers.

In this dwindling market for seafarers I contacted a variety of shipping companies for summer relief work. I received only one positive response. Stephenson Clarke Shipping, or Stevies as it was often called, proudly claimed to be the oldest collier company, established in 1732. Their reputation as an employer was not good. But it was a job.

My Seaman's Record and Discharge Book was out of date so on 14 July 1975, I went to the Mercantile Marine Office in London, commonly known as The Pool, to be issued with my new book, replete with bearded photograph, with EDH and radar certificates duly entered. According to the record, I flew up to Glasgow the same day. I had not been to sea since I had paid off *Silverharrier* in Melbourne, well over a year before. But it felt much longer than that. Student life was a complete contrast to my former life.

I lugged my kit up the gangway and cast a dyspeptic eye over the grimy and ancient *Ashington*, a traditional home-trade collier with accommodation amidships. Built in 1957 she lifted 5,600 tons of cargo. The train to Glasgow and taxi to the docks had swept me back into my old world. I had little time to adjust. Promotion to Second Mate. The navigator. Over couple of days I sorted out the charts and calculated courses and distances from Glasgow to Swansea, a short day and a half voyage; thence Swansea to Tunis. 2,162 miles at ten knots would, I calculated, take nine days. With the mate too busy to offer much advice and Captain Morris reckoning I should know my job without help, I had to flog my landlubber brain into action. The office claimed that they had been unable to find us a third officer as required on a foreign going voyage, and therefore the mate and I had to share the watches, working five on five off. We were paid shorthand money instead. Useful to this student.

We sailed lightship to Swansea where we loaded coal. I was looking forward to this trip but some of the crew was not. They were going too far away from their traditional home trade areas. I had not sailed in these waters since 1969 and it was good to pass familiar landmarks. Leaving the coast of Wales we shaped course down the Bristol Channel. Lundy Island, Hartland Point, and Longships Light off Land's End, where we set the autopilot to head across the dreaded Bay of Biscay, happily free of storms. Cape Tourinan, 20 miles north of Cape Finisterre, announced safe transit and we shadowed the Portuguese coast, altering course for the Straits of Gibraltar off Cabo de Sao Vicente.

Dawn flushed over the calm waters of the Tunis canal one early August morning as we steamed at slow speed and almost silently through a cloud of pink flamingos grazing the shallow waters to port and starboard.

A rickety steam crane puffed into life and swung its boom over the hold. Chuffing gouts of steam and black sooty smoke, it strained to lift the first grab load, then released a dusty cascade into the hopper with a sigh. We would be here for many, many days before our 5,000 tons of coal was discharged.

It was my summer holiday so made the most of the opportunity to explore. Boarding a commuter train we rattled for ten miles through suburban Tunis. I alighted at Carthage and walked among impressive ruins overlooking the azure sea. One could imagine sailors from long ago walking this very same street. A jumble of ancient stones revealed a canine graveyard, with inscriptions in Latin. *'Romani canes amabant?'* I wondered. The evidence suggests that they did so love them.

Waiting on the platform for the return trip a water boy offered me a mugful from his copper kettle. Mindful of my mistake in Bali, I declined the experience, more fearful of catching bugs than needful of refreshment. Standing on the peaceful platform I looked along the steel rail tracks curving round a distant bend. I tried to recall a vision of Roman armies tramping through the landscape but found it a challenge too far in such an industrial landscape. Carthage no longer resonated to the sound of iron studs on stone roads, but squealing wheels on iron rails.

I got off two miles on at the busy sea-side town of Sidi Bou Said. I drifted along narrow streets lined with white houses, interiors shielded from curious eyes by blue painted doors patterned with black studs and hinges. Ambling down a quiet lane I turned right into a busy marketplace. Noisy crowds pushed past colourful stalls piled high with sticky sweetmeats and brightly coloured material lifting in a light breeze. I succumbed to the temptation to buy a baklava, my first taste of that delicious sticky honey cake.

One evening Chris and I clattered down the gangway seeking supper. He was a lanky, longhaired radio officer and fellow pogonophile. We joined diners at long tables at an open air cafe and enjoyed an appetizing local dish in the warm Mediterranean air. I was mystified by the attitude of the other officers who were content to remain on board; too fixed in their ways to make the effort to explore this fascinating part of North Africa.

After two leisurely weeks in port we eventually completed discharge of our coal cargo and returned lightship to Newcastle.

The traffic separation scheme that came into force in 1967 became mandatory in 1971, but this was the first time I had experienced these segregated shipping lanes as we sailed up the English Channel. We joined the stream of north-going traffic in sight of the coast of France, the Cap de la Hague marking our change of course, before entering the crowded, narrow Straits of Dover off Cap Griz-Nez. Cutting across the southwest-bound traffic close to the coast of England, we headed up the east coast, rounded Cromer, Flamborough Head and Whitby Abbey, ruins prominent on the cliff top, until after ten relaxed days at sea, we sailed between the breakwaters of our home port, Newcastle.

Gangway

Laying down the courses and safely navigating 5,000 miles gave great professional satisfaction. This was a job I could do. But I was not tempted to remain at sea. On 26 August I paid off, my pockets filled with much needed cash. Six weeks work plus accrued leave at pay and a half was a fruitful summer job.

It was wonderful to be met by my wife and together we walked down the gangway, back to my life ashore. We made our leisurely way back to our home in Nottingham via Durham Cathedral where we stopped to appreciate the Norman architecture. A solid re-connection with my historic homeland.

The cartoon sellotaped to my cabin door of a deeply suffering hippy-ish character was not a man I recognised. How did I gain a reputation for reading The Times and drinking Earl Grey tea? A mystery to me. After another year of discussing the finer points of the Theory of Education with students who had had very little experience of life, it was good to enjoy the robust camaraderie of seafarers. The next year's summer vacation was aboard *MV Lobito Palm*, which I had joined in 1976 at Tilbury, thence coasted round to Liverpool during the month of August. She was a classic British ship, the accommodation block just aft of amidships topped by a green and black funnel. I was third mate, again. I enjoyed pleasant evenings in the bar after cargo work was over for the day; (London and Liverpool dockers rarely worked night shifts), playing darts, drinking beer, watching movies, enjoying sing-songs accompanied by guitar. There were plenty of officers and cadets on board to create opportunities for a happy gathering at the end of each watch even when at sea.

The second officer applied his cartoon talents to the rich human landscape before him. The dockers provided as much interest to me as I am sure I did to them.

My final summer relief post in 1977 was on board Cunard Brocklebank's *MV Samaria*. For this job I needed a new reefer jacket with Second Mates stripes so I went down to the London shop of Miller Rainer Haysom, Merchant Navy outfitters. A few adjustments were needed so I collected it the next morning after an overnight tailored fit, a standard service useful to mariners in transit.

I signed on as Second Mate on my first—and only—banana boat, in Dover on 9 July. We sailed lightship on my first trans-Atlantic crossing to Puerto Cortes in Honduras, Turbo in Colombia, (at anchor only for a few hours whilst loading from barges) Almirante and Panama.

The five holds and tween decks were loaded with banana boxes. Over 12,000 tonnes of them. Imagine that piled up in your local supermarket. A system of easily deployable roller tracks was rigged and dockers shot the boxes into neat lines and rapidly filled the holds.

On the nine day, 5,000 mile crossing of the Atlantic to Bremen I accompanied the fridge engineer when we went on "banana inspection". I stabbed a thin steel temperature probe though a thick green skin and read off the dial. 'Exactly 58°F. Perfect,' said Peter. On arrival in Bremen any bananas not still bright green were dumped on the deck for disposal at sea on the return voyage. I picked a banana from the huge pile; but really the quantity was overwhelming and I lost interest after one bite and threw the rest over the wall.

We returned lightship at best speed—23 knots—with orders to pass through the Panama Canal to load bananas on the west coast. Swinging on the pick off Cristobal, near the eastern entrance to the Canal, we waited. I was desperately keen to transit having never before done so. But I fretted as the August days slid away. My first child was due to be born early October. I had a personal deadline. If we had to go through the Canal I doubted that I would be home in time for the birth.

Taking the liberty boat ashore with a few off-duty officers we briefly explored Cristobal, sweating in tropical humidity. Not too impressed, we escaped to a bar by the harbour where we watched the sun set over the anchorage, supping a well-earned, refreshingly cold lager. In the anchorage beyond the palm trees the elegant outline of a four-masted sailing ship recalled an earlier age. Eventually, after four days of speculation, we heard that a late storm had blown away our potential crop. A change of orders sent us to Almirante, a mere six hours and one hundred and fifty miles west of Cristobal.

Samaria berthed at a single, long wooden jetty raised on piles driven into the tropical mud. It felt far too insubstantial to secure our large vessel. Once we had made fast for'ard and aft we waited in the heat for the gangs to come aboard and loading to begin. The bananas arrived by rail truck over lines which ran right up to the ship. Trestles and rollers were swung abroad and rigged into each space. Down the shoots sped the boxes and we were off! The spaces rapidly filled as rollers were re-directed into new areas. Finally each tween deck hatchway was filled out by hand.

After a quick lunch I went ashore. In the stifling tropical heat the fridge engineer and I squelched down a wide muddy track. This was the main street, edged with low, flimsy bungalows raised on stilts. Power lines and palm trees cluttered the skyline.

Crossing a bridge we discovered a community of riverside houses, also built on stilts. Palm trees and colourfully painted wooden shacks were perfectly reflected in the still waters. The scene was picture book tourism; attractive but for the locals, a life of poverty.

We met some cheerful children, over-topped by very tall jungle grasses. Laughing and pushing, they were keen to get in the picture. What did the future hold for them? We climbed a low hill and looked down on a town of low houses, *Samaria's* goal post masts and derricks towering over the rusty corrugated shed roofs. Her solid presence offered me security and hope. And my transport home. My future lay in making a success of my studies, becoming a schoolmaster and equipping the children who would shape England's future. That challenge seemed very remote from my present situation.

Suddenly I felt extremely dizzy and returned to the ship. Two salt tablets and several glasses of water later I felt back to normal. I was soon to feel more than dizzy as my life was turned upside down yet again.

Loading completed we battened down the hatches and made our way back across the Atlantic and up the English Channel to Rotterdam. At 23 knots we covered the 4900 mile voyage in just over eight days. I was in a hurry to get home.

A month after I ran down the gangway in Rotterdam my first child was born: Joanna Louise. The date of 11th October 1977 was burned into my memory. I was now a father. I was thrilled, delighted, amazed. I had extra responsibilities. I was even more determined to complete my course of studies and make a go of my second career.

Fifth Life

Return to sea

in

Stephenson Clarke Shipping

Scandinavian and European Routes

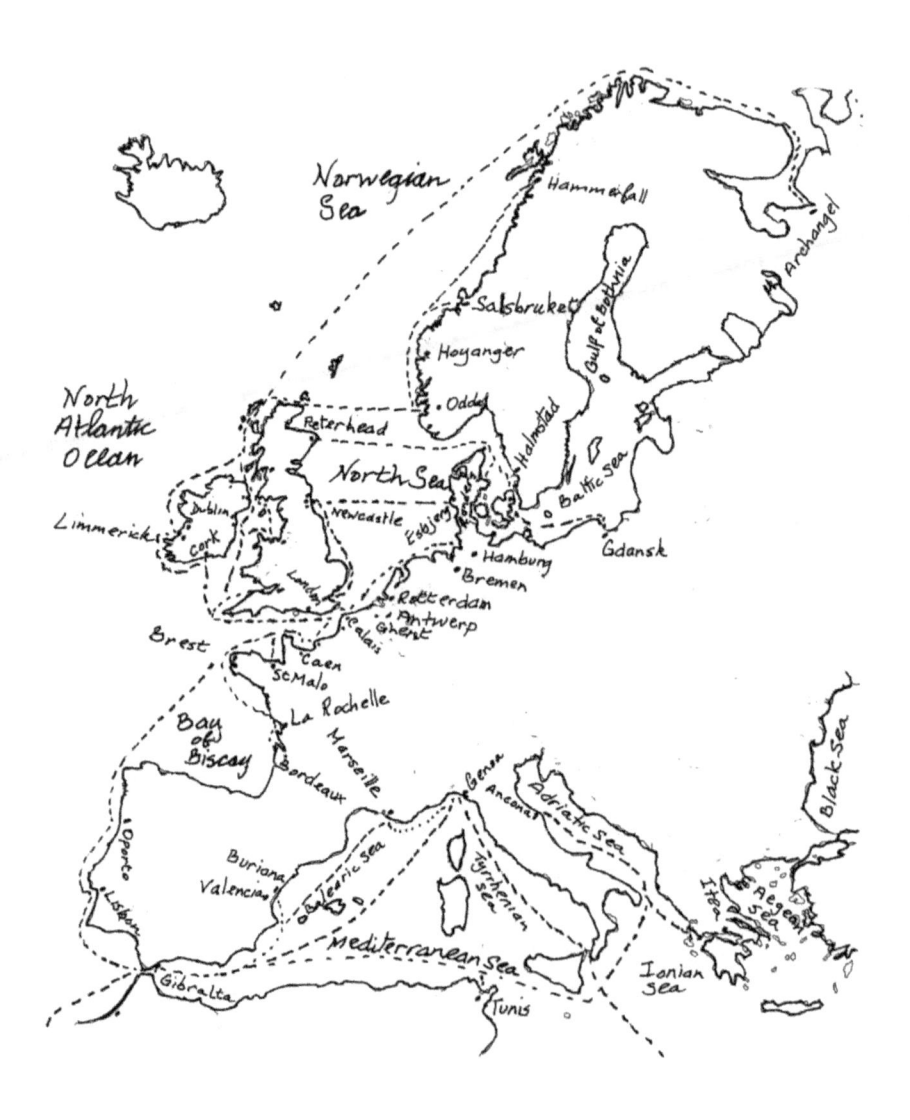

Chapter 27

NAVIGATOR

Lying in bed on Christmas morning I assessed my career options—yet again. I stared hard at the ceiling. There was no signpost upon its bare white surface to advise me which path to take. After nearly two years teaching at Loxwood Primary School, it was clear that my finances were in a mess. As Mr Micawber in *David Copperfield* put it, *"Annual income twenty pounds, annual expenditure twenty pounds nought and six, result misery."*

I had three choices. One: move the family back to Australia and make a new start. Two: move the family to Yorkshire, buy a cheaper house and teach there. Three: return to sea and keep the family in a known safe and familiar environment but suffer separation. I chose the last option. However, unknown to me, the Merchant Navy had been withering on the vine, suffering commercial atrophy. I applied to over thirty companies but only one had a vacancy. Stephenson Clarke Shipping. This home-and-middle-trade company had been engaged in the NE Coast collier trade since 1730. Ancient indeed and some of its ships were showing their age as I was to discover.

The troll took another bite.

Early morning 8 April 1980 I bid an emotional goodbye to my daughters (aged one, and two and a half) and my wife, at Gatwick airport. Staring out of the window on the flight to Aberdeen, I reflected with a sense of despair on the six wasted years in education; four years acquiring a B.Ed. degree and nearly two years teaching in a primary school. It was bitterly disappointing that my huge efforts to get a shore job had failed. My black thoughts matched the dismal granite of Aberdeen as I rattled and bumped along in the bus which dropped me in the middle of Peterhead. I grabbed a taxi down to the docks. I should have taken one all the way I grumbled to myself.

I boarded the smallest ship on which I had ever sailed—*MV Ferring*, a bulk carrier lifting about 2,800 tons of grain for Gdansk, Poland. A Sussex connection led to the tradition of naming ships after Sussex villages although in two cases, *Washington* and *Ashington*, there was also a connection with local towns near to Newcastle, our homeport. It felt very odd when calling up port control or a Coastal Radio Station, announcing the name of a very familiar Sussex village. 'Rogate, Rogate, Rogate, calling Cullercoats Radio.' It didn't sound very ship-like to an ear more used to African towns or Scottish glens.

In the fishing port of Peterhead the grain was delivered in big trucks, one by one, and it took five days to load via hopper and chute. I spent time exploring the busy fishing wharfs, watching the catches being landed and stored with a layer of ice. I was grateful to discover that the local Woolworths were able to supply a couple of uniform shirts as I had failed to get myself kitted out in London prior to joining up.

As second mate I had to calculate and lay off courses to our next port. Polishing up my rusty course preparation skills I successfully found the necessary charts from the chart catalogue to plan the passage to Gdansk in Poland. I set up my own Passage Distances Notebook. Looking back I see that my early layouts were very messy but over time I became more organised, with clear lists showing the length of course of each leg, course steered, and the distance to go. The 805 nautical mile passage total to Gdansk was just over three days at 10 knots.

On the sixth day *('and there was morning')* we battened down the McGregor steel hatches; watertight against disaster. Wet grain exerts huge forces as it expands. A steel hull is as vulnerable as a Hornblower prize vessel. I had no desire to become a sunken ship statistic. We sailed across the North Sea to the north of Denmark and rounded Skagen Point a day and a half later.

An unusual movement on the distant flat headland caught my eye. Checking with binoculars, I was astonished to see large rotating turbine blades mounted on tall white masts. My first offshore farm; commonplace nowadays off windy headlands.

We sailed south down the Sound, a narrow strip of water between Denmark and Sweden where the channel is only two and a half miles wide, giving me good views of Hamlet's Castle of Kronborg at Helsingor. Very dramatic.

The litany of lights continued: Kummelbank, Kullen, M1 Buoy, Ven Light, Lous, Falsterborev, Blenheim, Du Rozewie, Jastania, and Gdansk Pilot two days later.

We were guided on the final approach to Gdansk by Hel Light. I would have appreciated its warmth. Gdansk (the old Hanseatic port of Danzig) in May was still in the grip of winter, trees and shrubs still tightly budded. The docks were a grim, concrete industrial wasteland.

An unsmiling customs official dressed in a thick, dark coat opened up the heavy steel door of the duty-free bond. We idly perused shelves laden with heavy lead crystal and racks of leather coats. Fine if you were looking for the Stasi fashion look. I wasn't.

Having unloaded our grain we shifted berth and back loaded coal for Avonmouth, 1,400 miles and six days west. The pilot came aboard to take us out to sea. Waiting for a tug to lift us off the berth, I chatted to him on the bridge.

'Nice binoculars. Are they powerful?'

'Try it.'

I did. The image of the distant ship in the dock was bright and clear.

'Where are these made? They are very good.'

'You like? East German. Maybe I sell for good English pounds!' he chuckled.

He needed my hard currency to top up his pay. I thought £12 good value. He had a good business here each time he piloted a foreign ship.

Passing through the Skagerrak, north of Denmark, I decided to phone home. This is not an easy process; no satellite links and no mobile phones in 1980.

I called up the local VHF radio station on Channel 16:

'Skagen Radio, Skagen Radio, Skagen Radio. This is *Ferring, Ferring, Ferring*. Over.'

'Good afternoon, Ferring. This is Skagen Radio. How can we help you? Over.'

'Skagen Radio, this is Ferring. I would like a connection for a ship to shore telephone call. Over.'

'Ferring, Skagen Radio. Channel 28 please.

'Channel 28.'

And switched over.

'Skagen Radio. This is Ferring, Over.'

'Ferring, Skagen Radio. Receiving you loud and clear. What telephone number do you wish to call? Over.'

'Skagen Radio, Ferring. Please could you could put me through to England, telephone number (01403) 818081. Over.'

'Ferring, Skagen Radio. OK. Stand by in the queue until it is your turn.'

'Skagen Radio, Ferring standing by'.

Waiting in the queue I listened-in to the ongoing private conversation so as to know when it was over and thus my turn to go on. This was embarrassing and boring in equal measure. Eventually Skagen connected me and I heard the phone ringing.

'Hello?'

It was my wife. After a few words about my ETA and making arrangements to come home in a month's time she said,

'I will put Pippa on.'

'Hello Daddy. Where are you?'

'Hi Pippa. I'm off the top of Denmark '

'When are you coming hoooommme?' Pippa wailed.

Some domestic crisis called my wife away from the phone and I could not break the connection from my end. With the maritime community listening in, I tried to soothe my little girl, the misery of being an absent father pressing heavily upon me yet again.

We had some rough weather on the two day passage across the North Sea which slowed us down but eventually we headed through the Straits of Dover, the white cliffs bright on the starboard bow as we headed down the Channel. Careful to keep within the south-bound shipping lane prominent headlands, I checked off each landmark on our passage: Beachy Head, St Catherine's Light, Start Point, Lizard Point, rolling round Land's End and Longships Light. Here where the great open reach of the Atlantic Ocean funnelled into the Western Approaches the swell became short and steep and waves choppy. We skirted the edge of the Celtic Sea, altered course off Trevose Head and Hartland Point, rounded the coast of Devon at Morte Point and entered the narrowing Bristol Channel. The islands of Flat Holm off the coast of Wales and Steep Holm off the coast of England were like Guardians of the Sacred Lands beyond the Western Shore as from some ancient Norse tale.

Soon after docking in Avonmouth my wife and children came aboard to pick me up. After a very happy reunion we drove to stay with friends on their farm near Reading. It was a delightful, intense taste of normality. The next morning driving back to the ship was like being returned to prison. But with bills to pay and family stability paramount, needs must.

We sailed lightship to our next port of call, Llanddulas, which lay between Colwin Bay and Rhyl off the North Wales coast, with orders to load limestone for Odda, Norway.

Jutting out into the Irish Sea, open to elemental blasts from the north and west, loading limestone from the quarries at the Llanddulas Jetty was an original experience. The pilot did not come out to the ship but talked the Captain onto the correct line to the berth over the VHF. A night time approach was hazardous as the jetty only appeared out of the dazzling shore lights at the last minute. Onshore currents threatened to sweep us onto the jetty as we approached crablike until at the last moment we grounded for'ard on the rocky bottom. Single lines and springs fore and aft held us alongside. A distant roar grew ever louder till a heavy crash of rock on steel shook the hull. A stream of crushed limestone poured into the empty hold via conveyor belt and chute. Dust billowed out and covered the white paintwork in a scummy layer. I kept watch on the bridge ready for emergency engine manoeuvres. The crew remained at stations. De-ballasting had commenced well offshore and continued apace to match loading. The final load trim was about a foot by the stern. The shoreside loadmaster was in charge. But legal responsibility still lay with the Master. At the top of the tide five or six hours later the captain ordered: 'Let go fore and aft! Half speed astern!' and we came off smartish, full cargo or not. We had no desire to wait out a tide sitting on the bottom with a full cargo.

Hatches were rapidly battened down as *Ferring* set course for Odda on what became a regular route; up the Irish Sea, through the North Channel, and the delightfully named Rhum, Eigg and Muck to starboard. On subsequent voyages we often dogged behind these rocky islands to avoid the worst of frequent southwesterly storms. Eilean Glas on Scalpay kept us on course up the Little Minch as did the light atop the mighty cliffs of Cape Wrath. Built in 1828, this is another in the chain of remarkable Stephenson lighthouses. A solid 66 foot white tower, the light is a valuable and distinctive aid to navigation. Up until 1998 keepers kept watch round the clock. By then, like all the lights round the coast of the British Isles, its operation was automated. I explored the magnificent classical shell of the deserted Keepers' House of Eilean Glas nearly forty years later. The rotting bedding, mouldy snooker table and rusty washing-line poles spoke eloquently of a vanished era. The men and their families who had lived here and kept the light bright had abandoned the site in 1978. These amazing engineering marvels are now monitored remotely.

I much enjoyed the cruise along the dramatic coast line of the Pentland Firth, guarded on its eastern flank by the twin light towers of Muckle Skerry, before *Ferring* set out across the North Sea to the Skudenes Pilot, 21 miles south of Haugsund. The voyage had taken three and half days. Ships travel slowly. Time to be. Time to see. We cruised through spectacular fjords on a twelve hour 120 mile journey to Odda. Ferries criss-crossed the calm waters, stopping at remote jetties. The lower slopes of the steep mountain sides were smothered in a profusion of pink blossom of apple and cherry orchards. High above a glacier emerged clear of the snowfields. The two-mate watch routine, five hours on, five hours off, meant I had to drag myself away for some essential sleep but for once I looked forward to returning to the bridge.

Finally we turned south and entered Sor Fjord (Sørfjorden) for the last 24 mile run in. Coming alongside the quay at Odda was a simple operation. I directed mooring from my station aft. A heaving line was quickly lofted ashore and the polyprop headline followed.

'Take up the slack,' I called and a sailor quickly wrapped a couple of turns round the warp end of the winch as I operated the controls and heaved the line tight, cascading water from the fibres into the fjord. The stern drifted in. Up for'ard the crew had been equally efficient with heaving lines and ropes and brought the bow gently alongside. With a slight bump *Ferring* was in position. The sternline was stoppered off, and with a practiced figure-of-eight motion, the sailors made fast to the bitts.

Once we had made fast, the limestone was unloaded by single grab onto the conveyor belt. Discharge was completed in two days of steady work and the hatches swept clean. I learned later that our cargo was used in the process from making carbide, which in turn was used to make acetylene, a light and heat source.

Next we sailed to Egersund, just a short one day voyage beyond Haugersund, situated on the south-west coast of Norway. There we loaded silica-free rocks for Port Sunlight where it was ground into Vim for the kitchen sink. The voyage took us back through the Pentland Firth. Timing the passage to benefit from the twelve knot tides that surge through the Pentland is the ideal; a maritime 'jet stream'. Many years later I read, 'Blazing Paddles', the amazing adventures of Brian Wilson, who paddled a kayak around the north coast of Scotland. The wild whirlpools and tidal rips could easily have drowned him. I was glad to be safe aboard my sturdy steel motorship.

A lilting litany of Scottish headlands called out our course; Muckle Skerry, Stroma, Neist Point, Humla Rock, Ardnamurchan Light (most westerly point of the British mainland), Dutchman's Cap, Orsay, Altacarry, Crammay Head, Point of Ayre, finally, Liverpool Bar, after a 730 mile, three-day passage in generally fine weather. The dock water at Port Sunlight (the eponymous soap) stirred up by our berthing released a foul stink, a mixture of all the products sold to a housewife.

Another run from Llanddulas to Odda was followed by a two-day voyage with many hours pilotage through dramatic fjords up the coast of Norway to Hammerfall, 62.5° north. We nosed alongside a short jetty and prepared our hatches.

Although early summer in England here it was cool and damp. I strolled in the still air of the nearby forests. Red berries speckled skinny rowan trees, the deep silence broken by water dripping from thin branches of silver birch. No bird sang.

We loaded up with dolomite and three days later arrived at the southern Swedish city of Halmstad, berthing close to the city centre on the Halmstadvärgan. Exploring rural byways by bicycle I found woodland drifts of yellow winter aconites and white wood anemones. Later I sat in warm sunshine in the town square watching the world go by, enjoying a cup of coffee and local cake, a welcome contrast to plain ship's fare.

From sunny Halmstad we sailed back to Gdansk, a short day's voyage through the Baltic, where we loaded coal for Cork. The docks were too far from town to explore the city centre. There was something grim about the industrial port area that dissuaded me from exploring. Besides, I was busy preparing for the next voyage, digging out the thirty three charts needed, laying down the courses in pencil at least one mile off each headland and calculating distances to go. Each chart was manually updated in purple ink with a reference to the information from the Notices to Mariners and Light Lists; a task that required my full concentration. It was a pleasure to be fully absorbed in a useful but routine task.

Loading was completed after a day and we set sail to transit the Kiel Canal, 340 miles away. Coming alongside in the lock I saw a telephone box sitting enticingly close by. I had a few minutes to make a quick call home. I heard that a five pence coin was almost the weight of a one Mark coin. I leapt over the bulwark onto the lockside as the *Ferring* sank lower and lower. I repeatedly reinserted the maverick money as it slipped out of the slot. How frustrating! It was too light. To trick the phone box into making a connection required an old shilling piece. Before the Captain could yell his annoyance I leapt back aboard as the gangway door came level with the lock. Mission not accomplished. Having mobile phones at sea would have been wonderful in maintaining communication with home.

On arrival in Cork, 1,389 miles and six days later, we learned that there was no rush. Cargo work would start the next day. I boarded the bus to Blarney Castle, climbed the tower and kissed the famous Blarney Stone—upside down—trusting the guide to hold tight to my ankles. It was a long drop.

My first full tour of duty back at sea after six years was over. I flew home 10 July to enjoy six weeks' summer leave with my family. I had never been so long away from my wife, even when just married and sailing out of Sydney on two month tours of duty. I had a growing family now and the separation was even more painful. I was glad to have made it safely home.

Twelve years later, *Ferring* foundered off the north coast of Spain and sank.

Chapter 28

GEM TIMES

Piloting *Gem* down the busy Thames at night took all my concentration. p came the next buoy. I cross-checked it's flashing light against the chart; cross-referenced with a quick visual of the shape of the land echo on the radar. I adjusted the course to the next buoy with a twist of the control knob on 'George', the autopilot. The still water reflected a confusing kaleidoscope of red, green and white flashing lights in its oily black surface. I memorised the next course leg and when abeam of the turning mark, twisted the control knob again and brought *Gem* around on to the new heading, lining up with the next buoy. ('George' was more reliable than the helmsman at holding a steady course.)

It was August and I was the second mate, sailing from Northfleet. No third mate of course on the little ships. Vessels under 1600 grt were not required by regulation to carry a Thames Pilot. Doing my own pilotage was much more fun than watching somebody else do it? I was involved. I was in charge. I was successfully navigating a seagoing ship in the narrow confines of a busy river channel in all weathers and times of day or night. It was initially very intimidating but I enjoyed the satisfaction of honing my coastal navigational skills, sharply aware of dangers to shipping.

We were bound for Llanddulas, via the English Channel, round Longships light and up the Irish Sea. I was getting used to the rapid loading here and prepared the charts for our next stop, Odda again.

Once safely berthed in Odda and cargo operations sorted out for the next day the agent took two of us up to the snow line. Throwing slushy snowballs in September was childishly satisfying. There was no official Seaman's Club but a married couple had created a home from home for sailors, picked us up from the ship and took us back to their simple bar where we could play cards or table tennis and chat over a beer.

A short two-day voyage up the mountain-rimmed coast of Norway took us to Salsbruket, deep up the OplØfjord. We berthed at a very short jetty and ran long stern lines to bollards fixed into the rocky shoreline.

We loaded great blocks of processed paper, newsprint for Ancona, Italy. Going round the lumber mill in the eastern part of the village I watched with great interest as short, thin logs were tipped through one doorway and five ton bales came out the other. Various processes stripped off the bark, mashed the timber fibres and created a sludge which was pulled over giant rollers into vast sheets of paper. These were squeezed, folded, compressed and bound into large bales. A crane swung them aboard and dockers chocked each bale securely into position. It was a peaceful and unhurried operation. On completion, hatches were securely battened down; any water getting in would rapidly expand the bone dry bales, unleashing destructive forces on the hull plates.

We set sail down the peaceful OplØfjord bound for Ancona on the Adriatic Coast, a fifteen day voyage at ten knots. Reading book after book helped kill time. Between books I assembled and glued six brightly coloured little plastic aeroplanes; just one at a time to spin out the days. I hung them on strings to bob and sway as we rolled across the North Sea, down the English Channel, across the perilous Bay of Biscay, (just a stiff breeze), rounded Cape Trafalgar, leaving Gibraltar to port, on through the Mediterranean, turning north into the Adriatic Sea to halfway up the coast of Italy. No sextant was needed; just radar and coastal fixes to navigate the 3,800 miles.

Ancona. We slipped into our berth close to the entrance. Rising ground to the south cupped city and port in a hilly embrace. We made fast for'ard and aft and stopped the engine. Supping a celebratory beer in the sudden stillness was good, very good. Discharging cargo in Italy was even more relaxed than loading. Having arrived late on Friday cargo work would not begin till Monday and so I went to Rome for the weekend.

As the cargo of bulk newsprint was being discharged over a couple of days, we received orders to proceed to Itea, in Greece. I heaved out the heavy folios of paper charts, selected the required charts, sorted them into voyage order and laid down courses for the 552 mile voyage.

Soon after we left the bustling city of Ancona I noted the pretty town of Vieste to starboard, jutting out into the Adriatic Sea. Love to come back and explore it properly one day, I thought, and learn about its tragic past when 5,000 old people and children were killed by the Turks in 1500. Off Brindisi we dodged through the busy ferry traffic and encountered the magical beauty of the Ionian Islands as Fano Island rose out of the deep blue sea. The golden beaches no doubt full of tourist sunning themselves. The wedge of white cliffs of Cape Doukato lay to port, the dagger-shaped promontory like the incisor of a marine beast guarding the string of islands through which we had to safely navigate.

White sails dotted the blue as we pottered along at ten knots. To port lay the perfect little island of Oxia. The Ionian Sea narrowed into the island-rimmed Gulf of Patras as we sailed serenely through the Strait of Rion into the Gulf of Corinth, (the Labyrinth?) ferries criss-crossing the blue waters.

Continuing deeper into the Gulf the distinctive lantern-topped stone lighthouse of Ak Psaromita kept us on course, until, after our very pleasant two day cruise, we arrived at the sleepy port of Itea. We dropped anchor tantalisingly close to the hot shimmering town, the distant sweep of barren mountains and olive clad hills inviting exploration.

We berthed two days later and began to load dusty orange bauxite ore. By the end of the second day we had completed cargo but the paperwork was not ready. Time for another cold beer ashore. It wasn't until late the following morning that an apologetic agent puffed aboard, bearing gifts of local ceramic ware for the Captain and officers as a peace offering. The cargo clearance documents signed we duly set sail back to England, bound for Gravesend on the Thames.

Off the toe of Italy we hit a strong westerly gale. Soon we were slamming into heavy seas, which reduced our speed to 2 or 3 knots. I suggested to the Captain that we take a more northwesterly course; thankfully he agreed and although rolling heavily our speed increased up to seven or eight knots and we made better overall headway.

The next morning the Captain became very concerned about being so far from our original track, and thus too close to the Spanish coast. He directed that we head southwest, back into the teeth of the gale. The wind put the brakes back on as we slowed down to three knots and *Gem* slugged it out down the Mediterranean Sea, staggering through the narrow Strait of Gibraltar. It took longer of course and was extremely uncomfortable but Captains are in command whatever the advice of the navigator. Trying to snatch sleep when on a small ship pitching into a heavy sea and swell is not to be recommended.

With the wind on our port quarter we made good time up the Portuguese coast, across the Bay of Biscay again and entered the English Channel, where the joy of The Channels lifted our spirits. After twelve days of very mixed weather over 2,700 miles, *Gem* sailed up the Thames to berth snugly at Gravesend. Not being the mate cargo work details are not clear in my memory, but soon we were outward bound, piloting ourselves through the busy waters.

After a short run down to Shoreham I was delighted to pay off. I heaved my heavy suitcase down the gangway with a big smile on my face. I was on Ticket Leave for nine wonderful months. It was just over a month to go before Christmas and so a happy leave lay ahead with my wife and two gorgeous daughters. It was also my eighth wedding anniversary. A considerable amount of water had passed under several bridges since Sydney.

It was time to have another shot at that elusive Chief Mate's Certificate of Competence at Warsash Nautical College. It had been eleven years since the fourth attempt.

I was lucky to be going home. Thirteen years later *Gem* capsized and sank. Three of the crew of eleven were lost.

Chapter 29

NAUTICAL COLLEGE

'Let's have a gander?' pressed my classmate.

I lifted the flimsy bonnet of my little 2CV.

'Where is the engine?'

I pointed diffidently to the little two cylinder device towards the front of the compartment. The petrolhead lifted the bonnet of his E Type Jaguar. He pointed to the huge V12, 3.8 litre engine:

'Now that's what I call an engine!' he exclaimed with pride. His generator was about the size of my 2 stroke. Much laughter.

I had traded-in my much loved orange and white VW Caravanette for something at the opposite end of the spectrum—a blue Citroen 2CV. It could do 80 mph—downhill, cocking a leg rounding a bend. Very scary.

The academic term for the Chief Mate's course at Warsash, now more grandly called Warsash Maritime Academy and part of Southampton University, had started in early January 1982. I was looking forward to obtaining this Ticket having failed on previous attempts. But now I had motivation—my family. The study plan was to drive down to Warsash Monday morning bright and early, attend classes nine till four-thirty and then break for a restorative cuppa. Over to the library for extensive exam practise for three hours. Practise, practise, practise. Supper was at my mother's house in Portsmouth. More study. Then bed. On Friday, drive home and do no study at all. Pure family time.

The Chief Mate's syllabus consisted of two navigation papers, offshore and navigational equipment; also cargo work, ship stability, engineering and meteorology. Our lecturers were engaging, demanding and thorough. It was also a time of excellent banter. Our exuberant class—2C—flung paper aeroplanes across the classroom, sometimes during lessons, much to the annoyance of said lecturers. Our high spirits were a refreshing release from years of confinement at sea. I wore my 2C logoed sweat shirt with fond pride.

Colleagues in the classroom came from a wide variety of backgrounds and shipping companies. I particularly remember Roy and Warren, who served in the RFA. The next time those met each other was when Warren rescued Roy from San Carlos Water after he had been blown out of the *Sir Galahad* during the 1982 Falklands war. I heard the dramatic story from his own lips when we met up some time later.

'Grandad, grandad you're lovely' sang my classmates to me as I walked in to the classroom one day. Clive Dunn's hit was aimed at me, at 33 the oldest in the class. Granddad indeed! The song was already ten years old, so why then? Maybe because Clive Dunn was on children's TV at the time.

The dining hall had a grand view of Southampton Water. Through the windows early in February I saw a Sandringham circling and landing at Calshott. It was the last flying boat to serve Lord Howe Island. I had seen one twelve years before taking off from Rose Bay in Sydney Harbour on its way out to Lord Howe. Short and Harland created this civilian version of the Sunderland. The service ended two years later. End of another transport era. Looking up from my fish and chips one lunchtime, the large, slab-sided *Cunard Princess* set out on her maiden voyage. She was an impressive floating hotel. But in my eyes not a ship.

The time at college zipped by far too fast. On exam day we trooped nervously into the Board of Trade Examination Room in Southampton and nervously sat at little tables. School boys again. Over four days I completed five papers, each about two hours long. It was a nerve-wracking time. So much effort. So much need to succeed.

On Friday we sat the last paper. Outside the exam hall we shook hands goodbye, the camaraderie of the last six months quickly evaporating as we went our separate ways. I would have an anxious wait for several weeks before the results came through.

We took a holiday cottage for a long weekend in a nearby Sussex village, Bignor, under the South Downs. A time of relaxing walks with the family gave me many memories to treasure when I joined my next ship, the *Dallington*. Goodbyes are both tender and painful after so long ashore.

Chapter 30

COLLIERMAN

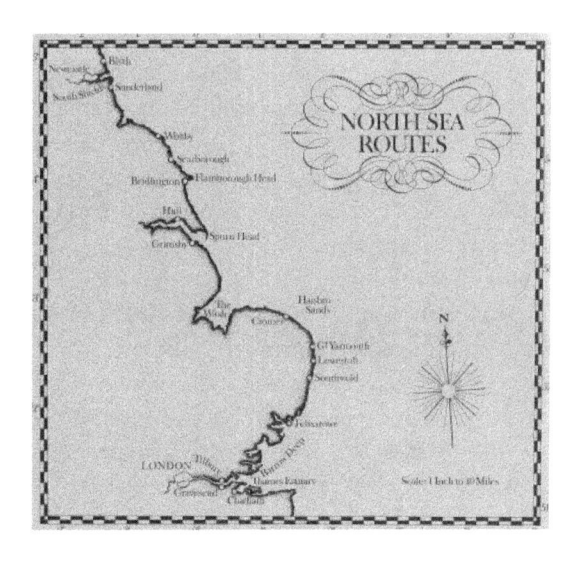

The folk of Blyth were vertically challenged. They dressed thirty years behind the times in caps and tweeds, car coats and sensible shoes. Blyth in 1981 was like Chipping Norton in the 1950s, my childhood Cotswold town. It was not a prosperous town. Coal mining was king but coal was dying. The mine extended about a mile underneath the North Sea and the coal was therefore expensive to extract. Water poured in all the time, continuously pumped out. It was a dangerous place. It was an early casualty of Margaret Thatcher's policy of closing the mines.

In early August I had been appointed second officer on one of the new D boats, *MV Dallington*, a 11,600 dwt collier on the run between Blyth and the Thames; a routine coal run which I endured for three months.

Arriving in back in Blyth on a Saturday night made for a welcome break because no cargo was loaded on Sundays. My fellow officers came either from Blyth or Newcastle and so went home for the night. As the only Southerner I stood duty shift but still went ashore. A little motorboat with a chugging diesel engine plied the ferry route between the berth and town. But not on Sundays. That meant a long walk round. I found a church and was given a friendly welcome during the four years that I was on the collier run.

The headlands on the northeast coast became familiar landmarks. Whitby Abbey starkly silhouetted on the high cliffs, the stubby white lighthouse tower not at all remarkable; Flamborough Head, Spurn Head, Haisbro Sands, the bold red and white horizontal stripes of the Happisburgh Light set low on the sandy foreshore; the round white tower of Southwold Light poking its head above the cluster of little houses gathered round its base; Orford Ness light, its foundations now under threat from the power of the sea.

The colliers of Stephenson Clarke carried coal for Kingsnorth, Thurrock and Tilbury Power stations on the Medway and the Thames. There was much waiting. Anchoring off in the Estuary on arrival we awaited berthing orders; only a few hours if we were lucky, days if not. Gone were the days of being entertained by guitar playing officers, movies, drinks at the bar, sailing through balmy nights under a swathe of glittering stars bright enough to read by. Just a TV with scratchy reception and a tin of beer.

Once on the berth a well-oiled operation swung into action. Hatches rumbled open. Crane booms swung over the hold. Twenty tonne grabs chewed bites out of the black stuff. The great maw gaped open, dropping a roaring torrent into an echoing steel funnel. Twelve thousand tonnes of dusty black coal trundled away on endless conveyor belts and was added to the tip of a growing mountain. The coal was ground to a fine dust then fired at speed into bright furnaces to boil water to make steam to turn a turbine to make electricity so folk could boil a kettle.

I was often able to get home for a night by hitching each way. This was a rather fraught time, worried as I was about not getting back in time and missing my ship; instant dismissal, but the homing instinct was powerful.

Once I set off from home carrying both sets of car keys in my pocket. A complete disaster. I endured a slow queue at the local post office to catch the post fearful of missing sailing time. Marilyn was not pleased.

West Thurrock ceased operations in 1993 and is now demolished. Kingsnorth closed in 2012, and demolition was completed by 2017. Tilbury closed in 2013, and the destruction of Tilbury will be completed in 2018. After forty nine years of creating electricity, coal has become a dirty word.

The 6th October 1981 was a notable day. I was allowed a quick trip up to London from the *Dallington* berthed at West Thurrock, to the Seething Lane office of the Department of Transport, the scene of a simple ceremony. I was handed a stiff folded black card. Having been found duly qualified, the Secretary of State was pleased to grant me a Certificate of Competency as First Mate of a Foreign-Going Ship. Number 6344. At last. It had been ten years since my first attempt in Sydney.

I enjoyed six weeks leave over November and early December and then re-joined the *Dallington* as second mate for another three months tour of duty. It would be Christmas at sea.

We sailed from Blyth after an overnight fall of six inches of snow which covered the decks and mooring gear. The cold steel deck bit through my thick socks and sea boots as I stood at standby on the fo'c'sle. Vigorous broom work cleared the bitts to reveal the second mooring line. The stiff polyprops were unwilling to release their grip. Eventually they were thrown off ashore and hauled in and coiled down. The wire headline was easy, wound in with the self-tensioning winches.

Soft white snow raced out of the bleak grey sky and died against the bridge windows and fell wetly to the deck. No land was visible. Marine dangers were hidden in the murk. The sweep of the radar painted bright orange blobs and a fuzzy outline of the coast; targets to track, collisions to avoid. I took radar bearings at fifteen minute intervals and plotted our position on the chart, keeping faithfully to the starboard side of narrow channels. I stared through the mesmerising flakes. Nothing to see. We arrived and anchored off Southend, joining a scattered fleet, all waiting, waiting for orders. It was Christmas Eve.

Coal stocks were high and work over the Christmas period was slow. My family were frustratingly close but we were condemned to spend a wintry and bleak Christmas swinging on the pick. There was not much jollification on board. We berthed the day after Boxing Day but the infamous Captain Potts refused to allow me a brief home leave. I'm sure it was nothing to do with him being a Northern Irish Protestant and me being a Southern English Catholic.

Relief came when he paid off the ship and the round, jovial figure of Captain Thompson walked up the gangway. He looked at my downcast face in amazement. "What are you doing here? It's Christmas time! Get yourself home for the night, now!" I obeyed and hitched home in record time.

A good break from the routine of carrying cargo is a few days in dry dock. It gives a different perspective. Literally. Instead of the view of the foredeck from the bridge I now had a view of the battered bulbous bow from the damp dock bottom. *Dallington* looked vulnerable and out of her natural element. By the time that we had replaced her cathodes, given her hull a new glossy coat of paint, she looked much snappier after her annual overhaul. The dry dock was flooded and we took her back to sea.

After three long, long months on board I went on paternity leave. Five days after paying off my son Robert was born. I had five more wonderful weeks of family life with the children, aged four, three and a new baby.

It was very hard to drag myself back to sea to join *MV Pearl*. A more misnamed ship I could not imagine.

Chapter 31

LIFE ASHORE IV

ROCK SCRAMBLING

One fine Sunday morning in the spring of 1980 I walked through the quiet streets of Odda to church. It was a simple Scandinavian structure, a crisp white cube. Unfiltered by stained glass, clear light flooded the space. A statue of Our Lady occupied a place of honour in one corner, the congregation in another. The Scripture readings were in Norwegian and English, for which I was most grateful. Having spent many Sundays at sea it was a relief to find a quiet spiritual time in community with others of the faith.

After lunch I went for a bike ride. The mate was not bothered. He'd seen it all before. Besides, the beer was cheaper on board ship. I pulled the ship's bicycle from the deck store and lugged it down the gangway. I swung my leg over and peddled hard out of Odda with a sense of release, escape at last. By Sandvevatnet Lake I cycled through meadows of bright yellow dandelions. Pale cream milkmaid on long stalks edged the banks. I rode up through the layers of glacial moraine edged with deep blue lakes. It was a geography field trip. I came to a magnificent foss, the water gushing with enormous force from a crevice high above. The rippling silver ribbon drew me into its endless flow. Mesmerised, I watched it splinter into shards of liquid light on the scattered rocks below.

Down and down I whizzed, coming to a halt on the flat at the entrance to a hidden valley. Almost lost in the Fylkesveg woods sat an ancient log-built church. The simple structure stood mute witness to the generations of faithful Christians. I did not want to return to the ship but time was passing. I puffed back up the steep hill, then down the other side. Crouched low over the handlebars, the wind blew hard in my face and my hair. I went faster and faster—too fast, so I back peddled to apply the hub brake. Nothing. A grinding noise. The chain had fallen off. The steep verge rushed by ever faster. I slapped one foot on the ground and twisted the handlebars, jerking the front wheel against the rocky bank, bang bang bang. At last I came to a juddering halt. I was breathless but relieved. With shaking fingers I replaced the errant chain. I returned to the silent ship in time for the evening meal. Nothing much had happened on board as I discovered when I went in to the saloon.

'We start discharge 0800 tomorrow,' I announced.

'Fine day forecast.'

'Orders have come through for Egersund, silica rock for Port Sunlight,' I continued.

'Oh yes, Egersund? About a day south?'

'Yeah. 'Bout that.'

Nobody was particularly interested in my explorations. Never mind, I had had an adventure.

Walking ashore in Port Sunlight I stumbled across a model village. Lord Lever was a philanthropist who, like Cadbury, built working men's houses for his workforce. At the centre of Port Sunlight was the magnificent classical building housing the Lady Leverhulme Art Gallery built for the education of his people. Each street of terraced homes was fronted by a foreman's house built in a grander style, the roof capped by mini turret. A clutter of parked cars edged the generous grassy swards. Money and taste combined with power can make a real difference to the living landscape I reflected on my way back to my simple tin box.

The little *Gem* provided big shore excursions. On arrival in Ancona on a Friday in September I was given weekend leave. Foregoing the local architectural attractions, I travelled by train across Italy to Rome. Such speed after our 10 knot plod. The journey rolled through mountain and pasture panoramas. I was met at the station by the same family friend I had visited ten years before when passing through on my way to Paris and home to England. The extended family had an entire apartment block to themselves, with the patriarch on the ground floor. Elvira Matzetti's family were on the second floor. The cool marble flooring and elegant furniture created an oasis of peace that I much appreciated after the long voyage. She was the same diminutive child at heart, with a zest for life, an intense curiosity about the world. It was good to re-establish our friendship. I was much refreshed by my time exploring Rome; going down to the beach for a few hours, eating and sleeping Italian style. Still groggy from my siesta, we wandered round an art gallery in the evening. The city was waking up for evening entertainments. Locals and tourists strolled along the streets as chattering diners spilled out of busy restaurants.

On Sunday I went by bus to St Peters and, having been instructed to enter by the rear of the basilica, joined 25,000 worshippers for a concelebrated mass, led by Pope John Paul II.

The Sistine Chapel choir tried valiantly but failed to fill the vast space with angelic sound, as a colourful procession of three hundred cardinals and bishops attending the Special Synod snaked between the faithful. A classic 'when-in-Rome' moment occurred when the Italian faithful stood on pews to take photographs of the Pope officiating at the magnificent high altar. I threw dignity out of the window and joined them. With my six foot two height advantage I obtained some memorable shots. I received Holy Communion and a Papal Blessing.

Duty called and on Tuesday morning I returned by train to Ancona, back to cargo and chartwork routine.

Our next port was Itea, Greece. With the usual lackadaisical Greek attitude to making progress, we lay several days at anchor before we could load our cargo of bauxite for England. Perusing the black-and-white detailed chart of the port (before such detail was removed from the new, coloured charts) the contour lines along the path to Delphi do not seem challenging. Chief Mate Chris Goddard and I decided we would walk the three miles to visit the Greek temples. I got on well with Chris. He was a cheerful Welshman but I found the continual flow of foul language wearisome on the ears. Too much profanity weakens its power.

Next morning the liberty boat dropped us at the jetty. The pavement was already heating up in the morning sun as we set off on our mission in the warm September sunshine. Puffing through the village we saw a Greek citizen standing on a wheelbarrow-like device treading several bunches of grapes through a sieve of bundled sticks. I was surprised by the basic winemaking equipment.

'Ello, welcome. Please, you like to try?' he invited us, holding out a glass of pure grape juice. It was warm, sweet and sticky, not at all refreshing.

'Very nice', we lied.

'Where you from?' he asked in thickly accented English.

'England. Our ship is at anchor off the port down there,' we pointed back.

'Ah! England! You know my brother, George? He lives in Baker Street, London.'

Umm… actually, no.

Carrying along the narrow track for a while we came to a dry river bed and came out through olive groves. Netting had been spread over the ground to catch the crop which was beginning to drop. The air was still, the intense heat reduced slightly by the shade of the ancient trees. The way ahead appeared to be blocked by a rocky cliff. Navigational charts do not make the best maps for exploration ashore. Undaunted, we scrambled up over the rocks and arrived breathless, hot and thirsty at the edge of the ancient town of Delphi. We had walked a good seven miles. Entering a simple tavern I drank deep of a welcome glass of cold beer and munched on a slice of local pie.

Thus refreshed Chris and I explored the impressive ruins. The Treasury had been restored to good order, as had many temples. We sat in the warm sun on the ancient stone seats near the top of the sweeping amphitheatre cut into the rocky hillside. A wash of blue-green hills and valleys faded to a pale stone horizon. Voices from the stage below floated clearly up to us high above. The Greek architects evidently understood the science of acoustics.

I was intrigued by the athletics track, not a continuous oval but a long straight stretch wide enough to take a broad front of about eight runners. I could imagine the oiled and naked Olympic athletes of long ago sprinting down the straight, encouraged on by the cheering masses, corralled by banks of stone seats hacked out of the hills.

As the warm September sun slipped towards the horizon we realised it was time to get back to the ship. Balham this was not. It was a much easier walk on the return. We were glad that we did not have long to wait on the jetty for the liberty boat to take us back to the ship; time to grab another cold beer and recall our adventures before supper.

Gem heading into Salsbruket

Gem loading bulk paper bales in Salsbruket

Chapter 32

JEWEL OF THE SEA

'Good Morning. Welcome aboard,' smiled the elegantly dressed lady, in a uniform of crisp white shirt and dark blue trousers. It was a cool and cloudy evening at London City Airport on 19 April 1982. Twenty passengers filed down the narrow aisle and slotted into slim seats.

'Would you like a newspaper? Sweets?' With another reassuring smile she walked back down the aisle to the cockpit, strapped herself in the pilot's seat and we took off.

'No need to use a hotel, Mr Quail, I have arranged for a clean cabin aboard your ship', promised Mr Field. The airport taxi did not stop at a comfy city hotel; instead we rattled over the cobbles of the grimy Antwerp docks. A short, two-hatch vessel lay quietly alongside. A dim light picked out the name on the bow: *PEARL*. Red rust dribbled through the dirty white lettering. I stumbled up the gangway and looked for signs of life. A dim light at the far end of the silent alleyway lead me to the Captain's cabin.

'Welcome aboard, but you're a day early,' he mumbled. The promised clean cabin was not awaiting me. The second mate had not left. Surprise, surprise. The bunk in the filthy, stuffy, cramped hospital was made up by a grumpy steward and at midnight I turned in for a few hours' sleep.

Next morning the *Pearl* 'beyond price' manoeuvred off the berth and made her way down the River Scheldt to the open sea. As soon as the aft mooring station was shipshape, I climbed the companionway to the bridge for my five hour watch. By now I had learned that the Captain was a two bottles of whisky a day alcoholic. The pilot was not at all amused by his dishevelled appearance on the bridge. Having cleared the harbour limits, the pilot, with a world weary shake of his head, handed over the con to the mate and scrambled down the wooden ladder to his waiting pilot boat and sped away.

I set course for Aalborg from where we were chartered to load 3,000 tonnes of silver sand for Antwerp. The Captain unsteadily made his way below, and after a brief chat to check I was ok on my first full day aboard, the mate also went to his cabin for a rest. He would soon be back to relieve me.

The engineers did not bother to change for breakfast but sat in the cramped duty mess in their dirty boiler suits, drank beer with their fry-up and toast and continued in like manner through the day. The crew seemed to be the most sober to me. That was not my only concern about this rusty tub. There was a worrying crack in the hull at the break of the accommodation and I wondered just when this 'jewel' would take me down.

Of the engineer officers, Jimmy was a particularly difficult character. Wiry, his deeply etched face was testimony to a hard life. I clearly see him now, his elbows planted aggressively on the table, thin arms covered in a mass of ancient tattoos. Small talk was non-existent. He cursed the engine and his fellow engineers, giving vent to a deeply embittered view of life. He had been a prisoner of war in Changi Jail.

In complete contrast was the diminutive chief engineer who hailed from Blyth, north of Newcastle. At sea he was permanently seasick; his pasty whey face was a picture of misery as he vainly fought off this debilitating sickness. He spent his hours off-watch leather working. He proudly showed me the results of his labours in carefully tooled belts and intricate models of leather men. How he concentrated when so ill impressed me; his steely resolve kept him at sea all his life.

Three repeat runs with silver sand allowed me several days to explore Antwerp; enjoying the architecture of the old quarter, art galleries and a movie (Peter Ustinov as Hercules Poirot in *'Death on the Nile'*) to celebrate my 34th birthday.

Over three months *Pearl* voyaged on to an interesting set of ports, sometimes twice; Egersund, Caen, Gdansk, Swansea, Drogheda, Leixoes and finally Garston. Egersund in is a natural harbour, framed by Norwegian mountains. Here I explored, losing myself in the back streets of the old town. Caen was approached via the Ouistreham Canal. The original lattice ironwork of the famous Pegasus Bridge lay rusting and forgotten on the bank; a new one swept open to permit our passage. We berthed a few minutes' walk from the city centre. I was soon ashore, exploring the ancient cathedrals. The mother of Duke William is buried in one; a blue stained glass window high above her tomb casts a dim light over stark Norman pillars. I learned how Caen had been completely restored after the shattering bomb damage achieved by the Allies in World War II. I recall a magnificent late lunch with a Captain on another trip. We had enjoyed lobster soup, a superb chicken stew, plenty of wine and had meandered in a happy haze back to our ship. Life aboard *Pearl* was in a different league.

In Swansea we berthed at the north side of King's Dock and loaded coal using the famous coal hoists. I watched amazed as, in uncanny silence, long lines of rail wagons, filled with coal mined from local pits, glided down a precise gradient, utilising only the force of gravity. With a roaring whoosh, a stream of fine coal was tipped into a long chute, which directed the black tide into the *Pearl's* empty hold, dust billowing around. Little did I know that I was watching the passing of an historical moment as by 1987 this method of loading coal ceased; Local mines were closed but imported coal was landed at this very same dock. A sad, sad reversal of fortune.

At last we escaped the confines of the near European coast and set off on a four day voyage across the Bay of Biscay to Leixoes, near the city of Oporto on the north coast of Portugal. On arrival, the agent came aboard with a message for the mate. His father was ill and Stevies were flying him back to Ireland immediately. The Mission to Seamen was very helpful in arranging a phone call home and confirming arrangements. This news meant that the ship would sail home without a mate on this two-mate ship. The alcoholic Captain would take his watch. I had a serious conversation with him. (His last name, like most officer's names, have fled the memory with the passage of time, as names were not often used, just the rank. This kept personal feelings and thus conflicts—hopefully—out of the chain of command.)

'I will only do this if you sober up,' I said very firmly. 'I need to be able to trust that you will keep a safe watch. I do not want to risk my life, nor the ship.' I was no mood to compromise on this.

'Oh I will, I will. You can trust me. Don't worry. I'll be fine. I won't drink a drop,' said the Captain soothingly.

I was not soothed.

On a warm summer's afternoon three days later I was hugely relieved when we rounded Great Orme's Head on the north coast of Wales and

170

made safe arrival at the Liverpool Bar Light. The pilot took us up the Mersey River. The famous landmarks were familiar from my youth as a cadet in Elder Dempster; the Royal Liver Building where I had sat my Morse code exam for my Second Mate's ticket; the Cunard Building and the Port of Liverpool Building. The long wooden Princes Landing Stage where I had berthed on *MV Aureol* was no more.

Pearl tied up at Garston, and as the tide ebbed she settled onto the muddy bottom. We were seven miles from the city centre. Looking out from the bridge wing watching our rocks from Portugal being lifted off grab by grab I could see a sliver of the Mersey to starboard and suburban houses to port, a contrast to the usual bleak dockland atmosphere.

It had been a long three months.

I paid off, tripping down the gangway with a light heart. I had survived *Pearl's* challenges. My leave coincided with the summer holidays. The highlight was the baptism of my son, Robert, in the modern chapel at Kingsland, Marilyn's childhood home; now a monastery. The wheel of life continued to turn up the unexpected.

Chapter 33

STAYIN' ALIVE

'Life goin' nowhere, somebody help me.' The lightship cavitational scream was almost too painful to be borne. The Bee Gees' words were bang on. My bunk was sited right aft and the stream of trapped air bubbles striking the half submerged propeller blades sent an intensely high pitched howl deep into my tired ears. No pillow could block out the sound. I was desperate for the oblivion of sleep but sleep proved elusive even after a five hour watch. I longed to be freed of these pinions of pain. Relief came on arrival at the next port. Finished with engines.

I had joined *MV Beeding* in Swansea as second officer. *Beeding* carried just over 3,000 tonnes of bulk cargo, similar to the *Gem* and *Birling* but she was a pig in a swell and rolled like a candle. She was built for the European inland canal waterways, not the high seas.

Normally bunks lie fore and aft so that even when rolling in a heavy seaway it is possible to sleep when gripping the mattress edges, one knee akimbo, the weight spread out. The body relaxes into slumber as it rises and then presses down into the mattress, like riding in a Willy Wonka lift which rapidly changes direction. The ship shuddering throughout her length when a big wave smashes into the hull makes the whole bunk vibrate, but even in sleep the hands maintain a good grip. On *Beeding* my bunk was set athwartships, port to starboard. Thus so was my body. One night rolling down the Irish Sea the effect was particularly vicious and I found myself standing one moment on my head and the next moment on my feet. The surging rush of blood was exhausting and made sleep impossible.

Stayin' Alive

As the ship rolled onto her beam ends and back, I timed its movements to drag my mattress out of the well of the bunk frame and flung it to the deck. There was little space to move. I lay down and grasped the mattress firmly on both sides, drew up one knee to brace myself against the extreme motion. Exhaustion took over and I found blessed relief in a sleep of the dead.

On two mate ships on the home and middle trade runs, the day is divided into five hour shifts with a four-hour shift to make up the hours. Thus over 24 hours one is asleep during what was the on-watch period previously. The longest I've ever kept rolling watches like this is twenty two days. Staying awake on watch is a battle. Even standing up with my head proud of the bridge dodger, to allow the full force of the gale to smash into my face, I have felt my knees buckle as sleep snared me in its grip. Banging my forehead repeatedly against the doorjamb didn't stop my eyes snapping shut nor even give me a headache.

There's only so much coffee you can drink in an hour. The trick is to think about something constructive but after weeks at sea the brain has analysed the political news, the family news, made holiday plans. Sean Connery starred in a film called 'The Wall.' He endured solitary confinement, forced to stand for hours on end, staring at the cell wall. Onto this cell wall he projected in his mind's eye the image of the house that he had been building at home. He reconstructed it joist by joist, brick by brick, nail by nail. I did the same on my solitary watch by reconstructing the garden shed I had built the previous leave. Sometimes I wondered how close I was to the edge of madness.

Beating up and down the south-west coast of Norway off Rekefjord on a night of vicious squalls whipping up high seas is not an experience I would wish to repeat. Obviously the pilot could not board the ship in those conditions. So we were sentenced to patrol up and down at slow speed with the wind off the port bow, trying to find our most comfortable position, retracing our course every few hours, ensuring that we were off the port at dawn the next morning. It was still too stormy for the pilot to board via the pilot ladder so we followed his launch through the narrow neck of cliffs which protected the inner harbour. Like a pheasant dashing for cover we shot through the rock-fringed entrance. (Amazingly, there is a video clip on YouTube of just such an entry dash.)

We made fast fore and aft and shut down the engines. The sudden silence and the comfort of a stable deck was not to last. Hatches banged open and with a roar reverberating through the empty steel holds the ship rapidly loaded with gravel. My mind was fully occupied in the safe loading of *Beeding* down to her marks. No time for sleep.

A few hours later we re-negotiated the tricky entrance and headed south butting through the last ravages of the storm. Rolling and pitching we made our way through the Skagerrak then edged the Kattegat towards Randers Fjord. I was operating on autopilot myself, never mind the ship. On picking up the pilot at the mouth of the fjord the sun came out and the wind died away. We wound through the flat, calm waterway towards the town. The evening light shed a golden glow over the osier beds. Winter green fields were dotted with horses and cows safely grazing. Mingled with a deep weariness was sheer relief at surviving a vicious storm followed by a fast loading. And professional pride because we were delivering our cargo safely to the next port. Job done. It was Christmas time and Denmark knows how to decorate a town. Its lights twinkled benignly and protectively over my deep slumbers.

I paid off *Beeding* in Rotterdam at the end of November. I had stayed alive. I was keen to get home and so pressed Mr Field to allow me to leave without waiting for my relief. I took an overnight ferry from the Hook of Holland to Harwich. I felt very emotional docking at dawn, back in England again. Trip trap ashore again.

Christmas was wonderful. My eldest daughter Joanna was growing up. Now she was five. With her little hand in mine, we walked together down the road early in January to her first day at primary school.
I dragged myself back to sea in the third week of January. Captain Allan signed me on articles as second mate on *MV Washington,* berthed at Kingsnorth Power Station. She was on the collier run between the Medway and the Thames. Built in Japan, *Washington* was only five years old and had quite a different feel to the rest of the fleet. The accommodation was roomy and her broad beam made her comfortable in most weathers. She lifted a solid 9,000 tons of coal, three times more than the *Beeding.*

But coal is coal and after three months of flogging up and down the northeast coast I was ready for leave, paying off at Kingsnorth. It was good to be home for my 35th birthday. The photo album is full of pictures of family picnics, walks, local explorations and birthday parties.

The crack of a bullet in the dark is sharp and fearsome. It echoes flatly against the cranes and ships in the silent coal dock. The scream of Land Rovers chasing shadows fade into the distance. Belfast at night is best avoided. I stepped away from the bulwark and went back inside. I had returned to the *Beeding*.

Next morning on a run ashore to get the morning paper and a few essential supplies all was quiet. It felt normal. It looked normal. But it was not.

The city centre was ringed by a bright red spiked steel fence. The gateway was guarded by armed police. A metal detector was pressed under my arms and between my legs. Satisfied, the gate was opened and I was allowed to pass through. People inside the security ring went about their shopping quite normally—if you discount the oddity of being stopped outside Woolworths by a guard who waved his detector wand over my body before letting me enter. I returned to my ship through the dock gates (more checks) and with relief climbed the gangway, back to my secure, separate maritime world. I was glad to be sailing the next day, away from this madness.

This trip was a typically busy loading schedule, carrying nine different cargos to thirteen different ports and six voyages lightship. We carried limestone (3x), petroleum coke, duff, grain gluten, silver sand, coal, scrap steel, limestone slag and cement clinker all round Europe, up and down the English Channel. From Belfast, Llanddulas (3x) to Ghent (2x), Rotterdam (2x), Newport, Calais, Cork Erith, Antwerp, Dublin, Workington, Limerick, Larne, and Drogheda (2x).

The spider grab pulled festoons of scrap steel from our hold and dropped them into the waiting hopper. We were alongside the Haulbowline Island Steelworks at Cobh, close to Cork. A conveyor belt carried the mess into a large shed. I followed the belt to track the process. A tangle of scrap fell in the large crucible and the crackling electric arc melted the mixture. A workman with a plastic visor covering his whole face pulled at the cauldron and tipped an iridescent flow of white hot steel into a narrow channel. It flowed swiftly away and cooled rapidly into mild steel bars ready for the next construction product. By 2001 it was all over. The steelworks had closed.

The mighty spire of St Colman's Cathedral dominated my view across the River Lee. I think that I took a little ferry over the river to explore. It may have been a bus. Cool, pink marble columns held up Gothic tracery. Here behind the high altar was a monument to the bishop who had commissioned it. And one to Pugin, the architect. A vast edifice for such a small town.

I discovered the plaque in memory of those who died in the sinking of the *Lusitania* by a German U-boat during the First World War, with the loss of 1,198 passengers and crew on 7 May 1915. It caused such shock and outrage in the United States that there was a popular clamour for America to enter the war. And it was from here, (then known as Queenstown) that the *Titanic* set sail on her final fatal voyage.

On the little ships in Stevie Clarke discipline was more relaxed than when in Elder Dempster. At all times on watch full attention should be given to keeping a good radar and visual lookout. And it was. However it was also important to stay awake. I found an effective stimulus was to listen to Radio 4. One bleak, black winter's night Malcolm McDowell was supremely convincing in a murder mystery story. I wedged myself firmly between the bulkhead and bridge console, buttressed against a rough sea and a howling wind. The radio waves transported me into a world of terror as the murderer stalked his victim on a night as black and as dreadful as mine. I had nowhere to hide from the insidious voice crawling into my head. I sought refuge on the windswept bridge wing and scanned the horizon for more tangible dangers.

At last 5 September arrived and I paid off the *Beeding* in Drogheda, Eire, flying home from Dublin to London for an extra six months' leave. Wonderful. It was time for that crack at my Master Mariner's Ticket.

I had stayed alive—this time. *Beeding* foundered off Turkey in 2003 with the loss of all hands.

Chapter 34

MASTER MARINER

I breathed in deeply. The crisp and cool early morning air blew in through the open window as I rolled along the winding A272 to Warsash. Autumn tints edged the green canopy cloaking the South Downs. I was on the weekly drive back to nautical college for another six months of study, this time for my Master Mariner's Certificate of Competency. I studied, in greater depth now, navigation, ship construction, engineering, metrology, and a new subject, ship master's business. All very challenging. I returned home on Friday evenings for a relaxing weekend with the family, as last time.

I revelled in the changing seasons in the glorious countryside of West Sussex. I enjoyed an excellent Christmas. But for the following two years I paid the price—Christmas at sea. In the spring we spent a memorable week on holiday in a simple cottage tucked under the high ridge of Offa's Dyke; walking the heights, damming rivers, building dens and playing the recorder.

The Chief Examiner of Master and Mates sent me a formal invitation to attend, 'punctually at 1100 on 15 March 1984', the Department of Trade Examination Centre in Southampton. It was all too soon. We trooped nervously into the examination classroom. For all of us a great deal of effort and hope had been invested in this enterprise. Success meant eventual promotion. Failure was not an option.

Four solid days of writing exam papers, each two and half hours long, was very taxing. Before returning to sea six weeks later I heard good news; I had passed four out of five papers, including the ocean navigation paper

I thought I had failed. Chart work had let me down again. I successful re-sat that paper the following November, after a three week revision class.

Thirteen months after starting college, on 25 April 1985 I stood at the counter of Mercantile Marine Office, Seething Lane, London. The busy but observant clerk handed me a gold-embossed certificate.

CERTIFICATE OF COMPETENCY
DECK OFFICER
CLASS 1

MASTER MARINER.

The clerk offered his hand, 'Well done,' he congratulated me with a warm smile. This simple gesture marked a significant milestone in my nautical career. I opened the folded black card and read my name, neatly handwritten. It felt surprisingly light. But solid. It represented many years of striving. I had reached the top of my professional hill. It had been a long, long slog.

Would Stephenson Clarke promote me to Master? Would I survive at sea for many more years? Would the company survive? Would the Merchant Navy survive? These were all deep imponderables as I returned to sea after this last long study leave. It was hard to let go—as always—of family life ashore.

Chapter 35

IN THE COURT OF KING NEPTUNE

Taking sun sights on a rapidly rolling ship is an extra challenge. Mill scale is flaky chips of hot rolled steel and is thus very dense and thus only loaded to a depth of a few feet in the hold. With a high centre of gravity, we ticked every six seconds like a grandfather clock, rolling our way across the South Atlantic to South Africa. Our special cargo was to be used as a catalyst in the process of distilling petrol from coal. It thus would mitigate the British-imposed trade embargo.

I had returned to sea as second officer on *MV Aldrington,* signing on in Dublin under Captain Ramsey, at the end of April 1984. Instead of the usual middle trade run around Europe, we had orders to carry mill scale from Liverpool to Durban. A proper tropical sunshine run at last. And, very importantly, because we were 'foreign going' (outside of middle trade limits) we carried a third officer and therefore enjoyed the more relaxed routine of three mate watches: four hours on, eight off.

Aldrington followed the 7,000 mile course that I had plotted: Liverpool Bar, South Stack, The Smalls, Bishop Rock, Cape Finisterre, Las Palmas, Cape Blanc, Cape Vert. Just south of the island of Sao Tome we crossed the Equator. King Neptune had to be placated with the sacrifice of a green first tripper in an extremely messy ritual. Though I had transited this great circle many times previously I had managed to avoid the Crossing the Line ceremony inflicted on 'first-timers' by claiming that I had been initiated on previous voyages. On an earlier occasion a terrified cadet had hidden in a locker, refusing to come out of hiding until the end of the day.

It was not so much the cold sea water douche as the indignity inflicted that caused victims to be unwilling.

For days the cook had been collecting food scraps in a large bucket; old gravy, sauces, vegetable peelings, slops in general. This gooey smelly mixture was placed handy on the poop deck.

'Let the revelries begin!' commanded King Neptune, waving a silver trident fastened to a mop pole. The Captain—and Mate—had unaccountably declined this honourable role. I sat enthroned in the Captain's Chair purloined from the bridge, my head covered with a silver crown, my face adorned with abundant quantities of cotton wool liberated from the first aid kit, and a beard fashioned from a floor mop. Over the whole I swathed myself in a counterpane stripped from my bunk. The crew joined in the dressing-up fun, covering their safety helmets in shiny cooking foil raided from the galley and creating cloaks from spare curtains borrowed from the linen locker.

The victim, a junior engineer, was brought onto the poop deck. Stripped to his swimming trunks, he sat on an after bollard. His face was plastered in a creamy mixture of yoghurt, toothpaste and shaving foam. The mess was briskly scraped off his cheeks with a wooden spoon. The Chief Steward had lovingly prepared a special tincture of rum, yoghurt, and sundry spices, which he pushed into the mouth of the suspicious culprit. His screwed up face said it all. The crew surrounded the hapless engineer and he, taking it all with resigned fortitude, allowed himself to be gunked with the filthy slops, to loud cheers and whoops from Neptune's acolytes. A fire hose swept him and the deck clean and sluiced the slops down the scuppers. We hoped that King Neptune had been mollified and would allow us safe passage through his domain.

Officers and crew gathered for a welcome barbecue cooked on half an oil drum and washed down with plenty of beer. We sailed on through the warm tropical evening trailing a band of silver foam behind us. I appreciated such camaraderie which broke up the monotony of crossing an empty ocean under a scorching sun.

The joy of being back in tropical waters after ten years was rekindled when watching flying fish flicker their silver wings in brilliant sun. Emerging from the deep blue in single shots, or in glittering shoals, they were airborne for a few vibrant seconds before crashing beneath the white-capped waves.

Dolphins leapt free of the water and surfed our bow wave, then dived below our barnacled hull, using it like a giant marine nit comb to scrape off their parasites. The pod emerged victorious on the other side and, with a final frolic, vanished as suddenly as they had appeared.

Onwards we inched across the small-scale chart of the South Atlantic, the noon positions marking the days, until we closed with the land off Cape Point forty miles south of Cape Town. *Aldrington* rounded Cape Agulhas and headed eastward, ticking off significant landmarks, counting down the miles to go: Cape St Francis, Hood Point, Rame Head, Cape Hermes, Point Shepstone and at long last, Durban.

On arrival, the VHF radio squawked disheartening orders: 'Anchor and await further instructions.' Our berth was full. We waited with mounting impatience as day followed day and no berthing news came. An occasional adventurer paddled out on his surfboard from the beach a mile off, said, 'Hi!' and paddled back to freedom. Through my binoculars I watched figures running or relaxing on the beach. At smoko time, engineers in dirty boiler suits heaved their weary frames up to the bridge to gulp tea from big white mugs, and gossiped.

After ten long days of checking anchor bearings we berthed on a Friday evening. No weekend work. I was given leave to visit relatives near Pietermaritzburg; a refreshing interlude.

Monday morning cranked the workforce into unhurried movement. Using a clamshell grab, a crane began the slow work of unloading our very dense mill scale into waiting rail trucks. As each truck was filled it was manhandled onwards and another pulled into position. Afrikaans overseers shouted in harsh accents at the sweating, slow moving African workers. The meaning behind the guttural sounds was blatantly clear. I recoiled from such racist attitudes.

Two days later we were empty, the ship's crew happy to earn cargo money sweeping out the holds. We shifted ship over to the coal berth. Several days later as June drew to a tired close, we set off on the return four week, 6,800 mile voyage. This time we were glad of the southeasterly Agulhas current, 6 knots at times off the coast between Durban and Port Elizabeth.

Rounding Ushant the deep emotional tug of The Channels set in. Home beckoned. Gratification had to be delayed as we crept up the Channel, leaving the White Cliffs of Dover far away to port. On to Ouistreham, where we picked up a pilot for the canal to Caen. Here I happily paid off to go on a much anticipated leave.

Crossing the Line Celebrations

King Neptune claims a victim

BBQ on the poop.
Enjoying a party at sea; happy faces, the author's arms outstretched
Note the Chief Engineer's wife, rare female company

Chapter 36

TAKING LEAVE

The first week is a week of adjustment. Tempers and strong views are held in check. Deferring to my wife is relearned. For three months I have been operating in a masculine, seafaring environment, used to taking decisions and applying them rapidly to satisfy the needs of the ship and the company. There was little discussion of options.

That is not the way families operate. Children mostly see things from their point of view. The female mind approaches problems quite differently from the male mind.

The beginning and end of my six week's leave between voyages was a painful time of readjustment for me and my family. Whilst I was away at sea the family did things together without me. Marilyn ran the household. When I came home there was one more person in the decision mix, one more person with a strong opinion, one more person to be fed, one more person to accommodate to family harmony.

As the end of leave approaches new tensions develop when one morning the phone rings. It's the call.

'Hello. Simon Quail speaking'

'Good morning, Mr Quail. Mr Field here. Hope you are having a good leave?'

'Morning, Mr Field. What have you got for me?'

'Okay, Mr Quail. You are flying out 7 September from London City Airport on the 1202 flight bound for Amsterdam. You are joining the *Rogate* as Second Mate. A taxi will meet you and take you to the ship. The mate will be going on leave five days later and I would like you to take over. I will send you an airline ticket in the post, as per usual.'

Now there is a pit of tension in my stomach. My time of freedom with my family has come to an end. I need to focus on the future and prepare for my new role, to check my stability knowledge prior to loading my first cargo. I dig out my uniform and new stripes, working gear, shore gear, heavy weather gear in case to go to the Baltic where winter comes early. I am not due home until January 1985. Three months. Three months without my lovely family. Stop it. Just think about getting ready. I get out my old ski salopettes, great for keeping me warm on the fo'c'sle during long standbys coming into port; a set of Damart longjohns and T shirt, thick waterproof coat, woolly hat, thick socks for my working boots. And just in case I get posted to the tropics during the voyage, a pair of shorts and one short-sleeved shirt. It will have to do. I lay it all out ready and add to it as I remember things. I remember to wrap up some Christmas presents and leave them secretly in the cupboard for Marilyn to give out later.

Departure tomorrow. Suitcase on the bed. Zip it open and look into its empty space. I fold each item and pack methodically. I add reading books, tape recorder, tapes, and radio; close the case and wait until the children have gone to bed before dragging the heavy load downstairs and place by the front door ready for the taxi in the morning. I make it a policy not to talk much about going back to sea. It's too hard.

Marilyn cooks a nice easy supper (sausages) for the family; three children aged seven, five and nearly three. Bath, read stories and put them to bed. Say prayers and kiss good night. And say goodbye quietly inside.

A great wailing noise wakes me from a deep sleep.

'Robert, what's the matter?'

'Daddy. You are going away... I don't want you to goooh,' he sobs.

It is 2 o'clock in the morning. Robert has woken, gone to the toilet and seen my big suitcase by the door. He has learnt what this signifies. 'I will come back soon,' I lie. 'Mummy is still here. Be a brave boy and look after Mummy, and your sisters.' I pick him up and comfort him.

Eventually he falls asleep and I go back to bed. Sleep does not come easily.

I am jerked in to wakefulness and slam off the alarm. 0600. Did I sleep? Dressing quickly I jaw away at a bowl of cereal. It is difficult to swallow. 0700. The children sleepily emerge in their pyjamas. The girls remember what this routine means. I pick up each one and kiss them goodbye.

I give Marilyn a big hug and kiss goodbye and drag myself away into the waiting taxi. It is a fine early September morning. I will not be home for Christmas.

Where will the next voyage take me?

Chapter 37

LIFE CHANGES

The *Rogate* was showing her age. The poor old thing, she was a leaky rust bucket. The leaks also came from the radiators in the mate's cabin; amazingly he was prepared to allow two inches of water to slosh about his cabin and do nothing about it. Dragging this well-oiled reprobate out of his pit so I could go back to mine was always a bit of a battle.

Five days later I had my first promotion to Chief Mate when he went on leave. The price was a short trip because they wanted to get me back to sea over Christmas. Now I was in charge of loading. Ship stability theory studied in the classroom was put into action. I consulted trim tables, made due allowance for ballast, fuel and stores, calculated draft and re-read the load line regulations. I took density readings by filling bucket with dock water and floating an hydrometer in it—a pocket-sized instrument with an outsized responsibility.

After six busy weeks sailing between Continental ports I paid off in Antwerp on 25 October for my usual leave. First I had to retake my Master's coastal navigation paper. This entailed three solid weeks' revision study back at Warsash Nautical College. As before, mid-week was spent in Portsmouth and the weekends at home. A difficult sacrifice, but it had to be done. I sat the paper in coastal navigation and took the remainder of my leave. The results would come in a few weeks' time.

I duly signed back on *Rogate* mid-December, this time as Mate. It was very cold and the heating ineffective. The radiator leak in my cabin had been reduced to a dribble. Rather different from the Elder Dempster chief officer's spacious office, dayroom and private cabin of twenty years before when I, a humble cadet on the way up, peered through his door. A lingering taste of ashes.

However, as we were discharging coal in Caen, life changed again. Returning from a few beers ashore we saw a Stevies ship, the *Ashington*, alongside and so of course we went aboard. It was not often we had the pleasure of visiting a company ship, to see if we could bum a few beers off them and indulge in a bit of gossip.

'Where are you off to?' I enquired as I sipped a cool tinny.

'Durban.' said Captain Patrickson.

'South Africa! Hot sun, tropical seas! I'm really jealous!' I exclaimed unthinkingly. I was not looking forward to sailing through the iced up Baltic to Gdansk in the depths of winter.

'Ohh,' he replied very casually, 'We are short of a second mate. Would you like to swap ships and come with us?' Quick internal debate: chief officer on freezing rust bucket going through the Baltic or second mate on a nice long ocean run to find summer sun in South Africa? I missed my deep sea days of the '60s and '70s and my trip to Durban on the *Aldrington* in April had whetted my appetite afresh. I decided to forego the cash and escape the cold.

'I'll come with you.'

'Good. I will contact Mr Field at the Office. He will be delighted. He will send the mate back to the *Rogate*. It *is* his ship. Go and get your gear and shift it aboard and I will sign you on.'

I then remembered that I had packed only one pair of shorts.

Donald Patrickson was one of the few captains whose name and character remain with me over the decades. He was a kindly, white-haired old salt who had sailed in Tate & Lyle's sugar ships. He knew how to run a ship, and how to keep up morale over long voyages. I didn't regret the transfer. Back to Durban again and another chance to visit my wife's relatives.

From Caen to Durban my Passage Planning Book tells me is 6,784 nautical miles; nearly twenty six days at sea at 11 knots. We left Caen on a cold day of biting wind in early January 1985 and headed down the English side of the English Channel, round the rocky Cherbourg peninsular, keeping to the traffic lanes as we headed towards Ushant's famous Créac'h Light, whose *Fl (2) W 10s* light warns ships away from lethal rocks, eighteen miles off the western coast of Brittany.

Having safely transited the Bay of Biscay without any troubles we stopped for bunkers in Las Palmas. Making a phone call home from the local Mission to Seamen's club I heard the excellent news that I had successfully cleared the hurdle of the coastal navigation exam on the second attempt and now I was the proud possessor of a Master Mariner's ticket. Hopefully promotion to Mate full time would follow on my next trip.

From Las Palmas we headed due south for Cape Corviero then on to Cape Blanc which marked the border between Spanish Sahara and Mauritania. As we sailed across our watery desert I reflected that due east of us lay the waterless wastes of the sandy interior of Africa. We rounded Cape Vert, hard by Dakar, capital of Senegal, where one day I would come ashore in unexpected circumstances. Now to port lay the hot humid river state of the Gambia which I had visited as a cadet. We struck away from the African coast at Liberia and set course 143° for landfall at Cape Point. Crossing some three and half thousand miles of the Southern Atlantic Ocean on this busy shipping route transited by thousands of vessels, it was a paradox that we very rarely saw craft of any sort. We were lost to each other in the vastness of the ocean.

As always, sparking flying fish, gambolling dolphins, colourful tropical sunrises, the taking of morning and noon sights enlivened otherwise mundane watches as we crawled south over the small-scale chart of the South Atlantic towards Cape Town.

One afternoon I came up on to the bridge for my 12 to 4 watch and stepped out onto the port bridge wing. There before me a massive solitary cumulonimbus cloud towered high into the sky. It was riven by brilliant flashes of fork lightning. There was no rumble or crash of thunder as the roiling mass made its way silently out to sea, propelled by an offshore wind. Uncanny.

At about latitude 5° north we entered the doldrums, an infamous area for sailing ships marked by a confused, multi-layered cloudscape, flat seas and still airs; the battle zone of the ITCZ, (the Inter-tropical Convergence Zone). Sailing ships could sit for days or even weeks praying for a wind to blow them out of their hot and windless hell. In our motor ship we powered easily through the Realm of King Neptune.

A film night once a week made a welcome break. The bulky and noisy 16mm projector was set up in the smoke room after the evening meal. I joined the day workers and off watch officers and grabbed a cold tinny. I pulled the ring tab with a satisfied shizzptt, savoured the first glug, and settled down to enjoy the movie.

Having just obtained my Master's Ticket I was confident that I could swing the compass at the equator. Ships built and operated in the northern hemisphere have had their magnetic compasses corrected for the effects of ship's magnetism only for that hemisphere. When entering the southern hemisphere, a ship needs to be swung 360° to obtain a complete set of corrections. However, Captain Patrickson wouldn't hear of it. He was far too fearful of a cock-up to allow anyone to fiddle with the magnetic compass. Its errors remained. And of course we relied on the electric gyro compass, which was steady and accurate.

In the tropics the engineers suffered grievously, working below in temperatures of 50°C. Every thirty minutes they would emerge wearily on deck to cool off in the tropical heat and glug down gallons of water. Tempers were short and we began to long for cooler southern airs. The air-conditioning kept failing. It was not built for tropical voyages.

I was pleased with my astro navigation when, two weeks after leaving Las Palmas, we made a good landfall off the rocky promontory of Cape Point, a mile east of the more famous Cape of Good Hope. Its sheer profile makes an excellent radar contact. The old light at 780 feet was far too often shrouded in low cloud, which hid it from passing ships, and caused the wrecking of the Portuguese *SS Lusitania* in 1911. Not to be confused with the *RMS Lusitania* (sunk off Ireland in 1915) this disaster led to the construction of the present lighthouse, sited 285 feet and so below cloud level.

My passage planning book confirms that it was another 775 miles and three more days to Durban. We berthed on arrival, late on a Friday afternoon. In the relaxed way of Durban, cargo work would begin on the Monday morning. I received permission from Captain Patrickson to take the weekend off. Hiring a zippy VW Beetle, I took off to visit the cousin's farm in the foothills of the Drakensberg Mountains.

On my return to duty three days later, the mate still didn't need me on cargo watch so I put my energies into planning the return voyage to Genoa.

The routine of passage planning was very soothing. Consulting the huge Admiralty chart catalogue I listed the required chart numbers in my planning book. Each chart was pulled out of large folio drawers from beneath the plotting table and arranged in the correct order. I drew compass arcs at least two miles off headlands, joined up the points and recorded each headland, lighthouse and course to steer in my notebook. Walking the brass dividers along the track I checked distance of each leg, measured off the vertical scale, and calculated distance to go. Having come out the same way, retracing our steps made course confirmation simple. In most cases it was just a matter of redrawing the same lines and re-labelling the direction. Plotting our course into the Mediterranean and up to Genoa was retracing familiar steps. I was absorbed in the task. So different from today's digital charts and satnav fixes.

The distance to Genoa was 6,720 nautical miles via the Cape of Good Hope. Four weeks at sea. Via the Suez Canal it was 5,795 miles, 745 miles shorter and three days quicker. I did not decide the route but I imagine the Suez Canal fees would have been too high. It had been nineteen years since I had transited that engineering marvel. It was not to be.

On 20 January the harbour pilot came aboard and we took our stations. I went to my station aft as usual.

'Single up to one and one,' squawked my walkie-talkie.

The men ashore threw off the second sternline. The motors of the self-tensioning winches growled into action and the sailors fed the polyprop directly onto the warp end, hauled it in and coiled it directly into the lazarette for deep-sea stowage.

'Singled up to one and one,' I reported to the bridge.

A few moments later: 'Let go aft!'

We slacked off the wire stern line and the wire spring, the shore gang tossed the eyes off the shore bollard and wandered off. Job done. The wire was quickly hauled in, directly onto the barrel. The water being now clear of lines which might foul the propeller, I reported to the bridge,

'All clear aft!'

The propeller thrashed out a wake, thrusting us against the for'ard spring and lifting our stern off the quay.

We cleared the berth and the pilot took us out to sea. The cutter came alongside, its powerful throbbing engines easily matching our slow speed. The pilot came down from the bridge and gave us a cheerful wave.

'Have a good voyage,' he wished us in a thick South African accent. I stood by and watched him make his way down the pilot ladder and safely to his boat. He returned to the land whilst we retraced our slow passage southwest, made good use of the Agulhas current, rounded Cape Point and headed north across the South Atlantic to Cape Vert. The rocky coastline of the Canary Islands slipped by in hazy sunshine and our bows lifted to the increasing northeasterly trades, as we shaped our course for the Mediterranean. As we transited the busy Straits, the misty mountains of Jebel Musa in Morocco were clearly visible to starboard, as was the dramatic sheer rock of Gibraltar to port.

March 20th dawned fine and clear as we approached a grey mountainous backdrop, the twinkling city lights fading to reveal the port city of Genoa. When we had made fast I looked over the side and saw a familiar face standing on the quay.

'What are you doing here?' I called down, mystified.

'Come to relieve you as Second Mate,' said my old shipmate. 'You are to go home on leave.'

I had no idea that I might go home. I don't think the Master did either. It took me thirty minutes to sign off, pack my bags and jump in my relief's taxi. Very soon I was at the airport and boarded the plane to Gatwick. The family was surprised but pleased to see me as I had not been expected back in the UK for at least three more weeks.

Joanna was now seven years old, Philippa was five and Robert three. They were growing fast and I was missing out on these vital early years. We enjoyed a wonderful spring holiday camping in France for two glorious weeks, exploring the châteaux of the Loire, sailing in local lakes and relaxing in the warm sun.

Chapter 38

THE ART OF NAVIGATION.

This chapter is of technical interest to landlubbers, ancient mariners and other seafarers in the grip of nostalgia; in fact to all those who wish learn how navigators found their way across busy coastal and ocean waters before the advent of the ubiquitous GPS. There are no signposts at sea, so how do ships navigate successfully across oceans devoid of landmarks? (The dedicated perfectionist is free to offer technical corrections and advice and so improve future editions of this book.)
If this is not for you, you are welcome to skip the chapter.

'Where are we? When will we get there'? The cry goes up from adults and children alike when travelling on long journeys. Road Atlases, signposts indicating road names and distances to go, ornate signs announcing the names of villages all provide reassurance that we are not lost and so will not be late arriving at our destination.

At sea, it is different. There are no highways, no dotted lines to follow, no signposts—just dangerous rocks lurking at the edge of vast ocean reaches. Keeping clear of threatening cliffs and headlands is the endeavour of every navigator, the nightmare of every ship's master. The Lighthouse Stevensons, among many others, saved the lives of countless seafarers over the centuries—and the ship owners several fortunes, which of course was much more important to the investor.

Satellite navigation (GPS) is used everywhere today; mobile phones, satnavs in cars and of course at sea. The mariner no longer has to wait for dawn and dusk to catch the fading stars in the mirrors of his sextant and pin them to the horizon to determine the ship's position. Now the mariner merely peers at the digital readout; the position of the ship may even be displayed on an electronic chart.

Fifty years ago the navigator had to master a variety of different methods and skills to find his way about the blank canvas of the ocean. The next few pages will describe in brief outline the navigational techniques used to find a vessel's way around the coasts and seaways of the world.

Coastal, or Inshore, Navigation

Navigating within sight of land provides the mariner with a variety of ways of fixing the ship's position. The old black and white charts contained considerable topographic details, used to identify prominent features, such as lights, cliffs and leading marks. They were a cartographer's delight. I have recorded elsewhere that information gleaned from a chart helped us explore ashore successfully and discover the ancient ruins of Delphi. Modern charts have much less detail, particularly inland. Colourful but bland. To turn the pages of the Admiralty Pilot Book for local coastal area was to enter a world of detailed landfall sketches, of headlands, of lighthouses. They provided vital visual clues which confirmed an arrival position off an unknown shore.

The usual method used to fix one's position on a coastal voyage is to take a bearing. To facilitate the taking of a compass bearing, a bearing ring is fitted to the steering or bridge wing compass. In ships built in the 1940s there was no gyro repeater and so use was made of the steering compass on the monkey island (the deck above the bridge deck). In a rolling seaway the dampened but still lively magnetic compass card made taking an accurate bearing difficult. When gyro electric compasses were later fitted, a gyro repeater on each wing made it so much easier. All one had to cope with was the rolling of the ship itself.

Taking a Compass Bearing on a lighthouse

First check that the bearing circle on the gyro repeater rotates freely. Line up the sighting vanes so the lighthouse appears behind the vertical wire in the far vane (like aiming a rifle). Drop your eyes to the prism at the base of the far vane, and then read off the bearing indicated by a hairline on the prism. Transfer the bearing to the chart, laid off from the charted object. The ship lies somewhere on that bearing.

The Three Point Fix
Take compass bearings of three widely spread objects, (lighthouse, known headland or coastal feature) and lay them down on the chart; the vessel is located somewhere within the plotted 'cocked hat'. The bearings must be taken quickly because the ship is maintaining course at ten or even twenty knots, which of course affects the accuracy of the fix.

A Transit bearing
Line up two charted objects such as a lighthouse and church steeple and your position lies somewhere on the plotted line on the chart. A transit plotted with a bearing of another object is more accurate than the three point fix.

Rising and Dipping
The distance from a lighthouse can be calculated by observing the moment its light is seen breaking the horizon. Using rising and dipping distances tables, apply 'height of eye' against height of the light, (from the chart or in the Admiralty List of Lights); read off the distance. Combined with a compass bearing of the light this gives a good fix.

Vertical Sextant Angles
The sextant is used to measure the angle between the horizon and the top of a charted object. Distance off can be calculated by trigonometry or by consulting a table for Distance off by Vertical Sextant Angle.

Radar
Today's polychromatic radar displays were to us navigating fifty years ago but science-fiction. Our Kelvin Hughes radar had an eight inch orange display. Below the screen we could use just two dials to vary gain and brightness. But it was sufficient to identify headlines to compare against the chart from which to plot bearings. And track which targets were on a collision course with us.

Echo Sounder
Using the echo sounder to determine depth and compare it with the depth on the chart was useful confirmation of position, particularly when approaching a steeply shelving coast or when crossing a bar at the

entrance of the river when the low-lying estuary offered few recognisable landmarks to fix a position.

Offshore, or Deep Sea Navigation

The technology available for fixing one's position out of sight of land in the 1960s and 1970s was basic but sufficient for the times. There were three radio direction finding systems, and navigation by the sun, moon, planets and stars—astro navigation.

Radio Direction Finder (DF)

The crossed grey rings of the DF loop were a prominent feature rising up out of the monkey island. Developed from technologies dating from 1888 and improved during World War II, it was still in use in the 1970s. Modern developments are still in use today.

Like a radio 'lighthouse', shore beacons transmitted a signal received by the ship's equipment. The frequency and Morse code call sign unique to each shore station was identified from a reference manual. The dial on the DF set was tuned for the strongest signal. The bearing was then plotted as a position line. Two more bearing from other stations resulted in a better fix. It was not uniformly trusted but was helpful to confirm a ship's position when poor weather prevented astro fixes.

LORAN C.

LORAN-C was an advanced system which used low frequency radio signals transmitted from land-based radio beacons. But it was expensive, thus when it was first introduced in 1957 only the US military could afford to use it.

Technological advances in the 1970s reduced costs and Loran-C became a widely used navigation system for large areas of North America, Europe, Japan, North Atlantic and North Pacific areas. Specialist navigational charts had to be purchased which were overprinted with position fixing lines, based on the measurement of the time difference between the receipt of signals from a pair of radio transmitters.

There has been much recent discussion amongst military planners about developing ELORAN as a backup in case of failure of GPS systems. Britain was actively supporting this policy until a sudden announcement of closure in a Notice to Mariners 1 December 2015.

But the companies on which I sailed never used it, preferring to rely on the Decca Navigator System.

Decca Navigator

The Decca Navigator System was a radio navigation system. Radio signals were received from fixed navigational beacons. The position was plotted on Decca charts overprinted with red, green and purple coloured lines. Readings taken from the radio receiver transferred to the chart gave more accurate fix than Loran-C in coastal waters.

This system is a rare example of an American invention failing to find backers in the USA military, being brought to England where it was successfully developed. First used by the Royal Navy in World War II, its use was expanded after the war around the UK and later deployed worldwide. Decca competed successfully against LORAN C but it was finally made redundant by GPS during the 1990s. When their patented receivers were replaced by more competitive designs, the company lost its place in the market and Decca Europe was shut down in 2000 and in Japan in 2001.

Returning from Africa I found the Decca Navigator useful approaching landfall off Portugal when star and planet observations provided a less certain position, for example when overcast or when the horizon was too hazy. In 2017 it was an unusual experience to sleep in a decommissioned Decca signal station at the Butt of Lewis, now a spacious and welcoming B&B.

Astro Navigation.

Voyages to the Far East via the South Atlantic and the empty reaches of the Indian Ocean provided far more opportunities for practising astro navigation than on the shorter runs to West Africa. The flash of a light or rocky landfall appearing on the horizon exactly as predicted after days or weeks sailing across an empty ocean felt good. Satisfying. A professional art mastered. Using the navigator's main instrument, the sextant, was, however, incredibly difficult and it took me several frustrating months to get the knack of it. It is indeed an art more than a science as, with the sextant telescope to eyeball, elbow clamped tightly to ribs, I learnt to move the body in a synchronised dance with the ship's motion, stabilising the movement of the sun or the stars to ensure an accurate observation. Another challenge was to remember the sextant's four adjustable errors which had to be checked for and removed: Perpendicularity Error, Side Error, Collimation Error and Index Error, and corrected in that order.

The wonderfully named Admiral Sir Cloudesley Shovell lost his fleet and two thousand men on the Isles of Scilly in 1707 because he had strayed too far east onto savage rocks. He did not know his longitude. Thanks to the brilliant invention of the marine chronometer by John Harrison in the late 18th century, the secret of calculating longitude was at last revealed and thus revolutionised navigation. Successfully tested on a voyage to Jamaica in 1761, and again eleven years later by Captain Cook on his second voyage, using the K1 version made by Larcum Kendall in 1769, the marine chronometer has proved its vital worth ever since in saving ships and lives, and of course, money. Straighter tracks make shorter voyages.

My memory tells me that our ship's chronometer was a Harrison. It may well have been a Thomas Mercer. Other mariners with better memories may know. For the clearest explanation of how knowing the correct time at the point of origin (Greenwich) and being able to compare it with the time at ship is the key to calculating a ship's longitude, I recommend Dava Sobel's absorbing and dramatic account, 'Longitude'.

Being on the 12 to 4 night watch did not absolve me from rising early for breakfast. At 0930 each morning I was required to take a morning sight of the sun. The second officer would plot the agreed observed latitude, crossed with the morning sight position line run-up to obtain the noon fix. When, ten years later, I became the navigator sailing deep sea, I found myself the only officer taking morning and noon sights of the sun. Manpower cuts and modernisation had taken its toll.

As we headed south to Durban on the first voyage, I brushed up these astro navigation skills, last used sailing west across the Atlantic to the Caribbean. I ran up my morning sight position line to cross it with the noon latitude to obtain our noon position and entered the latitude and longitude in the daily log book. I recalculated the course to go and adjusted the autopilot.

In the 1980s companies like ours on mainly middle and home trade voyages did not see the value in investing in satellite position fixing. GPS was in its infancy and fixes could only be obtained with two, maximum three, satellites. I had my own sextant and enjoyed the professional challenge of maintaining my skills through daily use. I am proud to be able to say that I was one of the last breed of professional navigators who relied exclusively on the sextant to find their way about the world's oceans.

Speaking to a newly qualified officer in 2015 I was not surprised to learn that the sextant was now very rarely used and officers would be hard-pressed to make effective use of it such was the reliance on GPS. A surprising development is that the US Navy has since 2015 decided to reintroduce teaching the skill of using the sextant as a backup against GPS failure resulting from terrorists hacking into computer systems.

When chief officer on the *Ashington*, en-route from Setubal in Portugal to Durban I fixed the ship's position from star sights observed at dawn and dusk. In the quiet final hour of the night as nautical twilight approached, I pre-calculated the altitude and bearing of several stars spread around the horizon so as to give a good cross. It gave such simple satisfaction when the bright white spark of a star glittered in the sextant telescope, aimed at the pre-computed spot in the heavens. Got you!

In the tropics the transition between night and day is swift and gives only a brief window of time in which to shoot the stars. Six observations gave a fix within a cocked hat of within a mile or two. I had more confidence in a position gained from several stars than in noon latitude crossed with a single position line run up from a morning sight.

With the progress of time no longer did I have to use five figure log tables, but a calculator and pre-calculated tabulated values from the Sight Reduction Tables for Air Navigation. This greatly speeded up the operation and in thirty minutes I could obtain a good plot.

But for much of the time my position fixes relied on radar or visual bearings around the challenging coastlines of Europe.

Chapter 39

COLLIER MATE

My long-awaited promotion arrived in the middle of May. I received orders to proceed to the power station at West Thurrock to join *MV Pulborough* as chief officer, or the mate as we were called on the collier run. She was sister ship to the *Rogate*, so I knew my way around. Built in 1965 at Blyth she represented the strong and continuing link between British shipping, British coal and British generation of gas and electricity. This link was beginning to fracture during the government of Margaret Thatcher as the contract between the Coal Board and the Southern Electricity Generating Board was opened up to competition. We sailed ever further afield to bring coal to the UK—to Rotterdam, Gdansk and Durban.

The tour of duty on the collier run followed the usual routine; two days loading coal in the northeast, then thirty hours sailing down to one of three power stations, West Thurrock, Kingsnorth or Tilbury. Depending on congestion we could spend a day or more waiting at anchor. It could take two or three days to discharge, depending on whether we were arriving at the weekend or the level of the stockpile; about a week per round-trip.

So after three months of that I was glad to pay off on Marilyn's birthday and go on leave. My project was to build bookshelves for the living room.

I joined *MV Wilmington* six weeks later, another collier, slightly bigger. In Captain Ramsay I met an old shipmate, with whom I had sailed in China Navigation fifteen years before. He was a thickset man, with powerful arms and legs, able to do one-arm press-ups, which he demonstrated with gusto.

She had a generous sized bridge and accommodation and, as chief officer, I was permitted, for the first and only time in my sea-going career, to take my family on board for a short voyage, from Birkenhead to Amsterdam and back.

With three little children in tow we took the train to Liverpool. Amazing how much luggage five people require for a week on board ship.

'Where is the blue suitcase?'

'You have it.'

'No, you have it.'

'It was under that seat'

'Well, it's not there now!'

It had been stolen before we had even left the train. Welcome to Liverpool. I spent a fruitless hour returning to the station, where I was taken to the train in its sidings to check that the suitcase was no longer on board. It had indeed been lifted. I was not happy. This delayed our arrival on board *Wilmington* but we arrived in time for the usual 1700 evening meal. The next day Marilyn went shopping for new clothes while I got to grips with cargo work.

The late night sailing from Liverpool meant that the children missed the departure fun. Sailing down the Irish Sea rough weather began to pick up; a good blow was forecast. The elements obligingly gave the family a proper maritime experience, a full gale at sea as we rounded Longships Lighthouse. The ship pitched violently enough to smash the plates in the galley and an extra-large twisting roll nearly tossed the children out of their bunks.

'This is nothing,' I heartlessly bragged. 'You should see a ship when she is really going!' Not helpful.

On arrival in Amsterdam, Captain Ramsey refused permission to accompany my family on a few hours jaunt ashore. There was not enough space to deploy the gangway so my three little ones and their nervous mother clambered awkwardly down the pilot ladder onto the coal black quayside and headed off into town. They explored the canals in a glass roofed river cruiser whilst I loaded coal bound for Birkenhead.

Back at sea we kept the children occupied by running races against the stopwatch in the narrow space between the bulwark and the hatch coamings. Luckily no child tripped over the numerous struts to fall overboard into the foaming wake.

During my morning watch the children came up to the bridge. They created their own logbook of life on board, a memento of an unusual episode in their childhood. They even steered the ship for a while. Not many can say that they have directed the course of a 9,000 tonne ship down the English Channel.

Liverpool stewards have a maverick reputation. I had many run-ins with one who was a disobliging Scouser, to say the least. I discovered that he had taken my middle daughter by the ankles and suspended her over the stairwell. She said she giggled and found it funny but I did not. It came to the crunch. I informed Captain Ramsay that either I left or the steward did. I didn't really care. The Scouser left but it didn't make me any happier. When my family went home leaving me to complete the remainder of my three month tour my morale was pretty low.

Back in Liverpool in mid-December, I paid off and dashed down the gangway before my relief had come on board and headed home. Sunday train journeys were slow and unreliable so I hired a car and sped along the motorways. The miles flicked by as I sang along to the radio, in control of my destination. I was going to have myself a merry little Christmas time.

The end of January found me back at sea as Mate on the *Rogate*—again—on the collier run between Tilbury and the Tyne. The only event of note in those months of traipsing thirty hours north and thirty hours south was that I was the last Mate and last man aboard before the *Rogate* was sold. After discharging her cargo for the final time on the Thames we took her back lightship to anchor midstream on the Tyne, our stern fixed to a buoy.

'Could I have the ship's bridge bell as a memento of our time aboard?' I asked the Marine Superintendent, Mr Campbell.

'No,' he said. 'There's a chance that *Rogate* will be sold for further trading.'

There would be no tangible mementos of my time as a collierman.

On 10 April Captain MacLeod, a dour, pipe-smoking man, paid off the crew and one by one everybody left the ship. It was the end of an era. In the darkening evening light I swung my leg over the bulwark and climbed down the pilot ladder. I tossed my bags into the waiting launch, stepped down onto the thwart and felt an astral thread shiver asunder. I looked up at the looming black hulk of her. After nineteen years of hard work on the collier run, *Rogate* had had enough. Her character, her trading history, the story of all her cargoes and crews floated away down river. The launch chugged back to port. *Rogate's* shadowy silhouette faded into the dark night. A vessel lying silent, deadship is an unnatural thing and I wondered if her future was prophetic for the company and for me. No longer a she, it was a rusting hulk fit only for the knackers yard. Razor blades. One month later she went to the breakers at Zeebrugge.

The Super was wrong about the bell.

The company history penned in 1980 listed a fleet of thirty one ships including two newbuilds. The old north-east collier days were coming to an end and Stevies traded further and further from home waters to find employment. Twenty six years after *Rogate's* demise the company no longer existed. Dry bulk freight rates had collapsed.

I enjoyed another happy spring leave during which time I built more bookshelves for the house. We returned to Llanthony, to the same simple Welsh cottage in a field by a stream under the ridge of Offa's Dyke. Three little walkers and relaxed parents happily explored distant vistas and followed footpaths weaving through the millions of trees planted by the poet Walter Savage Landor a hundred and seventy years before, now matured into the magnificent woodlands. All too soon it was time to climb a gangway and board another Sussex village.

Chapter 40

RUSSIAN ADVENTURES

Blue arcs flew, the acrid scorch of burnt metal sharp in my nostrils.

'Mr Wilcox, the Regs state that two bands of chains must be affixed to the for'ard timber tier. We must have more pads eyes,' I pressed the Marine Superintendent.

'No,' he grumpily replied, watching the welders, the pain of the expense watering his eyes. 'Far too expensive. Make do with one.'

Impervious to my logic. I lost that point. But I won the argument. The trip after I had left to go on leave, *Aldrington* departed Archangel and struck an early winter storm just off the northern coast of Norway. A solid wall of green water crashed over the for'ard face of the timber stow, snapped the thick chain and flung the timber planks like matchwood into the sea. I was glad not to be aboard to suffer that professional failure.

I had joined MV *Aldrington* as chief officer in Sunderland at the end of May. We had received orders to load a cargo of timber in Archangel (a new port for Stephenson Clarke) and ship it to Belfast and Newport. The holds would be filled out and then the decks and hatches covered with bulk timber two or three blocks high.

After her basic fit-out, *Aldrington* left Sunderland on a 2,000 mile, seven-day voyage. We tracked up the North Sea, the Orkneys and Shetlands to port, majestic Norwegian mountains to starboard, as we hugged the coast. The Arctic Circle is one of five major lines of latitude, so crossing latitude 66½° north was a significant moment. Now we were transiting the Arctic, land of the midnight sun.

One dank morning the brooding hulk of the Lofoten Islands emerged from the mist on our starboard side. Through the binoculars I spotted a smattering of grey blobs; houses almost lost in the landscape.

The Captain joined me on the bridge wing.

'What are you looking at, Mate?'

'Those houses, Captain. I was wondering what life is like for the locals in these extreme northern climes?'

'Very harsh. Fishing communities up here. That's a tough life. Too cold for much farming. Sheep maybe.'

'Pity we can't see what's going on. See their lives…'

'Steer well away from those rocks. A navigator's Nemesis. A graveyard for ships.'

The sailors' dilemma: the desire to see new lands; the fear of destruction on a lee shore.

A few miles to port lay the grey 1,000 foot bulk of Nordkapp (North Cape) and as the sun came out we entered the Barents Sea. (This area of open water was labelled 'Arctic Ocean' on the large globe in the courtroom of HQS *Wellington*, so I claimed another ocean 'scalp' to bring my tally to five.) In two decades at sea this was the furthest north I had ever sailed. Latitude 71°. An irresistible photo-op.

I thought about the hard life of those who made these rocky lands their home. Living in this dark and chilly landscape hemmed in by sea and mountain would produce an exceptionally hardy breed of individuals.

Compared to the lush, wooded landscape of West Sussex it seemed to me to be a very harsh environment. No wonder so many adventurous Scandinavians were keen to pillage our land hundreds of years ago.

Four days after leaving Sunderland we rounded the northern Russian coast and headed down into the infamous White Sea. As I looked over the side I thought of the thousands of Allied lives lost in these cold grey waters just forty one years earlier on the arctic convoys carrying vital war materiel for Russia.

We reported in to the authorities on arrival off Archangel. The pilot came on board and guided us to the outer harbour. The agent had given strict instructions not to photograph any potential military targets. I ignored this injunction and snapped huge rafts of logs floating down the river and logs stacks penned in by the river bank. I hid by a lifeboat and felt like a spy. In this frozen northern climate fir trees take a hundred years to reach maturity. This wreckage of an ancient landscape would take centuries to restore to good health; felled for cash just to provide construction timber for British house builders.

On dropping anchor near the edge of the harbour limits, we were told to await orders. And we waited. And we waited. And three weeks crawled by. We spent the time doing light maintenance on board in an attempt to keep the sailors gainfully occupied. The second mate checked his charts and prepared for the return voyage. I checked the deck stores and general paperwork and consulted with the bosun to create make-work schemes. On some afternoons, and most evenings, a liberty boat took the crew ashore.

After nearly three weeks at anchor, the crew were becoming depressed. And taking solace in drink. I watched as Paddy heaved himself stiffly on to the hatch coaming. He winced as he dropped a bag of tools noisily onto the steel top. Levering himself down stiffly, his fat bottom hit the surface with a rush and grunt. He looked round the deck breathing heavily, not seeing anything. With a shake of his head, he fumbled in the bag, found the chipping hammer and hefted it, testing its weight. One strike on a rusty patch. Pause. Lift. Strike. Not much noise and no dust. Pause. Another blow, followed by a few steady knocks. Pause.

'Look at the state of him, Bosun. He's just a waste of space. Captain has tried to pay him off, but the company won't wear it. Too expensive to repatriate him from Archangel, too much paper work.'

'Leave him be, Chief. At least he can't get at the bottle out here on deck. And I'll watch him like a hawk at smoko.'

'Do that, Bos. Try to get him home in one piece.'

'And we'll pay him off in the UK'

'We will indeed. We will indeed.'

The crew were always a source of trouble for any Mate. Always something. Drink, women, wives, family, AWOL on shore leave. Being stuck at anchor for days on end was difficult for morale and thus behaviour. As a plain without trees becomes dry and desolate so was our life without news.

On 23 July 1986 Prince Andrew and Sarah Ferguson were due to be married. The Captain asked the port authorities for permission to 'dress ship' in flag bunting in celebration. That night came belated orders to berth at 0800 the following morning. A subtle way to deny permission. Suddenly it was all action and I was hard at work with my fellow deck officers making sure that the timber was safely stowed in our three holds and securely lashed down on deck.

I noticed a movement below me on the bridge from where I was monitoring the timber packs being swung aboard and lowered into the hold. Focusing on a dark corner I saw two men behaving furtively behind the hatch slabs.

'What is...?' I muttered. 'Look at that! Swigging a bottle of whisky! What idiot sold these dockers our precious supplies?'

A disinterested mutter came from the second mate, busy with chartwork

'They won't be much use loading timber. More of a danger. Chase them off the ship, Peter!'

The Captain called me to his cabin as the stacks of timber built two then three high on the hatch tops. Neither of us had had any experience of loading timber. We were good bulk-rock men.

'All this timber on deck is going to raise our centre of gravity too high,' he fretted.

'Captain. I've done the calculations. Believe me. It's going to be fine. With the ballast and with full fuel tanks we have sufficient weight to keep centre of gravity low. What's important is that we lash this cargo down tightly, especially the front face.' I was worried about any rough weather we may meet on the way back to Belfast. I had sweated over the stability calculations, and was sure I was right…almost.

'Mmm. Keep me informed all times. Let me know how you get on with the final figures with the cargo surveyor.'

'Will do, Captain. We will be finishing cargo in a few hours. I will run up the figures.'

In twelve hours we completed loading. The crew finished off rigging deck lashings as the cargo surveyor ponderously climbed the steps to my day cabin. A bottle of whisky stood on the coffee table.

'Welcome Mr Surveyor. Do sit down. Would you like a glass?' I poured three inches as he lowered his bulk onto my settee, crushing it beneath his weight.

'T'ank you! Na Zdorovie! Good health, Mr Mate,' toasted the surveyor in thickly accented English and knocked back the glass in one.

'Nostrovia,' I toasted him.

'Please, more,' he demanded imperiously, holding out his glass.

I poured another three inches

'T'ank you again. Na Zdorovie!'

He mutely touched his glass again.

'Maybe we should have a look at the cargo survey documents and agree the figures first?' I suggested.

Agreement was rapidly achieved, signed off and toasted in another three inches of whisky. A very relaxed and contented surveyor made his way very carefully down the gangway and off the ship.

Luckily the bosun had plenty of experience securing this kind of cargo. I had found myself professionally stretched. But it was good to do something new. But a problem walked up to me.

'Chief, I have a little difficulty.'

'What is it now, Bosun?'

'The police want to question me about the money I changed for you and the crew on the black market. I am ordered to go with them to the station, *immediately*.'

'But we are sailing in a few hours! This could be nasty. Do the crew know what to do with the timber chains?'

'Yeah, I've got them up to speed now, they'll be fine.'

Though very worried, I didn't tell the Captain but continued to prepare for sea. One hour before sailing I was very relieved to see the bosun come up the gangway and give me the thumbs up. Crisis averted. I didn't ask how.

We were very happy to depart Archangel and retrace the 2,000 nautical miles to Belfast. Over seven days we transited the Arctic Ocean, the Norwegian Sea, the eastern edge of the Atlantic Ocean off Shetland, Cape Wrath light solid upon its high cliff. We were glad to reach the sheltered waters of the North Minch, in the lee of Lewis. Eilean Glas. The sheer cliffs of Skye at sunset brought a lump to my throat. Home waters. Over the horizon rose the evocatively named islands of Canna, Rum, Eigg and Muck; Arnamurchan Point, the huge lighthouse dominating the most westerly point of the British Mainland. I had cycled here in 1974 and stared out to sea. Now I was looking back at it. On between Coll and Mull, with memories of visiting Tobermory (whisky). Iona to starboard; Islay, (more whisky) Mull of Oa, Mull of Kintyre. (*Far have I travelled and much have I seen...*) Mull of Galloway lay hull-down far to the southeast. I was soaked in the history of Scotland written in whisky... on the rocks.

Now at last we entered the North Channel as *Aldrington* swung east into Belfast Lough. Blackhead Light led us in and we sailed into the calm waters of the River Usk.

All fast for'ard and aft. After a rumble of hatch lids, crane jibs swung hooks over the holds and began discharging our precious load of timber, bound for Belfast's many timber merchants, soon to be used for someone's house or fence.

I repeated the trip once more. Happily, we suffered only a few delays the second time. We berthed at Newport at 0400, seven days out of Archangel. Discharging this cargo would not be my responsibility! Off down the gangway I tripped. Driving along the dock road I was impressed by the imposing tracery of the Transporter Bridge, one of only six in the world still operating. The underslung platform winches its load of vehicles across the river high above boats of all sizes passing underneath. Impressive Edwardian engineering.

A taxi dropped me at the railway station at 0500. All was silent and still. I clattered my heavy suitcases up the steps to the deserted platform and sank wearily onto the hard seat. I was light-headed with lack of sleep, having been on duty since 0230, coming down from a high after the intense activity of berthing. I caught the first train to Horsham via London. I gazed out of the window at the late summer landscape, layered with rich-hued fields of gold and marshalled by thick woods of green. As the season changed to autumn, England looked perfect to my sore eyes.

Back home after three months away, I discovered the house locked up, nobody about. Dumping my bags I walked the village street, asking neighbours if they knew of the whereabouts of my family, who obviously were not expecting me. I tracked them down to the house of Marilyn's Godmother, enjoying Saturday lunch. Now I was home.

Passing the Isle of Skye homeward bound brought a lump to the throat

Chapter 41

LITTLE AND LARGE

It was Christmas Day. The officers assembled in the smoke room for a pre-lunch drink and light-hearted banter. We had earned our break from gruelling routine after several weeks transiting confined European waters. *Birling* had arrived in Bordeaux on Christmas Eve. No cargo would be worked for two days and so we relaxed at our berth in an industrial wasteland far from the city centre. Our recently promoted steward decided to do us proud for lunch the next day. He was shortly off ashore to work as a chef and was glad of the opportunity to hone his culinary skills. We were grateful guinea pigs.

Our little band of brothers sat down to a table invitingly spread with white napery, and forgot about the stark dock world outside. We lapped up the steward's delicious home-made tomato soup—made from real tomatoes. The memorable Beef Wellington was washed down with Bordeaux of course and sticky Christmas pudding with Armagnac. Officers and crew slept well that afternoon.

The dockers of Bordeaux came back to work on the day after Boxing Day and loaded us right to the hatch top with 4,000 tons of maize, destined to make Mars Bars.

I had joined the *Birling* at the end of October 1986, at Northfleet on the Thames. She and her sister ship *Emerald* had been constructed in 1978 by Clelands at Wallsend-on-Tyne. Another sister ship, *Steyning*, was the last vessel built in this yard, completed in 1983. Lack of orders by faithful companies such as Stephenson Clarke killed off this one hundred and twenty two year old yard in 1984.

We set sail for Liverpool Bar Light and boarded the pilot for the Manchester Ship Canal. Here, on an industrial berth on the outskirts of Manchester, my family joined me on New Year's Eve. I was very happy to see them but being a typical self-centred sailor, instead of staying on board, the Captain and I took advantage of the shipping agent's generosity of free footie tickets. We just had to watch our homeport Newcastle play Manchester United at Old Trafford. We had fantastic seats and saw great action but after Man U scored a fourth goal we decided to exit early to avoid the ecstatic crowds. Also I needed to make peace with my wife and family and share some shore time with them. They were not staying on board as *Birling* lacked space for overnight visitors.

I preferred the little ships with their varied cargoes picked up from the remote ports of Europe. After three months trading round these ports, on 22 January 1987, *Birling* sailed up Lough Foyle. An army rib boat powered alongside and shouted up that they were coming aboard. Protection squad. A camouflaged soldier joined me at my station aft, and squatted down, sheltered by the steel bulwark, leaving me a bright target in my white boiler suit. I felt rather vulnerable. We berthed in Londonderry, scene of much vicious tribal rivalry. Its reputation made me keen to pay off. Down the gangway I went and into a waiting taxi. After a short ride to the airport I was on a flight home. It was less than a month since Christmas and so we celebrated all over again.

In mid-March I went by train to Newcastle where I joined our newest build, the *Storrington*, as chief officer. A big ship. 12,000 tonnes dwt. Three times bigger than *Birling*. My own office, dayroom, cabin, shower. I rattled around in the impersonal surroundings. Being bigger meant longer loading and discharge times in port, more comfort at sea. But the same black stuff. After a few trips on the north-east coast collier run, I was transferred to the *Donnington* to take her on a quick hop across the North Sea to Esbjerg, on the west coast of Denmark. Manpower shortages. A flurry of paperwork completed and with only my overnight bag it was a strange interlude. I didn't have time to load or discharge before I was switched back to the *Storrington* which came alongside the next day.

We headed to Gdansk to load coal for the Thames. The Baltic in March was covered in ice about a foot thick. Icebreakers scored a crisscross of narrow channels through which we plotted our passage to Gdansk. The rising sun brilliantly illuminated the icy floes as they scraped our hull—a free scouring service.

After just over a month on the collier run I was sent home for a short leave, in time to celebrate my birthday with the family. On the cusp of my forth decade I wondered just how much longer I could endure life at sea. During my leave I applied to various London legal firms seeking an appointment as a wet salvage lawyer. I discovered that policy had changed. No longer were they turning master mariners into lawyers. It was easier to turn lawyers into master mariners—they thought. No job for me, then.

Chapter 42

LIFE ASHORE V

IRELAND TO AYR VIA DURBAN AND ARCHANGEL

Drogheda has two claims to fame, one as the site of the infamous Battle of the Boyne. I tramped lanes framed by high dense green hedges but failed to find the battle site so clearly marked on the map. The authorities had wisely decided not to draw attention to this highly contentious spot.

The second claim is New Grange, the famous passage tomb built by the ancient Beaker people. When on MV *Beeding*, I went with Captain Roger Francis in the shipping agent's car to this stunning 3,000 BC tomb. There were very few people about. Crawling deep within its ancient passages and sitting quietly in the sacred spaces was a deeply memorable experience. Now it is a World Heritage site and a big tourist attraction. Afterwards, I enjoyed a reflective two-hour stroll along quiet country lanes, back to the ship. The details of this visit were recalled afresh when I met Captain Francis at a lunch on the HQS Wellington thirty two years later.

Larne was different—on the edge of The Troubles. Walking ashore in the spring of 1982 from the *Pearl* was like walking back into my rural childhood. Big blowsy hedges smothered in white blackthorn blossom framed boxy fields. The narrow country lanes were deserted. Green hillsides sheltered little houses. But all has changed. The dock from where we used to ship cement now hosts a marina. The nearby Magheramorne quarry is now a film set for such as the Game of Thrones. Would you believe it, now?

We arrived at Durban in the *Aldrington* in May 1984, berthing on a Friday and no work till Monday. I hired a VW Beetle and roared off to a farm owned by distant relations in the foothills of the Drakenburgs just north of Pietermaritzburg. It was so refreshing to experience family life, to enjoy good food, stimulating conversation about South Africa, farming and family, and to sleep deeply in a comfortable, stationary, bed.

I was shown around the farm, met the African workers and saw what Cousin DP had done to provide houses, land for growing the inevitable maize for the family, a school and a shop for all their basic needs. Paternalistic but effective. He had recently hosted a group of white farmers on a fact-finding mission from Zimbabwe. They were curious about the bags of fertiliser in a shed. They didn't need fertiliser on their rich and fertile land in Zimbabwe. I weep for them now. Wild guinea fowl pecked contentedly at grain droppings at the edge of the maize field. Having lived in Australia I was interested to see the high windbreaks of majestic eucalyptus groves. A fast-growing but dangerous fire hazard.

DP was an artist and the view from his paddocks of the distant Drakensberg Mountains made excellent subject matter, especially when the peaks were picked out with a smattering of snow. His striking paintings effectively captured the light and vibrant colours of Africa.

I returned to Durban via the Valley of a Thousand Hills and stopped at a native village where tourists were invited to purchase local artefacts from dusky bare breasted maidens. Stuff of dreams when I returned to my steel prison.

The night before we sailed, a group of us spent a happy evening ashore. Walking among the evening revellers brought it home to us that on the morrow we would leave behind the bright lights and head back into the deep ocean on a four week voyage.

The Seamen's Club contained a vast room laid out with ten snooker tables, each equipped with brass and wood scoreboards and racks of snooker cues. Room for everyone. By each table was a bell which read, *Press for beer and food*. So we did, soaking up copious quantities of cold lager with platefuls of curry and rice. We rolled home happy but woke with sore heads.

I returned to Durban in the *Ashington* in early February 1985, and was delighted to visit the relatives again.

As I rolled again though the familiar Valley of a Thousand Hills I felt the deep peace of Africa seep into my soul. I came to a halt within the confines of a game sanctuary. Zebras grazed on thin dry grass. Stately giraffe sauntered by, swaying with their elegant long-legged gait. A laid back game park warden opened a gate in a high rusty wire fence and I drove through with great caution and stopped. Before my startled eyes, a family of lions ripped apart red-raw lumps of provided kill, blood dripping from their jaws. I stayed safe in my car with the windows wound up tight.

Cousin DP and Celia embraced me with another warm welcome. After a simple evening meal I luxuriated in the privacy of my static bed on a farm in Africa.

Monday morning saw me meandering back through the valleys and hills, heading down the wide but empty freeway towards the port. I handed back my freedom vehicle and reported back on board. I had not been missed. Nothing had happened. Tuesday morning we discharged our mill scale and off it went to help convert heavy oil into petrol. We shifted berth to load coal for Genoa, Italy.

'Party-time! Who wants to party?' came the offer from a junior engineer.

'Where, who with?'

'Old friends ashore, saw them last night. Come to our house for a party, they said!'

'Great! Let's do it!'

That evening four of us bundled into a taxi and stopped by a seedy booze shop with rusty wire mesh at the windows to buy beer for the evening. I felt very much out of my comfort zone as we entered a long low bungalow. G Plan furniture and a flat rug lay on the marble floor. Cool but clinical. So different from our familiar saloon. It took me a while to adjust.

Alcohol helped us to relax and enjoy conversation with new friends. Eventually food arrived but by midnight we were all shattered and desperate for sleep. We were invited to stay the night. 'Oh good,' I thought, 'Wonderful to crash out in a soft bed ashore.' Our hosts padded off to their bed with a cheery, 'Good night'. I looked around and realised with dismay that the warm, soft bed was only a rug on the floor. Pulling a thin blanket around my cold shoulders I tried to snatch some sleep. By 7 o'clock I gave up the struggle and hauled myself to my feet. I searched the kitchen cupboards for breakfast. I was starving. As I munched through a large bowl of cornflakes the others ambled in, groggy with lack of sleep. Tea and coffee was made and plans hatched for the day. They were gung-ho for driving to a local game park to see the wildlife. I was just not interested. The party had been a flop and sleep non-existent. I had no spare energy. My get up and go had got up and gone.

I took a bus downtown to find a church. There were blacks and whites on board but I hadn't a clue where I was supposed to sit so I took a seat near the front. Nobody kicked me out. I arrived at the church as the congregation spilled out, chatting and laughing. Having not been to church for months, I was very disappointed. I said as much to the priest outside and he very kindly invited me back in. I knelt at the rail as he said a few short prayers and gave me Holy Communion. Spiritually refreshed I set off back to the ship.

In June 1986 I arrived at the other end of the world: Archangel, Russia. I was Mate on the *Ashington*, awaiting a cargo of sawn timber. After a week at anchor, the agent invited us to watch Swan Lake, to be performed by the State Ballet Company of Siberia. I had been requested to bring my sailors. I sensed trouble ahead. The Captain had chickened out and remained safely on board.

I briefed our very British crew.

'Right lads, do try to behave. Queen, country, company and all that. Smile Jimmy, you might just enjoy it!'

'Ballet, Chief? Is that likely?'

'This is still a communist county. Behave or face jail. Take your pick,' I warned.

'Will there be any beer?'

Not yet, I hoped…

I worried about a diplomatic incident in this prickly Soviet nation. 'Drunken British crew run amok in Archangel. Chief Officer jailed for 2 years…' It had happened.

I led a subdued file down the gangway, jumped down in to the liberty motorboat and headed for the shore.

'Spasiba,' I thanked the boatman as we disembarked. 'Dos vedanya.' And received a brief smile in return.

We were taken by coach directly to the State Ballet Company Theatre, a solid concrete building in the Soviet style. We made our way to our seats, the buzz of anticipation from the audience failing to ignite any interest in the faces of my glum sailors. The situation made me nervous. A tug at my sleeve distracted me.

'May I introduce these girls from our local school?' said the ship's agent. The two pretty girls in the row in front of me were straight out of a Lewis Carroll illustration of Alice in Wonderland, dressed in long pinafores dresses with deep lacy shawls over their shoulders. Very Victorian.

'Hello,' they shyly greeted me. 'Have you come here to see the ballet before?'

Not bad English I thought. 'No, but I am very much looking forward to it,' I lied smoothly, ever the diplomat.

At last the curtains slowly lifted as the music struck up. From the back of the stage, a deeply offensive stink wafted over us, moistly redolent of Jeyes Fluid, damp concrete and sweaty unwashed bodies. The Corps de Ballet clumped noisily across the stage, the conductor keeping time by banging his batten on the podium. The red faced Prima Ballerina worked her way through her routine as the orchestra valiantly sawed away at the music. Snorts of derision and loud guffaws from the crew made the audience look round with hostile stares.

'Look at the state of that.'

'What about that beer, Chief? This is awful.'

'La da da da.' *Laughter.*

By the interval it was all too much to the corpsing crew.

'Get them out of here into a restaurant or bar somewhere, anywhere, before we get thrown out!' I instructed the bosun and the agent.

I learned later that strings had been pulled and a restaurant especially opened so they could dilute the beer with some food. Archangel was not blessed with sailor friendly pubs. I sat out the ballet to the bitter end and shuffled out as quickly as decency allowed. I was very glad to see the lads safely back at the liberty boat at the appointed time. I felt the tension in my shoulders drain away as we made the return journey to back to the sanctuary of our ship. I was not pleased with the Captain for dropping me in it.

My reward on the following day was to be taken ashore with the agent for a visit to the Imperial War Graves site in Archangel. A simple stone wall enclosed this dedicated space. Before me, amidst the rough mown grass, stood row upon row of clean white headstones, standard military pattern. These officers and men in their early twenties and late teens had come from all classes and conditions of men. Here in this 'foreign field' they were gathered as brothers. Each memorial, etched with name, rank and age, was eloquent, mute testimony to sacrifice for the greater good. As we confront Russia over Ukraine (2014) it would be nice if they remembered the lives laid down for this country over seven decades ago.

I was taken on to see a traditional onion-domed Russian Orthodox church. Damp lino and Jeyes fluid pervaded. The state of disrepair was sad to behold. Babushkas in printed pinafores, stockings tumbling down over bowed legs, looked bemusedly at our foreign faces.

Next on the agenda was a busy second-hand shop. Narrow aisles framed glass-topped cases full of bric-a-brac. Stuff hung from the walls. Customers vied for attention. My eye was caught by a bluey green balalaika. The agent translated and I handed over the princely sum of twelve roubles, pleased to get this unusual souvenir for my daughter. At the set exchange rate it cost £12. We got three times that on the black market, very useful when we went to the local seamen's club. Nemesis would catch up with the bosun later.

On the next evening ashore with colleagues we discovered the docklands residential area. We walked through atmospheric streets, stepping over rail tracks which wound between timber-clad apartment buildings. Each four-storey block was built on wooden rafts, the permafrost not suitable for deep foundations. The chilly and sinister atmosphere was evocatively captured in Robert Harris' thriller, 'Archangel.'

After waiting at the stop as advised, we boarded a tram through the side door. We pushed our way through strap hanging Russian peasants who warily yielded space, staring at us aliens from another planet. I looked in vain for a conductor to give him my kopecs for the fare. Nobody helped. Nobody shouted at us when we jumped off on arrival in town.

We made our way to the seamen's club and found the bar.

'Ello!' greeted a friendly sailor.' Where you from? What eez your sheep?

'Hi. I'm from London. My ship is the *Ashington*, out at anchor waiting to load timber.'

'OK. I from Tallinn.'

'Italy? That's a long way.'

'Noo, no Italy; Tallinn, capital of Estonia, nice place. Not far.'

Indeed it was as I discovered some thirty years later when I visited on a cruise ship and explored the mediaeval old town. No longer part of the Soviet Union.

We played table tennis and drank warm champagne when the cold beer ran out. I disgraced myself singing rugby songs on the tram going back to the ship. I felt ashamed the next morning when I woke with a thick head and furry mouth. 'Haven't done that for a long time.' I thought. 'Need to get loaded and out of here.'

Thank goodness for Prince Andrew and Sarah Ferguson. Their nuptial celebrations had got us onto a berth and back out to sea.

Nearly a year later I joined the *Ashington* in Ayr. It was a quiet Saturday in port and not a lot to do. I mooched aimlessly ashore. At the bridge over the wide river I was confronted by a seemingly impenetrable barrier. A thick, black cloud of midges writhed before me. Covering my nose and mouth, I forced my way through and into town.

Just off the high street I spotted a little model shop and halted outside the window, transfixed. I was transported back to the Meccano kits, the aeroplanes of balsa and plastic of my youth. The seed of an idea grew in my mind; a creative activity to carry me across oceans of time.

I opened the door and entered the cool interior. Stacked on a multitude of shelving was a disconcerting amount of choice. I had to be able to carry my purchases back to the ship—and to take the completed models safely home. I explained the situation to the helpful man behind the counter.

'I know just the thing. Follow me.' He swept his arm over a tempting display. 'These aircraft are really simple to make.'

'And,' he continued, 'they are made of brightly coloured plastic so no worries about needing a dozen tiny paint tins. Just glue.'

'Ah, yes. Good point.'

I spent a happy ten minutes selecting six Airfix kits of fighter planes. Now equipped with a hobby for the voyage to the tropics I carried my treasures back to the ship.

Chapter 43

MATE ON A SAILING SHIP

a e a direcção do vento, tornando-o «mais leve» e económi[c]

I stared up at the carbuncle atop the funnel. Three thin fins like vast window blinds stretched skywards. What were they for? Would they be of any use?

This was a Walker Wing Sail. It was designed to save at least ten percent of fuel costs and its genesis was in the 1970s fuel spike. To prove its worth it needed long continuous voyages blessed by steady trade winds. But on our short sea trades it was destined to be a sad failure and so it proved. It was removed two years later. However, monitoring its operation and supporting the development engineers gave me hours of interest, and a free dinner ashore in La Rochelle courtesy of Walker's commissioning engineer.

Three days after celebrating my birthday, I had re-joined *Ashington* in Ayr, this time as chief officer. I was proud to see LONDON painted on our stern; our port of registration. It is rare to see this in the world's merchant fleets in 2017 when so many ship owners, especially cruise ship owners, register their vessels in places like Barbados, the Isle of Man or Hong Kong (till 1997). This allowed them to carry a defaced Red Ensign and fool the passengers into thinking they were sailing with a British company. LONDON meant that British regulations applied in ship construction, safety and manning. We were that rare breed, a British ship crewed with British officers and men.

Ashington had been built by Swan Hunters in 1979 on the old Clelands shipyard at Wallsend-on-Tyne. It was the largest ship ever built by the yard. Eight years later she was showing signs of wear and tear and struggling with the tropical voyages on which I was to take her over the next nine months.

A short, thirty-six hour trip with a load of bauxite took us to Aughinnish, an island on the south shore of Galway Bay. A welcome change was a four day run south to Setubal, Portugal. Here I met the press for the first time. A journalist from the local paper came aboard, intrigued by our Walker Wing Sail. So I was duly interviewed and the next morning the agent brought aboard a copy of the local paper. I eagerly scanned the pages, but the story was all in Portuguese.

Next orders were for South Africa; Durban again for coal. Three weeks and nearly 6,000 miles. We sailed south of the Canaries into the smooth subtropical waters of the South Atlantic. I was becoming less keen on these extended trips away.

Once at sea out of sight of land, routine on board settled into a simple pattern. Star fixes at dawn and dusk as usual. After a quiet 4 to 8 morning watch I enjoyed breakfast; cereal, fried eggs and bacon, fruit juice and two cups of strong tea.

I walked the decks with the bosun, finding jobs for the day.

'Chief, I thought we would paint up the for'ard store. Tidy up a bit, before like.'

'Good idea Bosun. Keep the men going till 1600 at least, please. It's a bit annoying to see them sloping off so early nowadays.'

'Have a heart, Chief. Got to give the lads time to clean up. You could always give them a bit of overtime. Always popular, overtime.'

'I'll think about it, Bosun. Can't keep splashing the company money about, you know.'

I rarely dealt directly with the sailors themselves. I somehow lacked the common touch, that ability to give orders while not seeming to order people about bossily. Most bosuns had thick skins inured to crabby sailors with their moaning, complaining workshy attitudes. They knew when to push and when to ease off. I drifted off into the duty mess. Time for tea.

'What news, Chief, managed to find out where we were this morning?'

'You keep the engines going, Bill and I'll point us in the right direction and get us there.'

'But when?'

Coffee time with engineers on day working duties was a time to rehash expected ETA, engine problems, company politics.

Lunchtime was a meal to which I looked forward. It broke up the monotony of the day. Except when the cook was Dr Death, the nickname we gave the cook who dribbled nasal fluids into the soup with a dash of cigarette ash from the ever present rollup hanging from his bottom lip.

Duty engineers ate in the working mess where dirty overalls were allowed. All other officers dressed in clean uniform, usually but not always wearing epaulettes of rank, gathered in the officers' saloon. The meal was served by the steward dressed in a clean white T-shirt. Sometimes.

'Aircon just holding out, thank goodness.'

'Just keep that bridge wing door shut! Just sweat and suffer like us engineers.'

'Making better speed now with this tail wind. Should knock off a couple of hours.'

Soup spoons clattered against china bowls. The distant chatter and guffaws of laughter from the crew's mess filtered through the saloon bulkhead and thickened the silence.

After lunch a settled peace descended over the ship. The huge Sulzer engine thrashed away at over 500 rpm delivering an average ten knots, slowly oh so slowly, eating up the miles to Durban.

I made my way for'ard and leant weary arms on the fo'c'sle taffrail. The bows rose and fell with hypnotic regularity. The rumble of the engine was hidden by the hiss of the bulbous bow slicing the swell into white foam. No dolphins today. The blue sea was clean of any mark to the flat horizon, save only the whipped wake boiling from our stern. High overhead, a bright sun beat down hard upon my skull.

A flying fish flashed across the surface and vanished abruptly. I peered around at the endless empty ocean. No ships. The rolling swell was as ignorant and uncaring of our presence as the rest of the world hidden below the horizon. Long, long days stretched endlessly before me.

What to do with my empty head?

I drifted aft and clunked up the metal companionway to the officers' deck. Heaving hard against the spring weighted storm door I stepped over the lintel into cool air. Peace reigned. Off duty officers and sailors snoozed behind closed doors. Distant banging and shouting floated up from far below as engineers grappled with recalcitrant machinery.

Padding quietly along the lino I came to my door: 'Chief Officer'. I had climbed the greasy pole all my life to get this far and what had I achieved?

An open door means come in at any time. A door on the hook means knock before entering. A shut door means do not enter. I shut the door, secure in my own space.

Time to play. I pulled out the Airfix kit from its safe stowage and set out all my gear and equipment on a nonslip mat with surgical precision. With the deliberate actions of one aware of infinite time but finite resources I turned the box over and over, reading all the small print. 'Nice graphics,' I thought, caressing the edges of the shiny new carton.

I lifted the end flap and, like a child opening a Christmas present, pulled out the transparent plastic bag. It bulged with mysterious, mummified contents. I peeled open the sealed edge and slid out the parts. I laid them in neat rows on my desk. Unfolding the vital secret code, the parts and order list, I checked them off against the detailed exploded diagram. Coloured squiggles of plastic lay expectantly within grasp, awaiting the slice of the surgical knife. A quick snip released each fiddly part and I laid them out ready for assembly. Picking up the tube of plastic glue, (quick sniff, illegal intoxicant), I deftly unscrewed the cap and with a slow squeeze of its sides, enticed a glistening drop to the tip of the bright metal nozzle. With metal tweezers filched from the medical cabinet, I grasped a fragile part, applied a sliver of adhesive to the contact surfaces, brought them together and held them under pressure; one elephant two elephant three elephant.

When my allotted thirty minutes of creative activity were up I admired progress so far, before, with iron self-discipline, I carefully re-stowed all materials and equipment until the next day's allotted treat.

That took care of two weeks at sea.

I felt a deep loss when these half dozen brightly coloured planes had been completed. What now? Lose myself in another book and while away the dragging hours, until lost in sleep's forgetfulness.

The completed planes were later made into a mobile, gathered dust for many years until banished to the attic and, over time, disintegrated.

All was not well in the engine room. A ship which was designed to operate in cool northern European waters was struggling to cope in the challenging heat of the tropics. High scavenge temperatures reduced our speed to 6 ½ knots, (down from our usual 10 ½ knots). The air-conditioning kept failing and tempers were short.

Ashington ploughed south through the silk smooth waters of the doldrums, the oppressive heat not only overheating the engine but my fractious body. I had another manufacturing idea. I could sleep outside on a cool deck. I would rig a hammock. I would stitch my own. The bosun's prototype was too short. I searched him out in his for'ard locker store.

'Thanks Bosun. I tried out your first idea but it was too short for my long legs. I'd like to give it a go myself. Give us a bolt of green canvas, sailmakers twine and sailmakers needle and palm, boat lacing, a hank of lashing robe, a couple of thimbles and shackles.'

'Is that all?'

'That should do it.'

I spent many happy afternoons fashioning a traditional hammock. Wielding hammer and punch I thumped out eyelets to take the rigging lines. With a sailmaker's palm and needle I sewed several reinforced holes and doubled hems, stitch upon stitch. I set up a spread of lines, carried back to the shackles fitted at each end. I cut and shaped two wooden stretchers to keep the hammock open.

Great was my satisfaction when I rigged the completed hammock on the monkey island atop of the bridge. Carrying book, dark glasses and sun cream to my eyrie, I settled myself into its soft folds as *Ashington* laid a wake across the tropical South Atlantic. Rocked by the gentle rolling swell, I was lulled to sleep.

We arrived off Durban at dawn. The pilot boarded and took us straight into a coal berth. No time to explore ashore. Due to our delayed arrival the shippers were keen to get us turned round and back to England.

Two days later on 10 July we headed back to Blyth, hoping that the better conditions experienced in the South Atlantic would continue and that the tropics would not have a serious impact on our average speed. We all wanted to get home for the summer holidays. We should be home in thirty days. The engineers had worked extremely hard to make the best repairs they could. Needs must. The company were not prepared to fly out any spare parts.

The long days at sea were made bearable by the challenge of Astro navigation at dawn and dusk, eking out model making time and dozing afternoons away in my hammock.

Approaching the West African coast towards the end of a long watch and looking forward to my breakfast I felt a looming presence. Visibility dropped rapidly to two hundred yards, the temperature fell from 31° to 24° C. Lightning flickered dimly through rapidly spreading thick black clouds. A ferocious squall lashed the placid seas into a froth of spume dragged down wind. Everywhere white horses galloped across the thrashing surface of the sea. A quick check of the radar's orange scope showed a screen empty of targets, just the sharp leading edge of the storm front. The ferocity of the attack abated after twenty minutes as the torrential rain eased off to light northerly winds. The thick shroud of cloud lifted to reveal a fat, dark, curling underbelly of cumulonimbus which stretched to the horizon. Jagged flashes of searing-bright forked lightning carved up the sky, and stabbed again and again—and again, punching the sea. Too close for comfort. Extra brilliant flashes brought thunderclaps audible above the constant beat of the engine. This was nature on parade, producing an awesome West African Storm.

But the engine was not happy.

Chapter 44

LIFE ASHORE VI

MOUNTAINS AND BEACHES

Journal Entry

Monday, 19 October 1987
Ashington, at Odda.
We had cruised up the majestic Sørfjorden between snow-capped mountains. Leaving the second officer monitoring cargo operations, I walked up the twisting roads, passed new houses perched on vertical rock faces and set deeply into the rocky mountain. Norwegian engineering skills never ceased to amaze me. The narrow tarmac dead-ended abruptly in front of an impenetrable wall of firs. Pushing my way through painful, spiky dead branches I emerged Narnia-like into a world of tall silent trees. *'Isn't it good? Norwegian Wood.'* In the confined space, the litter of pine needles crunched loudly underfoot. I picked my way over boulders, across slippery slopes, through rocky gullies until I emerged high above a farm. Looking down, I could see a group of buildings clad in winter-worn planking. They sheltered under a grove of skinny trees. Silver birch. Such an isolated spot. All was quiet. 'Where is the footpath?' I thought. My English reserve, used to keeping to legal, rights-of-way footpaths, made me worry about the farmer's reaction if I just walked across his land. Still nobody about. I strolled diffidently across a pocket-sized field, bordered with scrappy hedges, pleased when I pushed through a gap to emerge

onto tarmac. Continuing along I came to a broad, blue lake. Ahead I saw a bench sheltered by tall fir trees. Here I rested with a sigh and stretched out my tired legs. I needed to take more strenuous exercise, obviously. A great expanse of silk-smooth water was framed by mountains which rose sheer to 5,000 feet or more, steep but distant; two or three miles away I guessed.

Sudden laughter, happy voices jolted me out of my daydreams. A noisy group of youngsters clattered by on short roller skis. Silence. A deeper quality to it now. Another new experience. I followed the rural road downhill through the gloaming towards the welcoming lights of the town, stars guiding me home.

Wednesday, 21 October
After breakfast I hired a mountain bike from the tourist office (£2) and set off through the town. I peddled alongside a glacier lake edged by flat water meadows. Handel's 'Nelson Mass' filled my ears through my Walkman headphones, its soaring music complementing the marvellous mountain views. Freedom.

I stopped at Latefoss waterfalls, drank refreshing cold water from cupped hands and munched a sugary biscuit. Rushing water tumbled everywhere. On and on, up and up, sometimes walking, sometimes cycling, I forged my way up the steep main road, views grander with each step. Pastoral Symphony. A sandwich and beer lunch by the Odda river (narrow and quiet at this point) re-energised failing limbs. A time to think—hopes for a shore job, life with my family.

Concerned with cargo work progress I set off back to the ship, whizzing down at great speed. Tenth gear still not high enough. Zipped round corners. Exhilarating. Stopped briefly to drink in mountain views and listen to the everlasting music of the waterfalls. Back into town in one hour. A brief break away from the ship; tired legs, refreshed spirit. Next stop St Malo.

St Malo. 31 October 1987
Berthed at 1400 on a fine autumn day. I was back in a town of which I had grown quite fond. It was a Saturday. Time to go ashore and stretch my legs. The familiar landmarks welcomed me back. I changed money and checked out the restaurants. I strolled down to the beach and gazed upon a golden afternoon scene. The sky was a deep, deep blue. Boats glided on a gilded sea. Castellated clouds drifted over the sandy island of Grande Bé,

a few hundred yards out. Relaxing on the beach in the warm sun I felt the stress of 5-on-5 off watch-keeping begin to evaporate.

I suddenly felt extremely tired. I had been on the go for twelve hours. I heaved up my weary body; time to return to the ship. I clambered back up the gangway, padded along the alleyway to my own little space and fell onto my day bed. I slept solidly for two hours.

At eight I went ashore to find a place for supper. But first I phoned home and caught up with family news.

'We are all in Portsmouth for Bonfire Night. Your brother Julian is here on leave from Jeddah.'

'How was the trip?

'Miss you so much.'

Me, too.

I found an appealing restaurant, sat down and ordered oysters—we *were* in a fishing port. Very disappointing. Poached salmon. Nice but not enough. Filled up with three cheeses and a bottle of wine. (£13). I walked down to the beach—susurration of the sea and all that—kicked off shoes and socks and relished the sensation of wriggling my toes in the soft sand. Starlit sky filled my vision above, monumental walls of mediaeval town lay behind me, soft sea before me. Such scenes are for sharing.

I stopped for a large Grand Marnier in the quiet square on the way back to the ship. I staggered up the gangway just before midnight. No sign of the nightwatchman.

Sunday 1st November 1987

I woke at 0600. Far too early. Not refreshed. It was Sunday, a new month. Autumn proper. I went to the 9 a.m. Mass at the Cathedral. All Saints Day. Sung Latin liturgy. Anthem from Handel's Messiah sung as a processional; 'Blessing and Honour and Glory and Power'. 'Ode to Joy' as Communion Hymn. Very good Bach Organ Voluntary at the end.

Much refreshed in heart and soul I walked around the town walls and along the beach. I remembered my inebriated walk of night before, especially when I walked round the edge of the swimming pool. Luckily I had not fallen in. I can just see the headlines…

A throng of elegantly dressed people strolled along the cobbled streets, objects of interest to the café crowd. Sunday best. Beautiful ocean-going yachts lined up in the marina, steel stays beating out a call to go a-roving. Checking my wallet I discovered that I had run out of cash and so had to forego the pleasure of coffee in a local café, watching the world go by. Instead I sipped a cup of instant in the confines of my cabin. I dozed in my chair after lunch awaiting visitors who failed to turn up.

A fast late afternoon walk about St Servan Beach and along the heavily wooded promontory cleared my muggy head. Stacks of trees had been blown over by recent storms, scattered like spillikins. I sat on a mound in the shadow of an ancient castle of classic proportions. Before me spread a serene panorama of moored boats, silver water lapping the rocks below; the late sun flushed pink on cumulus clouds drifting eastwards. Houses perched on wooded slopes merged into the distant horizon.

After a pleasant two days in port, it was time to load our next cargo and proceed back to sea.

Chapter 45

DRAMAS AT SEA

Journal Entry

MV Ashington. Thursday, 29 July 1987
At anchor one mile off Dakar, Senegal.
Today we anchored due to engine failure, caused by overheating. The Master quite rightly refused to countenance the idea of sailing thousands of miles home when further breakdown was liable to occur at any moment. *Ashington* would be at the mercy of the elements and the many rocky coasts on route. No effort has been made by Stevies to obtain spares when we originally reported the problem a week ago, steaming north at only six knots. I am sure they were simply hoping we would struggle home and save them the bother and expense of flying out the vital spares.

1500. Telegram from Stephenson Clarke Shipping:

ENGINE SPARES AS ORDERED AT PRESENT IN TRANSIT BY AIR TO DAKAR AIRPORT. EXPECTED ARRIVAL TONIGHT.

Huge cheers from exhausted engineers and crew greeted this news.

Friday, 30 July. At anchor, Dakar.
0800 VHF call: 'Good morning, Captain. This is your Dakar Agent here. Our apologies but we are trying very hard to get your engine spares cleared through our local customs. We hope to have them out to you tonight.'

It took twenty eight hours to clear customs at Dakar Airport and transport the vital engine spares to the ship. The engineers worked through much of the night stripping down the engine and fitting the new parts.

Saturday, 1 August. At anchor, Dakar.
On 4-8 morning watch. Uneventful. At first. I checked anchor bearings and watched the pink dawn flush the eastern sky. I walked down from the bridge, along the length of the foredeck and wearily climbed up the companionway to the forecastle deck.

Something was missing.

Wet footprints laid a trail from an empty pallet to the hawse pipe. The pallet had contained several hundred feet of polypropylene mooring line. Not anymore. Skinny thieves had shimmied up the anchor cable, wriggled through the hawsepipe and liberated a very expensive headline. Oh dear. I was going to have to fill out lots of paperwork.

The engineers continued all Saturday sweating copiously in 50° heat to repair the engine. Much cursing floated up through the engine room skylights.

Looking through my binoculars I could see two fishing boats close inshore. Low scrubby landscape merged into the grey mudflats. A group of fuzzy huts dotted the flat land. All was still in the muggy air.

Unusually I had enjoyed a good lunch. I dragged my hammock for'ard to the fo'c'sle deck and rigged it between two strong, vertical posts. A light breeze blew fitfully over the bulwark bringing welcome relief to my baked flesh. The anchor cable clanked in the hawse pipe as *Ashington* rolled in a gentle swell, swaying me to sleep under the hot tropical sun. Sweat oozed from every pore and dripped stickily into the green canvas of the hammock of my own laboured construction. 'The History of the Waring Scots' fought for my attention against the distractions of my heavily weighted eyelids. A couple of pre-lunch cool scoops added to my post-prandial weariness. The book slipped to the deck and I dozed.

The results of the engines trials late in the afternoon failed. We will not be speeding home at 11½ knots. The new exhaust valves did not work. The four day wait at anchor in the middle of nowhere has been for nothing. Futile. It is deeply depressing because all we want to do is go home. ETA more like 19 August. If that. We are deeply discouraged and disappointed. In our various ways the whole crew is trying to come to terms with these depressing facts.

The engineers went to bed exhausted. They will try out new ideas in further trials tomorrow. I feel a helpless observer of their tribulations but grateful for their dedication.

Sunday, 2 August. At anchor, Dakar.
More engine trials today; result: engine no better and the engineers cannot discover where the fault lies. I know there are many others praying for the strength to cope with the ups and downs of hopes raised and dashed. So wishing to be home by the 16th for a family day with my Godfather. Tomorrow is Marilyn's birthday. It had all changed for the worse when we received new orders for Conakry. This has turned out to be a disastrous trip and not even home yet! The second crate from Stephenson Clarke in London is due tomorrow. We hope.

Monday, 3 August. At anchor off Dakar
0630. On anchor watch. Not a lot to do other than check anchor bearings to confirm that the anchor is not dragging. Peaceful on the bridge. Wrote letters home whilst dawn broke over the calm sea. Marilyn is forty one today and so I wrote a long letter, explaining that further delays due to engine repairs, slow steaming could take until 21 August, dangerously close to the French holiday starting 20th, and also missing a couple of important engagements. Wrote telling children how much I missed them.

1600. Surprise telegram from Stephenson Clarke Shipping:
PHONE MR FIELDS RE MR QUAIL'S RELIEF AT DAKAR

I made a call on the VHF radio to the shore station, requesting a connection to Portishead Radio in Somerset and was connected to Head Office in Newcastle.

Mr Field: 'We would like to fly you home so that you would be back in time for your holidays in France. Your wife has been in touch and gave us the latest situation.'

Me: 'This is all a big surprise. Will come back to you as soon as we can. Over and out'.

Me: 'What a load of rubbish. What they really want is to save money on employing three deck officers! Fourteen days return journey, maybe more—you guys doing 5-on-5 off seems to me to be grossly unfair.'

Third Mate: 'You're an idiot. Don't worry about us. We would certainly not worry about you!'

Me: 'I can't leave you in the lurch like this. This really is not fair on you guys. I want to go home but...'

Second Mate: Simon, this is your opportunity. Take it. However, if you are having such a fantastic time here and really do not want to go home then I will go home instead!'

Mr Field claimed that Dakar sits on the edge of middle trade limits and that maritime regulations only required two watch keeping officers on the bridge; back to twelve hours days, five on five off instead of eight hours a day four on eight off. By sending me home early, ostensibly to ensure that I got home for my vacation in France, Stevies were saying they were helping me out. They were also saving themselves a salary of a third watch keeping officer. Roy Fenton in his book, "Coasters" explains (p8) that after WWII middle trade limits were introduced, extending from Bergen to Santander. Dakar is 2000 miles further south...

I was persuaded to go. At 1800 I rang Mr Field in Newcastle again to accept. Three hours later I got through on the VHF phone to tell Marilyn the good news. Not good news for my fellow officers...

Huge prayers of thanks raised to God for answering a prayer I had not dared to ask. What a change in the mood the last few hours have brought.

Tuesday, 4 August. Dakar to England
It took a whole day for the agent to organise air fares and transport but at 1800 a launch came alongside. I dropped my suitcase into the cockpit aft of the wheelhouse and followed it down the stiff planks of the pilot ladder. I felt embarrassed leaving my shipmates in the lurch, no doubt jealous at my escape. The crew gathered at the taffrail and waved me off. I never did hear how long they stayed or how long it took them to limp home with a damaged engine.

Ashington and the stress of the last three months receded from view. I turned my thought to home, and getting out of Dakar. We entered the busy harbour, the berths lined with a variety of ships and boats nudging alongside at the harbour steps. I jumped ashore, my suitcase tossed up to the agent's driver, climbed into the waiting car and we set off. We stopped outside shabby offices into which the agent disappeared.

'Wait here. Won't be long.'

Where would I go? In the gathering tropical dusk I felt vulnerable. The agent had my passport. I was in a strange African country. I was on my own. I had left my ship behind and missed its comforting presence.

Relief. The agent returned after forty long minutes.

'Passport stamped OK. Now we go to the airport.'

We set off across town. Driving rules were non-existent. Traffic merged across a huge muddy intersection with little regard for any recognisable rule of the road. A free for all.

On arrival at Dakar airport, a quick handshake;

'Good bye. Safe trip.'

'Er. Bye. Thanks.' And he was gone. I was on my own again.

Lining up at the airline check-in I was feeling hot, sticky and rather hungry. It was late at night and I had no local currency. Patience. I kept clear of the armed soldiers patrolling the echoing corridors.

At 0005 we lifted off into the black African night, leaving behind the turmoil of a deeply frustrating trip. Huge relief. I was free. I was homeward bound. Ninety minutes later we flew over Tenerife, Mount Teide thrusting 12,000 feet into our sky. A lifetime before it had reared up from sea level out of the haze. After a very welcome meal and a glass or two of wine, I smiled hopefully at the Sabena Airlines hostess, flourishing my red Seamen's ID Book, and my Master Mariner's Certificate.

'Any chance of a visit to the cockpit please? I am a professional navigator on my way home on leave.'

'Just one moment, sir. I will talk to the Captain and see what can be arranged'.

A few minutes later I found myself sitting on the jump seat discussing navigation techniques with the co-pilot.

'We use these five TV screens to monitor the aircraft's flight conditions, navigating by GPS and radar,' explained the co-pilot.

I pointed out of the cockpit windows, 'See the constellation of the plough and the planet Jupiter, the brightest light in the black night sky?

Over a month ago I was plodding south at ten knots, navigating by these stars on our way to South Africa. Now I am aboard an aeroplane at 33,000 feet winging my way home at over 500 miles an hour! Hard to believe.'

'Welcome to our world!'

Over the last few years I had sat in the jump seat for a landing and had visited the cockpit during a flight at least twice. This was to be the last time. Security today has taken away that great pleasure.

I landed at Gatwick at 0800. Pushing my trolley through the exit gate and looking around the sea of faces pressed around the barriers, I unexpectedly saw Marilyn. It was a very emotional welcome home. It was good to be back in England on a lovely summer's day.

Marilyn was working as physiotherapist part time. Now it was my turn to look after the children. We had a marvellous, revitalizing two-week holiday in France, camping in the Loire Valley, visiting many châteaux. We spent five days in the Dordogne at Uncle John's farm. It was idyllic. They kept ducklings, hens, geese and guinea fowl. We went boating on the pond, ate long lunches outside under the shade of a spreading tree. We relaxed in the warmth, space and peace.

Chapter 46

TEMPTING FATE

I gave the children a big hug goodbye, then embraced Marilyn. Another emotional farewell. My six weeks leave was up. Marilyn has to put up with a great deal, bringing up the family single handed. I felt very blessed to have married such a strong, loving wife and mother.

I travelled by train through a pastoral landscape on a bright and sunny September day. Better than gloomy rain. I watched tiny tractors crawl across the landscape. Preparing to sow winter wheat, I thought.

I arrived at Habrough at midday, pleased to be met by a taxi (unexpected but appreciated) which took me to my usual ship, the

Ashington, by lunchtime. She was berthed at the Immingham Docks not far from the Humber River estuary. Also not far from Grimsby where I had berthed when on the little ships. And just forty miles from Lincoln where I had taken my education degree nine years before. *Plus ça change, plus c'est la même chose.* Things change but make little difference, I thought.

The chief officer already gone of course. Second Officer Neil Williams handed over and I completed loading coal by late afternoon in spite of delays due to continual belt breakdowns. After a brief phone call home, *Ashington* set sail for St Malo at 1757, the precise time confirmed by my diary. Back to the old routine.

Three thousand miles of Atlantic Ocean funnelled into the Western Approaches and on up the narrow neck of the English Channel produces a steep swell. The sea bed depth rises from 600 feet at the western edge to 150 feet in the central portion. Introduce into that Michael Fish's 1987 super storm and the powerful winds created seriously rough seas. The front edge of that tempest made its presence felt, whipping up short seas into long feathered drifts of foam, the spume blown downwind along the crests of a lumpy and rising swell.

On Thursday, 15 October 1987 *Ashington* was on passage to Boulogne heading north. I was on watch, and at 0630 I tuned in to the BBC weather forecasts—gale warnings for sea areas in the English Channel. At 1030 this had been upgraded to warnings of severe gales.

When the plastic corrugated awnings on the boat deck whipped away like cornflakes with a crack that made me jump I knew that we were in for a serious blow. And this was just the entrée. Never was Boulogne Harbour a more welcome sight as we skittered in smartish, moored alongside, safe for the night.

At 2235 GMT winds of Force 10 were forecast. I went to bed, glad to be snug alongside in port.

The nightwatchman called me in the middle of the night, somewhat tardily concerned about the safety of the ship. We rigged extra mooring lines but I had a feeling that the worst of the storm had blown through. It was later that I heard about the effects of the violence in the woods and hedgerows of Sussex and in my home village. I was relieved all was well. It could have been a great deal worse. We heard later about the disasters at sea. As well as many smaller craft being wrecked, a Sealink cross-channel ferry, *MV Hengist*, was driven ashore at Folkestone and the bulk carrier *MV Sumnea* capsized at Dover, Kent.

October in Odda. Snow-capped mountains towered above me; grand, imposing, sharp against the blue sky. Little ferries plied between jetties tucked into hidden coves. Isolated communities nestled within the narrow strips of land which ran down to the fjord. Rows of fruit trees climbed up the lower slopes. With the pilot in charge I took my ease. Rounding the final promontory we sailed the last few cables to the head of the fjord where Odda sat snugly in a glacial valley between the high steep mountains. *Ashington* nosed her bow close to the jetty.

'Heaving line as soon as you can,' I called and a strong-armed sailor flung the coil of rope, the monkey's fist supplying sufficient weight and momentum to carry it successfully to the waiting shore gang. With deft movements the shipboard end was secured with a bowline to the polypropylene headline, hauled ashore and dropped over the bollard. The heavy and awkward manila or sisal ropes in use twenty years ago had long been replaced by these light buoyant mooring ropes.

'Take up the slack.' The bosun clicked over the winch controls and heaved the line tight.

'Easy. Let the bow swing out.'

Down aft the stern was brought gently alongside, wire spring lines were run fore and aft, self-tensioning winches set, the ship secured and engines rung off.

Securing cleats had already been thrown off at each of our three hatch lids on the way up the fjord so all the bosun had to do was to start the hatch motors and pull a lever to engage the drive gears. The chains grew taut, towing back the heavy steel hatch slabs with thunderous crashes as they rolled into the storage position at the aft end of each hatch. Not a time to carelessly put out a steadying hand in the wrong place. I loved the feeling of power it gave when I took the controls, and with absolutely no effort on my part, powered the lids into position. Twenty years before the operation to prepare the ship for loading took a crew of twenty cadets half a day. Then, we tottered along narrow beams hefting six foot hatch boards. I had felt like a circus performer as we balanced over holds without any safety lines or harness; gaping maws eager to devour the unwary. Now it took five minutes with one man.

'Welcome back, Mr Mate.'

'Hello again! Start at Number 2, hatch, OK?'

'Fine.'

After a short consultation with the shoreside foreman we commenced discharge. Twenty tonne grabs of coal dropped their loads directly into hoppers which fed into rumbling conveyor belts. The line of black dust hummed away into the distance. We would discharge 6,500 tonnes in about three days. The second mate took over the routine operation. After lunch I decided to escape ashore. I needed to breath deep and blow the cobwebs from my mind.

Early next morning thunderous crashes woke me from my slumbers. The ship vibrated to the sound of hollow steel struck violently by gigantic hammers. It was the bosun opening hatches closed against overnight rain and preparing for the day's work. All went quiet. Time to roll out of my bunk before sleep dragged me under again.

Donning my dirty white boiler suit adorned with its SC Shield logo I went out on deck. Hauling myself up a handy hatch step I peered over the coaming. Looking down, I saw that steady bites of the grab had chewed away huge black hollows in the number two hold. Time to shift to number one where the waiting coal was filled to the brim. Maybe complete discharge tomorrow. I walked along the quay to check the draft, for'ard and aft. Trim OK.

I stripped off my boiler suit, donned uniform and headed to the saloon.

'Morning.'

'Morning.'

'Fine day.'

'Enjoy your walk ashore yesterday?

'Yes thanks. Found a little farm just tucked away into a...'

'Pass the sugar.'

I drank my too-cold juice, munched of a bowl of cereal, a plate of eggs and bacon, treated myself to a slice of toast, all washed down with a strong cup of tea.

'Excuse me'

Silence.

I went out on deck to talk to the bosun about the day's work.

'Morning, Bos'. Fine day for it.'

'Morning, Chief. I thought I would set the lads on greasing the dogs on the storm doors and roller fairleads. Wash down the poop deck and touch up any rusty bits.'

'Fine by me. Could you get someone to look at the bottom gangway step? Looks a bit stiff to me. Bit of oil should free it up.'

And so the day's tasks are set up. Bulk carrier maintenance is much simpler than on a cargo ship equipped with four derricks per hatch plus the heavy lift derrick.

The crane cranked into action, biting away at the shrinking mound. I chatted to the shore foreman about my brief foray ashore and watched the grab yawn open its steel jaws and with a soft roar drop a stream of dusty coal onto the hopper. The ship rose steadily out of the water. The sun climbed in the sky and set. Cargo work ceased for the night. Clang. Two days later—discharge complete.

We followed the usual routine for departure. The holds swept out, the last few shovelfuls of coal dust thrown into a waiting grab and hauled ashore. The hatch wheels tracked along the runner with a steel-on-steel rumbling and grumbling as chains pulled the heavy hatch lids into position with a final clang. A distant subterranean echo arose from the empty holds. The lids were quickly cleated down. Ready for sea.

The pilot came up the gangway with a cheery 'Good evening!' and I took him up to the bridge to meet the Captain. The crew wound in the gangway and stowed it away.

'Crew to standby,' squawked my walkie talkie.

I took up my position on the fo'c'sle.

'Testing testing, fo'c'sle to bridge.'

'Bridge to fo'c'sle, loud and clear. Single up to one and one.'

The second headline was thrown off the bollard shore and quickly hauled in. The automatic tensioning winch held on to the spring leading aft.

'Singled up to one and one.'

'Roger that.'

'Let go head line!'

'Let go head line.'

The polyprop rope was quickly hauled in onto the winch barrel and coiled down. *Ashington* strained ahead against the wire spring, forcing the stern off the quay.

'Let go the spring!'

The bow thruster kicked in, pushing the bow away from the berth and we swung round and headed out to sea. In the last of the evening light the grey waters of the fjord stretched ahead, darkening mountains closing in on both sides. I unwound while the pilot navigated us safely a hundred and twenty miles back to the coast. A familiar voyage and cargo discharge had been made memorable by the mountains.

We were bound for Hoyanger, 150 miles north, deep into fjord country. Sailing up to the sound the mighty mountains towered high above us. Grey-green rock swept steeply down and plunged into the waters, shimmering in our wake ripples. Tall silos marked the position of our berth. We slipped alongside easily, made fast and rang down finished with engines.

Survey complete, loading alumina for St Malo began. No fuss, little noise. I went for a stroll, climbing high above the town. *Ashington* lay below me, a stream of white powder pouring into her open holds. The aeronautical wingsail dominated her profile. Hopefully the second officer was keeping a good cargo watch.

I continued higher and higher into the mountains. The town houses spread far below were lined up in serried ranks like a child's toy blocks. Meadows of late season wildflowers filled the foreground in glorious colour, the still blue water of the fjord far below, bound by snow-capped peaks.

I ambled back to the ship in good time to complete loading down to her marks. I flung a tin bucket into the fjord, set the hydrometer spinning, read off the density and corrected the draft. Scribbling rapidly at the office desk I finished the final survey calculations. I agreed the figures with the shore surveyor and signed off the loading documents while the crew battened down the hatches.

'Let go for'ard and aft!'

And we were off back down the fjord. I looked back at the mountain so recently explored. A hidden gem.

A passage of just under four days took us down the rocky coast of Norway, across the North Sea, through the crowded Straits of Dover, merging with the southbound separation zone traffic close to the English coast. The White Cliffs were sharply beautiful against the blue sky. The family were one hour's drive north from Brighton, ten miles off on my starboard bow.

Plodding southwest down the English Channel, we rounded the coast at Cap de la Hague threading through the Channel Islands and entered the

Golfe de St Malo. The great town walls rose up to welcome us, our arrival marking the last day of October 1987.

Why do we always arrive in port at mealtimes? I snatched a quick lunch and went for'ard to my station on the fo'c'sle. It was a lovely autumn day. The arms of the breakwaters embraced us as the pilot guided us to our berth. Tensioning winches were set, two additional mooring lines run out and I returned to the bridge.

'All fast, Chief, finished with engines,' I reported to the engine room. The agent was standing on the quay ready to brief the Captain and me about cargo operations. It was a Saturday afternoon and no work would begin until Monday. Time to go ashore and explore.

Monday morning brought a little activity. The shore foreman came aboard with a relaxed Gallic attitude to work and eventually began to discharge our cargo. White powder was grabbed ashore, *Ashington* rose out of the water and by Tuesday afternoon we were empty. The crew turned-to to clean out the holds as we prepared for sea. Late afternoon the pilot came aboard and we took our stations for'ard and aft once again. We were bound for Brest, a mere one hundred and seventy miles away which at twelve knots should take us fifteen hours. In the fading light we caught a glimpse of the imposing coastline; a clear echo on the radar, good for navigation fixes.

Brest is a major naval port. We arrived at a tucked away berth at breakfast time. I had great difficulty in communicating with the loading stevedore. In sailing to sixty countries around the world I found that English is the lingua franca. Not in France. And certainly not in this corner of it. But with my schoolboy French we muddled by.

In less than twenty four hours we loaded 6,000 tonnes of pre-slung bags of wheat flour, a deck cargo of containers filled with army uniforms, and army trucks bound for Nouakchott in Mauritania. It was the first time I had carried mixed deck cargo in over twenty years. It all needed lashing down with rope reinforced with a steel wire core. Nearly forty years later a piece of it holds up my hammock in the garden.

We sailed from Brest mid-November on a voyage of 2,000 nautical miles back to the tropics. It would take eight days at 10.5 knots. A little jaunt away from winter in Europe was a pleasant prospect. We were due home to England and home leave just before Christmas. All were looking forward to that.

I should have realised that the Fates are beyond the control of sailors.

Chapter 47

WAWA II

Ashington headed south across the Bay of Biscay, now quiescent, unlike my stormy crossing twenty one years before. This stretch of the north coast of Spain, known locally as the Costa da Morte, is the site of numerous shipwrecks and founderings. Not me this time. Another nineteenth century maritime marvel, Cabo Finisterre lighthouse is a strong stone tower clasped by a large Keepers' House. Its flashing beam visible for twenty three nautical miles kept us safe.

The familiar landmasses in the Canary Islands rose faintly on the horizon; the looming bulk of Mount Teide, Tenerife, was barely visible in the heat haze. At over 12,000 feet it is the third highest active volcano in the world. It was not erupting, unlike Mount Etna that I had seen trailing a plume of black ash two decades earlier.

Cabo Blanco, or Cap Blanc as I better knew it, hides a big secret. Its two names testify to colonial territorial land grabs over the centuries. Spanish Sahara had been occupied and ruled as a territory by Spain between 1884 and 1975. Mauritania had been part of the larger French colony of French West Africa.

The town of Nouadhibou which has grown up on the peninsula was originally named Port-Étienne by French merchants who settled there shortly before World War I. That's how I knew it. Its bay holds the largest ships' graveyard in the world. Ship owners pay bribes to dump unwanted hulks in the harbour. After nearly three decades of this, Nouadhibou's coastline is scared with the silhouettes of over three hundred rust heaps rotting away their existence. Not a good end.

It's not all bad news. The collection of semi-sunken vessels of all shapes and sizes has created artificial reefs for fish and other wildlife, stimulating a local fishing industry that had previously been decimated from years of over-fishing in the area. The metal hulls have become breeding grounds for fish, replenishing the local supply. Birds have settled on the largely-unmolested offshore barges, and in some cases complete ecosystems have taken over the wrecks.

All that was hidden from me as we rounded Cabo Blanco and entered Nouadhibou Port. We looked forward to a quick discharge of cargo here, on to Nouakchott then on to Bissau then Conakry then home. It was just over a month to go before Christmas. 3,179 nautical miles, just over thirteen days to Blyth. We had two weeks to complete what should be no more than seven days cargo work. Easy. We only had to get this port behind us.

According to a letter written home on 24 November we discharged our jeeps, trucks, containers and bags of flour, crates and earthmoving machinery. There were lots of discharge problems due to the shore cranes being too weak. I found it strange that after twenty years I was back on the West African coast but in very different working conditions. My ship had no swimming pool, no teak taffrails, no teak promenade decks, and no bar run by an obliging second steward. With no derricks to maintain and more efficient hatches and engine room gear, our crew levels were less half those which I had experienced in Elder Dempsters.

I was impressed with the gentleness of the local dockers. They were very helpful, but worked with no sense of urgency. No doubt they did not suffer from ulcers like Westerners. Dressed in flowing robes and wearing turbans like the Touregs, they were a tall and graceful people, much given to holding hands. If there was a cargo problem on deck, the headman would come and take my hand and lead me to the hatchside to explain the situation. I felt the pressure to complete the cargo that night so we could sail early in the morning. There the army was eagerly awaiting its jeeps, trucks and containers full of uniforms and boots ready for the Independence Day celebrations due at the beginning of October. France was giving a nod to its colonial history by providing food and equipment for the Army so that the Mauritanians could put on a good show.

Just as it was looking that we might indeed get away in time the stevedores ran out of trucks to take away our bags of flour. This added to the Captain's already anxious state of mind. He badly wanted to get ashore, to leave the sea. He had recently lost an opportunity to buy a fish and chip shop when the owner decided not to sell after all. So, as I reported home, he was not a happy man.

We finally completed unloading our mixed cargo and sailed at 1200 the next day for Nouakchott, 200 miles and less than a day to the south. Nouakchott is the capital and the largest city of Mauritania, the hub of Mauritanian economy and is home to a port that handles 500,000 tonnes of cargo per year. It's a big place. We were expecting a big dock area within a lock system to protect us from the ocean rollers.

Oh no. There was no breakwater. The jetty jutted out from the coast completely open to the huge swell of the Atlantic Ocean.

The dockers ambled up the gangway. A crane trundled along the quay and took up position opposite number 2 hold. We carefully unloaded the precious celebratory cargo and cleared off the hatch tops and decks. With a sound like rumbling thunder, the three lids opened to reveal the neat stowage of sacks, our five thousand tonnes of grain, destined to feed the population. The crane hook was slipped into the protruding pre-slung loops and the first cargo swung ashore.

WAWA II

Dunnage had been laid to prevent the grain sacks from touching the side of the cold steel hull and thus being spoiled by condensation. To people living in a country denuded of its forests this scarce building material was worth more than grain. Stacked in piles on the deck inviting avaricious eyes, the canny bosun saw the makings of a deal. They had no cash. What did *we* need? The local fishing boats gave him a clue. The bosun, chief stevedore and I gathered in a huddle by the gangway.

'You want the timber. What will you give us?'

'What you want?'

'What about seafood?'

'We give you one large bag of king prawns.'

'Two,' said Bosun.

A nod of the head signified agreement. Hands were shaken.

Later that afternoon a large Mauritanian came on board, biceps bulging, hefting two huge plastic sacks of dirty, grey prawns. They were not a pretty sight and I wondered who had got the best of the bargain. We handed over the prawns to the cook, Dr Death himself, with strict instructions to do a good job and not to ruin this special treat.

A working party gathered after dinner to shell the cooked prawns, now looking a healthy pink colour. Layer upon layer was set between sheets of greaseproof paper and stored in the freezers. On the way home we ate prawns with everything.

The timber was rapidly cleared from the deck and walked up the quay. Very handy two tonne woven slings similarly went ashore to make a very flexible construction material. I still use one in the garden at home.

We occupied the biggest jetty. The local fishing craft and tugs therefore lashed up alongside us. But we were surging up and down the jetty on the Atlantic swell. Self-tensioning winches burnt out their brakes trying to steady the ship, encumbered by the marine parasites clamped to our hull. We broke three wire springs during a two-day stay. Worth maybe £4,000. More paperwork. It is difficult to explain to a man sitting in a cold grey Newcastle office the complexities of managing a ship thousands of miles away in a Third World country.

Our next port was 478 nautical miles south to Bissau, in Guinea-Bissau, a two day passage. Just before we sailed a pretty woman came swinging down the long jetty, followed by many hungry eyes. She came boldly up the gangway and asked to speak to the Captain. 'I have come to ask the Captain a favour.' she informed me enigmatically. A soft continental accent. Dressed in a simple T-shirt and short skirt, big hair and big brown eyes, who could resist her request? Escorting her to the Captain's cabin down the long alleyway I was immensely curious about this visitor. The silence and the cool contrasted with the heat and noise outside. But amplified her female presence. I knocked on the Captain's cabin door and left him to it.

Captain Jung came out to find me on deck. A rare consultation indeed.

'I have a problem,' he explained. 'The lady is travelling through West Africa. Road transport down to Bissau is extremely difficult. She wants— is begging me!—for a ride south. If I ask Head Office, they will say no. If we take her without permission and the authorities in Bissau refuse to allow her to disembark we will have a passenger stuck with us for the rest the voyage back to England.'

Big risk.

'What's the problem?' I replied, free of the responsibility. 'If she has to come back to England with us, I am sure we could find some suitable work for her to do.'

Her big brown eyes won the day. We sailed away from dusty Nouakchott and headed for the humid attractions of Bissau. The atmosphere on board lightened as the officers were charmed. Like bees round a honeypot, we all vied to gain her attention. I do not remember her name. Two days later we arrived safely off Bissau, eager to get alongside, eager to get home.

'Get on the VHF, Chief, tell them we are here.'

'Bissau port control, this is *Ashington, Ashington, Ashington*. What are our orders please?'

'Good afternoon, Captain. Please proceed to the anchorage one mile off the jetty and await further orders. There are other boats on the jetty discharging cargo. When they have completed you will be next on.'

We all groaned at the news. As we approach the anchorage I took my station for'ard with the bosun.

The walkie talkie barked an order.

'Let go starboard anchor!'

With a roar and a smothering plume of choking dust we paid out five shackles of cable and I waited patiently until we were brought up.

'Anchor up and down, Captain.'

'Aye aye. Make secure and come back to the bridge.'

I set up three anchor bearings, picking out features with difficulty within the low scrubby landscape.

And we waited for further orders.

And we waited.

Journal entry
Monday 14 December 1987. Bissau Anchorage, Guinea-Bissau.
We anchored about a mile off the jetty at 1348 on 29 November, sixteen long days ago. We have just one thousand tons of bagged grain on board which no-one seems too anxious to receive. Both jetties are at present occupied. The light of hope—of imminent berthing news—has been repeatedly lit, then snuffed out.

The hitch-hiker has escaped in a launch, lucky girl.

We arrived on a day of excessive humidity and heat and the air-conditioning immediately packed up. Five days of unremitting work by the engineers totally rebuilt the air-conditioning compressor, bits being cannibalised from the old unit, spare O-rings glued to fit and cut to size. Being able to enjoy a cool sleep made a huge difference after sweaty nights of tossing and turning.

Daily temperatures of up to 32° C, 25° in the evening and 21° at night. Paradoxically, for four days after the AC was fixed the temperatures were down to 24/18°, skies overcast.

Three engineers, the radio officer and I played cards, Monopoly or Scrabble in the evenings. Beer was in very short supply so we drank cold white wine to while away the hours. While stocks last.

Initially we were due back in Blyth on 22 December. Each day the ETA slips back, so hopes of Christmas at home are quashed, not only for me. I was particularly aware of the morale of two sailors, one with a family of toddlers like myself. He was taking the interminable delays very badly. Tempers were becoming frayed, especially when Bill, the second mate, woke up the chief engineer at 0430, operating the noisy spin dryer. His was a classic case of obsessive-compulsive disorder. He was a short, thin man with a drawn, deeply etched grey face, and did not mix with anyone. When not in the laundry room battling the spin dryer, he kept to his cabin and read his Bible, fighting inner demons.

My days were spent reading and doing karate exercises during each watch, relieving my aggressions by punching the air. Off watch I walked rapidly for half-hour walk around the hatch top lids, topping up my suntan. A walk round the ship with the Bosun sorted out the make-work tasks for the crew. After a plain bun for lunch I caught up on my sleep with a two hour nap. I avoided lunch in the saloon. Inedible.

Thank God the crew seem to get on okay. However, Captain Jung is a loud, boorish man, given to walking the bridge in his underpants. He appears to have no shorts in his possession. He is given to pontificating loudly, making categorical pronouncements on what he will NOT do. Which later he does. He 'doth protest too much, methinks.' He hates being crossed or contradicted. A difficult man to advise when he is so often wrong. I have never seen him take a drink. A reformed alcoholic.

Three days ago on Saturday morning I phoned Marilyn. All the crew have been given a free phone call. It is a sign of the extraordinary delay that our parsimonious company have made this deep concession. We make the connections through the VHF via the local radio station, keeping the radio officer busy. We exchanged news and hopes.

We are still here, one mile off shore. Will we be home by New Year even? I made another call at 1900 this evening. A poor connection meant a distorted conversation with the children. I am acutely aware that people waiting in the phone queue can hear all we say.

'Hello, Daddy. Missing you loads. Where are you? Will you be home for Christmas?'

'Missing you too. We are at anchor thousands of miles away in West Africa. We are trying to get into port but it seems that they do not want us just yet. So probably not. Sorry.'

Marilyn: 'There is some good news. There are some prospects of a teaching job, as a supply teacher.'

'That could be good. Stevie's may go foreign flag soon and thus pay redundancy money.'

The VHF is a very difficult way to communicate emotions and feelings. Each must remember to wait for the other person to stop speaking before responding. Any interruption cuts out the other person who is of course unaware that they have been cut off. Much repetition is necessary. And patience.

As dawn broke at 0644 we swung yet again to another tide. A painted ship upon a painted ocean. I wait in hope of berthing orders, to offloading our paltry one thousand tonnes of flour and then on to Conakry to load alumina for Blyth. ETA 1988. This year, next year, sometime. Never…

Tuesday 15th of December 1987. Day 17 at anchor off Guinea-Bissau.

Feeling very low when I got up at 0350 to go on watch. I tried not to be a 'God Bother-er', but who else can I turn to, in this seemingly hopeless situation? I sank to my knees, and prayed long and hard that this limbo, nay, this Purgatory may end, that we may berth, tonight.

0600. The VHF burst unexpectedly into life.

'*Ashington, Ashington*, Bissau Port Control. Come in please.'

I jumped at the VHF and grabbed the hand mike.

'Bissau Port Control, this is *Ashington* over.'

'Good morning *Ashington*. Good news for you. The berth is now free. The pilot will be out in one hour.'

Heart thumping, I knocked on the Captain's door and woke him to give the good news. There was a flurry of activity as the engineers prepared the engine, the crew roused out and the pilot ladder put over the side. The pilot clambered aboard and I took him to the bridge then went for'ard to my station to weigh anchor. After seventeen days large clods of thick, black claggy mud gripped the cable. Water and mud flew free as the washer sprayed the cable, clanking shackle by shackle up the hawse pipe and settling into the cable locker with a loud clatter. Peering over the bulwark I saw patches of faded white paint on the joining shackle as they emerged clear of the murky water.

'Anchor aweigh, Captain,' I report into the walkie talkie.

With a thud the anchor shuddered fully into the hawse pipe and clamped itself tight against the hull. Anchor home. The bosun gave the windlass brake an extra tug.

'All secure, Chief.'

'Aye, Aye, Bosun.'

We made our way across the bay towards the jetty. Soon we'll be alongside, I thought. It took twenty four hours to load six thousand tons, so I am sure this one thousand tonnes will be offloaded in a few hours. Two days max.

The fierce tropical sun beat down relentlessly. No sign of any shore crane on the quayside. Our hatches lay open, ready for a rapid discharge of our cargo. Two battered trucks filled the cramped access road, ready to load the slings of grain sacks. I watched in weary resignation from my high vantage point on the bridge wing as a single, battered Coles crane trundled down the ancient jetty towards us and parked parallel to the number two hatch.

The driver dropped stiffly down from his cab and began the laborious process of rigging four stabilisers. Satisfied at last he swung round his crane boom, extended to maximum reach and slowly lowered the hook into the hold till it reached the top of the cargo. A docker slipped the first strop on the hook, and with a rattling, revving heave forcing out a belch of black smoke from the rusting exhaust pipe, the first two ton load was slowly hauled out. Slewing the boom outboard, the sling dropped down,

down, down towards the waiting truck. The axles creaked under the load. 998 tonnes to go.

The evening thirst came upon me at about 1800. Leaving the second officer keeping an eye on the creaking crane, a few of us drifted down a dusty quay lined up with trucks waiting to take our grain. Ignoring the stares of idlers, we stopped at a simple bar at the end of the jetty. Soon we were seated outside on white plastic patio chairs, clutching cold bottles of local lager. The first long swallow tasted good. Really good. It was good to relax ashore, particularly after the last agonising days confined at anchor.

A revving, roaring engine jolted us out of our reveries. Our Coles crane, our sole discharging crane, trundled away down the road and off into the distance. We would not see it again until the morning.

Breakdowns and lengthy repairs became the norm. Our grain took six whole days to discharge. 166 tonnes per day.

It was ten days before Christmas. There was time to explore ashore. I wandered around the hot and dusty streets of Bissau, lined with tired colonial buildings.

The Portuguese had set up trading posts in the sixteenth century along this coast. By the nineteenth century these colonisers regarded the country and much of the area around as part of their empire. Neither here nor in any of their conquests had they ever set up a reliable civil administration nor supplied an efficient education system such as the British had done in Sierra Leone, Nigeria and Ghana. And it showed. My experiences in those countries were quite different to those here. Guinea-Bissau had only been independent fourteen years when we sailed in. Its chaotic political and civil life since then explained the soul-destroying delays we had experienced.

A beautiful fan palm stood sentinel outside the faded elegance of a bank building. Coming to a crossroads and looking south down a long tree-lined avenue I was surprised by the sight of the tall grey flutes of *Ashington's* Walker Wing Sail. The days of sail had returned in a most unexpected way.

The Roman Catholic Cathedral looked mediaeval but was in fact only completed in 1950. Its white facade dazzled in the morning light. Situated over a hundred feet above in a tower I could just see the light that had flashed it warning (*fl. green 2s, every 7s*) to us out at the anchorage. In a photograph outside its Romanesque door, I look like a stork; long brown legs sticking out from under a pair of swimming trunks, my only shorts. An Englishman ashore.

Chapter 48

LIFELINE

Journal Entry

Thursday, 17 December 1987
Right on 1530 the VHF boomed out without warning, making me jump.
'*Ashington, Ashington, Ashington*; this is Bissau Radio. Come in please.'
I had booked a VHF phone call via Portishead Radio to Marilyn. I was waiting for an update on a shore job. This was a longed for opportunity. Would it be good news? I walked nervously about the bridge in earshot of the VHF. It was hot and sticky outside. The work of discharging our grain cargo continued at a grindingly slow pace.
I snatched up the handset, heart beating madly.
'Bissau Radio, this is *Ashington*. Loud and clear.'
'*Ashington*, Channel 27, please.'
'Channel 27, switching over.'
'*Ashington*, Bissau Radio. You have a telephone call from England. Putting you through.'
'Hello Simon! Marilyn here. I have good news!'
'Wonderful. Tell me more. Over.'
'Hi, yes, good news. You have been offered a job at your old school, Loxwood. Teaching three days a week as a supply teacher. £55 a day; £11,000 per year.' Pro rata, of course.
How odd! Back to where I had started my teaching career eight years before.
'Excellent news! Thanks for setting it up. I will fit back in just fine. When do I start? Over.'

'Hello, yes. There is a staff meeting on Wednesday, 6 January. You start teaching your new class the next day.'

Three weeks away. Will we get home in time?

Immediately I begin to make lesson plans, teaching maths, English, football, PE, handwriting, spelling. Music. I knew nothing about music. I will be home every evening! I will spend holidays with the children! I calculated that with Marilyn's salary and with a fractional pay increase due we can just afford to live on two salaries and not just my one. It is for only three days a week but it is a start. It is a foot in the door. I feel very grateful to God for answering my prayer.

Captain Jung arrived on the bridge, showing a brief interest in the progress of cargo work. I took the plunge.

'Captain, you have my resignation from Stephenson Clarke, effective as soon as we arrive back in England.'

'Ahrummph.'

Maybe he was pleased that I was leaving but not pleased for my good fortune.

Everybody on board was glad for me in getting a shore job and out of this game. They wished me well, wistfully hoping that they too could escape. All sailors miss home. In whatever job or career we find ourselves it is never easy to break out of the rut and seek new pastures. We do what we know. There are frustrations in every job but sometimes they boil over and become insupportable. Something has to give.

Two days later I go back to the bridge after breakfast for a quick phone call home. At 0800 the temperature was a cool 20°. Ten minutes conversation costs me £17.20. Excitement at the future made me extravagant. Details of the job were clarified. I am to teach a class of thirty five 9 to 11-year-olds. Two year groups in one class. Quite a responsibility.

Chapter 49

A White Christmas in Africa

The crane roared and grumbled for the last time as with a plume of purple smoke the final sling of grain was swung ashore. At last. Now we can get on to Conakry, 364 nautical miles down the coast in Guinea. Just one and a half days.

Whilst I finished off the paperwork, the engineers topped up water ballast, the bosun took final ballast tank soundings and the crew cleaned out the last of our three hatches, ready for loading. Naturally, being Guinea-Bissau, it took a while for the pilot to appear. Once on board we took our stations.

'Let go for'ard!'

'Let go aft!'

Captain Jung, now wearing his uniform, applied full power on the bow thruster, swinging our bow off the quay and we headed out to sea. Once the pilot had climbed down the pilot ladder into his launch and turned back to shore we wound up to full power and proceeded south at 10.5 knots. There was a great feeling of relief among the crew as we headed towards our final destination, before heading north for home at long, long last.

'Conakry Port Control, Conakry Port Control. This is *Ashington*, *Ashington*, *Ashington*. Come in please'

'Good morning *Ashington*, this is Conakry Port Control. Please proceed to anchorage and await orders.'

Oh dear, oh dear. Or words to that effect. I walked to the fo'c'sle with the bosun and dropped the anchor. Here we are again in another hot and sticky anchorage at the mercy of another port control. It is two days before Christmas.

Journal Entry
Christmas Eve. At anchor off Conakry.
0700. The long-silent VHF speakers filled the bridge with Good News.
'*Ashington, Ashington, Ashington* Conakry Port Control. Please proceed to the berth immediately. Your cargo is waiting for you. The pilot is coming out to you now.'
0936 All fast for'ard and aft.
1130 Commence load alumina after a busy lightship survey.

The depth that a vessel floats in water depends on the density of that water. Freshwater has a density of 1,000. Salt water has a density of 1025. Obviously a ship floats more deeply in fresh water. To discover the density of water locally I attach a heaving line to the handle of a tin bucket. Next I throw the bucket over the side of the ship, encouraging it to sink into the water with a shake of the line. (It's amazing how stubborn a tin bucket can be, refusing to sink when you want it to.) I check to make sure that the bucket is not sitting underneath the engine room cooling water discharge, and heave it back in. From my office drawer I take the sacred hydrometer. Like a one legged man with a pot belly, it is composed of a shiny sphere the size of a golf ball below which is attached a weighted scale. Protruding above its 'stomach' is a long, graduated column. Grasping this neck, I gently lower the stem into the bucket of water, and give it a gentle spin. I wait for the bobbing to cease and, making allowance for the meniscus, read off the density from the bottom of the curve.

Next the surveyor and I agree the draft read from the draft marks on the stem and stern posts. We carefully observe the rise and fall of the water resulting from the lop on the surface of the harbour. Sometimes it takes much discussion to agree on our reading.

To the draft we apply a correction for density taken from the ship's data book.

Making allowances for remaining ballast, fuel, stores we arrive at an agreed lightship displacement figure. This will be compared with the final draft on completion of cargo loading, followed by yet another density dance with a tin bucket and hey presto we can agree how much cargo we have actually lifted. I have done this in dozens of ports from Archangel to Durban for the last four years. This will be the last time I do it.

Alumina is a fine white powder easily blown on the wind. In European ports it is loaded down an enclosed chute and restrained by rubber skirts fitted at the tube mouth. This can be guided to the exact spot the loading mate wishes to place it. At all times the height of the cargo mountain pouring into each hold can be monitored and the trim of the ship kept within comfortable limits.

In Conakry they do things differently. The alumina arrived on an open conveyor belt from the plant a considerable distance away. It took twenty minutes to arrive at the ship. It took twenty minutes to stop the cargo flowing. It took another twenty minutes to restart the flow. Deciding when to move the chute required patience and an intuitive sense of timing. The chute mouth did not have a constraining skirt. The powder fell from a great height and enveloped the whole ship in white dusty drifts. The white fog was so thick at times that I could not see where the alumina was flowing. My cabin was covered in a thick layer of dust because I failed to hammer down the porthole dogs. A white Christmas indeed.

Peering over the hatch coaming, I saw a white mountain emerge though the thick swirl. Its height had to be guessed at. If too low, the cargo would have to be restarted. If too high, the hatch lids could not be closed and the crew would have to be turned out to level it with shovels. Neither the Captain nor the shore stevedore would appreciate unnecessary cargo stoppages. I constantly monitored the ship's draft and calculated the remaining tonnage to be loaded in each hold. It was a tense time.

I took a breather, grab a quick lunch and looked at my very welcome post from home. I had received two Christmas cards. They were much appreciated here in hot, sweaty Conakry.

In the distance I saw palm trees, and fancied a long drink of coconut milk. There was no chance to nip ashore so I bartered with a local docker—two beers for two coconuts. He was very pleased with his side of the bargain. The milk was deliciously refreshing and relieved my parched throat.

With the trim aft getting quite severe I moved the chute to the number one hatch for the final time. The applied lever (the distance from the aft end of number three hold to the for'ard end of number one hold) should quickly make a difference. I was relieved to see the trim rapidly ease towards a more even keel. I liked the ship to be trimmed about a foot deeper by the stern. I was close to being loaded down to my marks but in the dark it was very difficult to be sure. A strong flashlight helped but a stiff lop made the draft marks quite tricky to read.

I continued to worry in case I overloaded. There were no cranes to remove excess cargo. The alumina poured on, hatch coamings mere ghostly outlines in the weak gleams of the cargo lights as the white mist swirled around. Eventually at 2330 I call a halt. I would just have to convince the surveyor that we are indeed loaded to our marks.

The dust cleared away and revealed a white peak prominent above the number one hatch coaming. Not good. The third mate and I grabbed shovels and as midnight heralded Christmas Day we sweated to level piles of powder. I was up to my hocks in hot white drifts. Weird. The peak diminished until I was sure that the hatch lids would close. We thankfully flung our shovels on deck and I sent the 3/0 to call out the crew to prepare the ship for sea.

I staggered off to my cabin, broke out the best Scotch and called in the third engineer and the radio officer. They were awaiting departure, keen to leave. We toasted each other. I was hot and sticky, coated in white dust. Traditional carols broadcast on the BBC World Service floated distortedly on the ether. A white Christmas in Africa. A Christmas Eve to remember.

Chapter 50

ON OUR WAY BACK HOME

Journal Entry
Christmas Day, 1987. Conakry.
0220. Cargo loading figures completed, ready to agree the data with the shore surveyor. Still no sign of him. Chasing paper, getting nowhere. Postcards and letters home have been sent off. At the end of a twenty three hour day I was on a nervous high. I survived by keeping very quiet, buttoning up my thoughts and emotions. Not the sort of Christmas I had planned. We all think that this is the craziest Christmas ever. At 0300 I grabbed some sleep before being roused out for standby at 0700.

We gave up waiting for the surveyor and sailed at 0918. Showered. Captain Jung had refused my request for two bottles of white wine from his bond for lunch. Our relationship had badly deteriorated. I didn't think it could get any worse. He does not speak to me. I poured myself a gin and martini and toasted my family, feeling somewhat emotional. *Ashington* was at last steaming north, home to England.

At 1130 we assembled in the smoke room for a pre-lunch Christmas drink. The third mate was on watch, the second mate, suffering another attack of malaria, had gone to bed. The captain was covering his watch. The rest of us dressed up in white shirts, black trousers and ties (Red Sea Rig), with the chief engineer and the radio officer in full whites, and all had epaulettes shipped.

We went through into the dining saloon and discovered that the Captain had indeed supplied two bottles of white wine and a case of beer. Why didn't he tell me about the wine? Banquo's ghost stood shirtless in the saloon doorway, dressed in blue shorts and flip-flops, and silently scanned his assembled officers.

'I am not coming in for lunch,' he announced and left.

So five of us sat down for a quiet meal: prawn cocktail, tomato soup (very good) Turkey or beef with all the trimmings. I have no memory of what it tasted like. I left most of it, washed down with lots of white wine. Plum duff with rum sauce. Very rum indeed.

I slept very heavily for two hours then staggered up for my watch. The third mate came up to relieve me for tea; mince pies, fruitcake, sausage rolls, ham salad and sardines on toast.

At 1915 I got on the VHF for a brief call home; another poor connection. Very emotional lump in the throat. Miss the family terribly.

I survived to the end of my watch and went below, where I tried to unwind for an hour but had a very restless night.

Boxing Day 1987. At Sea.
Another unforgettable day. I had a row with the Master. He was an overbearing martinet who trusts no one to do the job and interferes irritatingly in matters that really should be delegated. The Chief Engineer had quite clearly set the control knob which governs the revolutions as being maximum for these tropical conditions. The engine is a delicate creature which needs precise handling.

'Do not touch these controls at all at any time,' the Chief commanded. 'If you increase the revolutions we won't get there any faster. The engine will simply come to a grinding halt. And we do not want that do we?' he finished with a warning glare at all of us on the bridge, including the Captain, who scowled back.

I came on watch as usual at 0400 and enjoyed a peaceful tropical night. As the bright stars began to fade and the eastern horizon took solid shape, I obtained a good fix from six stars and adjusted our course fractionally. With no ships on the horizon and the radar clear of echoes I quietly paced out the ten steps of space on the leeward bridge wing.

The Captain came into the wheelhouse and immediately a knot of tension tied itself in my stomach. I saw him fiddling with the forbidden control knob. I knew what he was doing. He was in such a hurry to get home that he could not resist fractionally increasing the revs thinking nobody would notice the difference. I noticed. I cared about rolling helplessly dead ship as the engineers tried to repair—again—a broken marine engine; an unreliable, cussed, obtuse beast. Just like the Master. Also I didn't want the engineers put through all the agony of sweating in 50° heat as they wrestled with the monster because of the bloody-mindedness of one man.

I wearily slid open the bridge door and walked over to him. 'You know the Chief asked you not to fiddle with that, Captain? It will only make things worse, wont it? Just leave it alone.'

Captain Jung looked up and gave me one of his special maniacal stares. 'Come with me,' he commanded. And took me out onto the wing of the bridge and with great deliberation, slid the door shut. He thrust his big ugly face into mine.

'Don't you dare tell me what to do. I will alter the controls if I so chose.'

I stood my ground. I looked him straight in the eyes and held his gaze. I felt unafraid for once. After all, I had nothing to lose because I had already resigned. I was leaving. I was going home.

'Captain, just delegate. Let the Chief and Sparky do their jobs. They are qualified. You are over reacting and being unreasonable.'

The Master did not like being stood up to and walked off in a huff. He would not talk to me except on business. Good thing. Kept him out of my hair and off the bridge.

Friday, 1 January 1988. New Year's Day. At sea. Conakry to Blyth.
Position at midnight: 31° 15" north. 13° 55" west; between the Canary Islands and Madeira. Course 017° True. Speed 9.5 knots. Wind north by

east 6. Pitching and rolling in choppy swell and a generally overcast sky lit by a full moon.

I plodded up the bridge stairs ten minutes before my watch at 0400. I shook hands with the lookout and the Second Mate, now recovered from his malarial episode. 'Happy New Year everybody. Let's hope it's a good one.'

With tight smiles of agreement, tiredness called them back to their bunks, leaving me to a peaceful watch. We rumbled on through the night, the automatic pilot holding us steady to our northerly course.

I have great hopes for 1988. A return to life ashore, and to a teaching career which should last another twenty years. I feel that my life over the last eight years has been like that of a mere floating truck driver, doomed like the wandering albatross to float for ever on the wind, never to make fast to a fixed abode. But now I have broken free of my chains.

Ashington is labouring home, far behind the flying thoughts of all aboard who long for an early and safe arrival after such an eventful voyage. Please God we get to Blyth before midday, 8 January. I will miss the start date in my new job by one day.

Saturday, 2 January 1988. At Sea.
I booked a VHF call to phone Marilyn at 0840 to update our ETA.

'We hope to berth by Friday, so I will be late for school. We are at the mercy of the elements—and our engine—and there is nothing I can do about it. Please pass the information to Loxwood that I am sailing home as fast as I can. Tell them not to give up on me!'

The call is brief. Hopefully this will be our last stilted VHF conversation and we can get back to talking normally.

Now we are reaching deeper into northern latitudes, leaving behind the heat of the tropics. After lunch I carried a chair onto the poop deck and found a place to park it between the bitts. I sat for half an hour in the warm sun and let my thoughts drift. It was a time to rein in thoughts of the future. A moment to savour the present, before clouds covered up the sun's warmth and a chill wind sent me back inside.

My eye was drawn deep into the madly thrashing wake—a fading cappuccino ribbon the only mark of our passing. A solitary gull stalled, dropped and fished. White-tufted cumulus clouds drifted across the sky in serried ranks slow marching towards the flat horizon. The ship rolled in the growing northwesterly swell, an echo of a storm far out in the Atlantic.

The engine rumbled beneath my feet, its reassuring power propelling us slowly homeward. How many fish have been minced in our marine blender? I wondered. Across how many thousands of miles of ocean have I sailed? How often have I seen such seascapes?

My seafaring life began twenty two years ago. I have experienced all climates: temperate, tropical, maritime; all winds: gales, trades, doldrums, West African storms, and tornadoes in the South China Seas. I have voyaged from Africa to Australia, Caribbean to Archangel, Norway to Greece, North East England to the Thames many, many times. All over Northern Europe.

Some ports have left more positive memories; Odda at the head of a classical fjord. St Malo, a gem of an old French town. Historic, rebuilt Caen. Drogheda home of the Beaker people and the Battle of the Boyne. I have walked through olive groves to Delphi, taken train journeys across England, Italy and Australia. I have flown to join ships all over the world. There have been extraordinary shore excursions in Archangel, Central America, Oceania, the Far East, South Africa. And drab Blyth, thirty years behind the times.

A strange fate to be leaving the sea from dying Blyth, fading away like the Merchant Navy, for which it had constructed so many vessels. Including the *Rogate*, I her last Mate. Difficult though the life has been I am proud to have been part of that ancient tradition: the Collier Mate.

I am leaving with one major ambition achieved—my Master's Ticket. Although I never obtained my own command, it is not one I would want in Stevies. Gone are the days when a master sailed to the ends of the earth with almost no contact with the office back in the UK. Telegrams and VHF calls keep the captain on a short leash.

On Monday I resume my career in teaching, two days short of the anniversary date on which I joined the Merchant Navy twenty two years ago in Liverpool, an indentured Apprentice with Elder Dempster Lines.

I will be forty in May this year. A good age to settle down to twenty or so years of steady work. Teaching will provide an interesting and challenging and socially useful job, a good career structure with good prospects, pension and adequate financial reward. I am determined to make a go of it, so help me God.

I went on watch in good time at 1550 as usual, taking over from Peter, who quickly retired below, no doubt to make further use of the laundry. At 1749, I tuned in the LW radio. Almost back in home waters. A freshening breeze and increasing southwesterly swell lifted our port quarter and threatened trouble ahead.

'And now the Shipping Forecast, issued by the Met Office at 1700 today.'

The warm, feminine voice reached across the airwaves, calling us home.

'There are warnings of gales in all areas except Trafalgar. The general synopsis at 1700. Low 200 miles south of Iceland 960 drifting slowly east and filling. Low 250 miles north-east of Faroes 956 moving steadily north and deepening, 940 by 1700 Sunday. High Trafalgar 1033 slowly moving with little change.

Using a chinagraph pencil on the glass-covered map of the shipping forecast areas, I rapidly plotted the lows and highs.

Her clear tones continued to recite the litany:

'The area forecast for the next 24 hours. Viking, North and South Utsire, Forties…'Biscay: southerly 6 to gale 8 occasionally rain. Moderate or poor…'

The white chinagraph crayon told its tale in wind arrows dashed across the glass.

'Trafalgar. Southwesterly 4 or 5, drizzle, moderate or good. Finisterre. Southwesterly 6 to 8, occasionally 9. Moderate or poor.'

At least we now know what we are in for and can prepare ourselves accordingly. The rough weather will inevitably reduce our passage speed. The ETA will need to be adjusted. Downwards.

We pass Cabo di Sao Vicente well out to sea, running up the coast of Portugal and shaping up to enter the Bay of Biscay off Cabo Tourinan, clearly marked by its tall white lighthouse, Cabo Ortegal way off to starboard.

Ushant again. Now we are indeed *Homeward Bound* and the emotion of 'The Channels' sets in strongly for all of us. Cap de la Hague, Cap Griz Nez, cutting across the busy Dover Straits, the White Cliffs of Dover bringing a deep lump to the throat. Such an ache to be home. Two more days to go as we battled up the North Sea, tangential to the flat coast at Lowestoft, the white stone lighthouse at Cromer, *(Fl W 5s)* a reassuring presence 276 feet above sea level. We head towards familiar Flamborough Head, the ruins of Whitby Abbey clear on the cliff top, Sunderland,

Newcastle, till at long last, in humble little Blyth, we tied up at the Alcan berth on the north side of the river.

All fast for'ard and aft.

Friday, 8 January 1988. *Blyth.*
Captain Jung paid me off by inserting a final entry in my Seamen's Discharge Book.

MV Ashington, London, 379883, GT 4334. Date and place of leaving ship: 8.1.88. Blyth. Capacity: Chief Officer. Description of Voyage: Unlimited. Conduct: VG. Signature of Master: G Jung. Official or Company Stamp: Stephenson Clarke Shipping Ltd, Europe House, World Trade Centre, London.

I went back to my cabin to finish my final packing. I felt a bit numb and unfocused as I cleared all my belongings from cupboards and drawers and checked the shelves clear. I unlashed my radio sitting on the porthole sill and disconnected the long wire aerial from the outside world. My sturdy radio and tape player had been my faithful friend over thousands of sea miles, keeping me up-to-date with news and entertainment and bringing balm to my soul. It would have pride of place in a new setting.

The chief officer who would be taking over from me had not yet arrived and so I had no formal handing over duties to do. The paperwork was all shipshape and the second mate was on cargo watch. A low humming from the extractor tube was the only sound to indicate cargo activity as white powder was sucked ashore, destined for the Alcan Aluminium Smelting Works.

The taxi arrived to take me to Newcastle station. I looked around to bid goodbye to my erstwhile shipmates but the deck was deserted. Dragging my heavy suitcase behind me, I clattered down the gangway, out of the Merchant Navy, into the waiting taxi and drove away. Trip trap again. Had I slayed the troll?

The following month I opened a letter from Stephenson Clarke Shipping. I pulled out a folded flimsy sheet. It was my final payslip. I peered into the envelope. It was empty.

I had finally left the sea.

SIXTH LIFE

LIVERYMAN

Epilogue

I braced my foot against the brass rail at the base of the bar as the ship rocked suddenly in the wake of a passing ferry. The cool, clear surface of my white wine shivered invitingly. I took a deep refreshing sip from the dew-dropped glass. Through the porthole the river scene shifted and settled. Glancing around I took in the nautical decorations in the wardroom; original navigation charts, a framed selection of maritime knot work, an ornate coat of arms worked in wire thread and photographs of a variety of warships and merchantmen. I was enjoying the comforts of the wardroom aboard *HQS Wellington*.

I reflected on the wheel of life that had brought me back into the marine world after twenty one years in the classroom as a schoolmaster and deputy headmaster. I had had a successful teaching career. I had made the transition from sea to shore.

In July 2015 I had received the Freedom of the City of London by Redemption. The Clerk to the Chamberlain received my declaration and presented me with my Certificate as a Citizen and Master Mariner of London. It was a very special day. It marked another milestone in my continuing connection with the British Merchant Navy.

The following February I made my Declaration as a Liveryman of the Honourable Company of Master Mariners. I had returned to the fold. I was a member of the Company by right of holding a Master Mariner's Certificate of Competency. I had served my apprenticeship in the ancient calling of the sea. Now I could offer back to the sea through service to others all that had it had taught me.

The Honourable Company was formed in 1926. In 1928 Edward, Prince of Wales, was the first Master. King George V bestowed the rare title of 'Honourable' on the Company in recognition of the sacrifice made by thousands of Merchant Navy officers who perished in WWI. In 1932 the Court of Aldermen of the City of London conferred the status of Livery, the first 'modern' Livery Company, number 78 in order of precedence. A further thirty two companies have been formed since then. All these companies wish to be part of an ancient tradition reaching centuries back.

Built in 1934, *HMS Wellington*, was a sloop of war and is the only surviving North Atlantic convoy warship in British waters, and still afloat. I believe that there are others in Canada and South America, but in a dry dock. Moored at Temple Steps on the Thames since 1948, *HQS Wellington* is a link with my past, where I can share salty tales with like-minded members over a drink in the wardroom. Together we can recall the great days of the British Merchant Navy. We are of course guilty of selective recall when the painful past is largely forgotten. It was part of the experience of life. Dealing successfully with that impostor failure is an essential element in maturing into a better man or woman.

Wellington provides both a connection with my past and focus for the future. Seeking life has brought me thus far. My lifelong search for variety, for something new and interesting, for a satisfying occupation, for companionship, has been rewarded at many waypoints in my life; life at sea, life in port, marriage, family, lay minister, school master, Master of Arts, Master Mariner. All have been transformative. All make me who I am—a seeker after life.

BIBLIOGRAPHY

1. Chang, Jung, *Wild Swans* (London 1991).
2. Cowden, James, and Duffy, John, *The Elder Dempster Fleet History 1852-1985* (n.p. 1986).
3. Cox, Peter, *A Link with Tradition: the Story of Stevenson Clark Shipping Ltd 1730 – 1980* (n.d. [c.1980]).
4. Fenton, Roy, *Coasters: an Illustrated History* (Barnsley 2011).
5. Gregory's, *Gregory's Sydney Street Directory, 36th Edition* (Sydney 1973).
6. Munro, AD, *HMS/HQS Wellington* (London 2006).
7. Newby, Eric, *The Last Grain Race* (London 1972).
8. Brown, Charles and H, *Nicholls' Seamanship & Nautical Knowledge* (Glasgow 1961).
9. Sim, Norma, *the Sixty Miler* (Pier 9, Sydney and London 2005).
10. Tse-Tung, Mao, *Quotations from Mao Tse-Tung* (Peking 1967).
11. Woodman, Richard, *Fiddler's Green: The Great Squandering, 1921-2010* (Stroud 2010).

Acknowledgments

Many people have guided me over the last seven years through the process of creating this autobiographical maritime adventure. The writing course at Horsham Library in 2011 was motivational in re-starting a stalled project. The 2015 Arvon course in Devon was inspirational. I was fired up by our fellow writers and by the daily sessions lead by our two published authors, Olivia Laing and Alexander Masters, who guided and encouraged us to be more creative in our writing. I deeply appreciate the support of my friends and family, and fellow Liverymen of the Honourable Company of Master Mariners who guided me in many constructive ways. Ian Kay was a sharp-eyed proof reader and I am most grateful to him. Special thanks are due to Captain Richard Woodman for his helpful advice.

Any errors remaining are entirely my own.

I am indebted to you all.

Simon Quail
Rudgwick, Autumn 2019

CPSIA information can be obtained
at www.ICGtesting.com
Printed in the USA
LVHW081258040220
645804LV00017B/647